Routledge Revivals

Razos and Troubadour Songs

Razos and Troubadour Songs

translated by
WILLIAM E. BURGWINKLE

Volume 71
Series B

First published in 1990 by Garland Publishing, Inc.

This edition first published in 2018 by Routledge
2 Park Square, Milton Park, Abingdon, Oxon, OX14 4RN
and by Routledge
52 Vanderbilt Avenue, New York, NY 10017, USA

Routledge is an imprint of the Taylor & Francis Group, an informa business

© 1990 by William E. Burgwinkle

All rights reserved. No part of this book may be reprinted or reproduced or utilised in any form or by any electronic, mechanical, or other means, now known or hereafter invented, including photocopying and recording, or in any information storage or retrieval system, without permission in writing from the publishers.

Publisher's Note
The publisher has gone to great lengths to ensure the quality of this reprint but points out that some imperfections in the original copies may be apparent.

Disclaimer
The publisher has made every effort to trace copyright holders and welcomes correspondence from those they have been unable to contact.
A Library of Congress record exists under ISBN:

ISBN 13: 978-0-367-17918-2 (hbk)
ISBN 13: 978-0-367-17922-9 (pbk)
ISBN 13: 978-0-429-05847-9 (ebk)

The Garland Library of Medieval Literature

General Editors
James J. Wilhelm, Rutgers University
Lowry Nelson, Jr., Yale University

Literary Advisors
Ingeborg Glier, Yale University
William W. Kibler, University of Texas
Norris J. Lacy, Washington University
Giuseppe Mazzotta, Yale University
Fred C. Robinson, Yale University
Aldo Scaglione, University of North Carolina

Art Advisor
Elizabeth Parker McLachlan, Rutgers University

Music Advisor
Hendrik van der Werf, Eastman School of Music

Razos and
Troubadour Songs

translated by
WILLIAM E. BURGWINKLE

Volume 71
Series B
GARLAND LIBRARY OF MEDIEVAL LITERATURE

Garland Publishing, Inc.
New York & London
1990

© 1990 William E. Burgwinkle
All rights reserved

Library of Congress Cataloging-in-Publication Data
Razos and troubadour songs.

Garland library of medieval literature ; v. 71,
ser. B)
Includes bibliographical references.
1. Provençal poetry—Translations into English.
2. English poetry—Translations from Provençal.
3. Provençal poetry—History and criticism. 4. Troubadours. I. Burgwinkle, William E., 1951–
II. Series: Garland library of medieval literature ;
v. 71.
PC3365.E3R39   1990   849'.1208   90-3951
ISBN 0-8240-5346-X

Printed on acid-free, 250-year-life paper
Manufactured in the United States of America

Dedicated to the memory of

Mary Julia Quinn McNamara

and

Dorothy Burgwinkle

Preface of the General Editors

The Garland Library of Medieval Literature was established to make available to the general reader modern translations of texts in editions that conform to the highest academic standards. All of the translations are originals, and were created especially for this series. The translations attempt to render the foreign works in a natural idiom that remains faithful to the originals.

The Library is divided into two sections: Series A, texts and translations; and Series B, translations alone. Those volumes containing texts have been prepared after consultation of the major previous editions and manuscripts. The aim in the edition has been to offer a reliable text with a minimum of editorial intervention. Significant variants accompany the original, and important problems are discussed in the Textual Notes. Volumes without texts contain translations based on the most scholarly texts available, which have been updated in terms of recent scholarship.

Most volumes contain Introductions with the following features: (1) a biography of the author or a discussion of the problem of authorship, with any pertinent historical or legendary information; (2) an objective discussion of the literary style of the original, emphasizing any individual features; (3) a consideration of sources for the work and its influence; and (4) a statement of the editorial policy for each edition and translation. There is also a Select Bibliography, which emphasizes recent criticism on the works. Critical writings are often accompanied by brief descriptions of their importance. Selective glossaries, indices, and footnotes are included where appropriate.

The Library covers a broad range of linguistic areas, including all of the major European languages. All of the important literary forms and genres are considered, sometimes in anthologies or selections.

The General Editors hope that these volumes will bring the general reader a closer awareness of a richly diversified area that has for too long been closed to everyone except those with precise academic training, an area that is well worth study and reflection.

James J. Wilhelm
Rutgers University

Lowry Nelson, Jr.
Yale University

Contents

Acknowledgments		*xv*
Introduction		*xvii*
Glossary		*xxxvii*
Manuscripts Cited		*xxxix*
Bibliography		*xli*
1.	Bernart de Ventadorn 70, 43	3
	Song 70, 43	3
2.	Bernart de Ventadorn 70, 6	6
	Song 70, 6	6
3./ 80b.	Bernart de Ventadorn 70, 1 and	
	Guillem de Cabestaing 213, 5	310
	Song 70, 1	315
	Song 213, 5	318
4.	Arnaut de Mareuil 30, 19	9
	Song 30, 19	10
5.	Guiraut de Borneill 242, 69	12
	Song 242, 69	14
6a.	Guiraut de Borneill 242, 36	17
6b.	Guiraut de Borneill 242, 36	18
	Song 242, 36	19
7.	Guiraut de Borneill 242, 51	22
	Song 242, 51	23
8.	Guiraut de Borneill 242, 73	25
	Song 242, 73	26
9.	Guiraut de Borneill 242, 46	30
	Song 242, 46	30
10.	Guiraut de Borneill 242, 55	35
	Song 242, 55	35
11.	Arnaut Daniel 29, 2	38
	Song 29, 2	40

12.	Bertran de Born 80, 37	42
	Song 80, 37	44
13.	Bertran de Born 80, 12	46
	Song 80, 12	47
14.	Bertran de Born 80, 1 and 15	50
	Song 80, 1	50
	Song 80, 15	52
15.	Bertran de Born 80, 38	54
	Song 80, 38	56
16.	Bertran de Born 80, 19	60
	Song 80, 19	61
17.	Bertran de Born 80, 44	62
	Song 80, 44	63
18.	Bertran de Born 80, 32	65
	Song 80, 32	70
19.	Bertran de Born 80, 20 and 32	68
	Song 80, 20	74
	Song 80, 32	70
20.	Bertran de Born 80, 20	73
	Song 80, 20	74
21.	Bertran de Born 80, 33	75
	Song 80, 33	77
22.	Bertran de Born 80, 21	78
	Song 80, 21	80
23.	Bertran de Born 80, 13	83
	Song 80, 13	84
24.	Bertran de Born 80, 26	85
	Song 80, 26	86
25.	Bertran de Born 80, 35 and Guillem de Berguedan 210, 10	88
	Song 210, 10	89
	Song 80, 35	90
26.	Bertran de Born 80, 39	93
	Song 80, 39	93
27.	Bertran de Born 80, 36	96
	Song 80, 36	96
28.	Bertran de Born 80, 31	98
	Song 80, 31	101
29.	Bertran de Born 80, 2	103
	Song 80, 2	104
30.	Bertran de Born 80, 29	106
	Song 80, 29	107

31.	Bertran de Born 80, 8	109
	Song 80, 8	110
32.	Bertran de Born 80, 34	112
	Song 80, 34	113
33.	Bertran de Born 80, 28	115
	Song 80, 28	117
34.	Bertran de Born lo fills 81,1	119
	Song 81, 1	121
35.	Richart de Berbezill 421, 2	123
	Song 421, 2	126
36.	Raimon Jordan 404, 9 and 12	128
	Song 404, 9	131
	Song 404, 12	132
37.	Gaucelm Faidit 167, 43 and 59	134
	Song 167, 59	138
	Song 167, 43	141
38.	Gaucelm Faidit 167, 52	143
	Song 167, 52	145
39.	Gaucelm Faidit 167, 33	147
	Song 167, 33	148
40.	Gaucelm Faidit 167, 40 and 15	151
	Song 167, 40	153
	Song 167, 15	155
41.	Gaucelm Faidit 167, 13 and Elias d'Uisel 136, 2	157
	Song 167, 13 and 136, 2	157
42.	Gui d'Uisel 194, 2 and 19	159
	Song 194, 2	160
	Song 194, 19	163
43.	Gui d'Uisel 194, 9 and Maria de Ventadorn 295, 1	165
	Song 194, 9 and 295, 1	168
44.	Peire d'Uisel 361, 1	166
	Song 361, 1	166
45.	Maria de Ventadorn 295, 1	167
	Song 194, 9 and 295, 1	168
46.	Savaric de Malleo 432, 3	170
	Song 432, 3	172
47.	Savaric de Malleo 432, 2	175
	Song 432,2	175
48.	Uc de Saint Circ 457, 4	178
	Song 457, 4	180

49.	Uc de Saint Circ 457, 18	182
	Song 457, 18	183
50.	Uc de Saint Circ 457, 33 and Coms de Rodes 185, 3	185
	Songs 457, 33 and 185, 3	185
51.	Guillem de Saint Leidier 234, 16	186
	Song 234, 16	188
52.	Guillem de Saint Leidier 234, 7	190
	Song 234, 7	192
53.	Dalfi d'Alvergne 119, 4 and Robert, Bishop of Clermont 95, 3	195
	Songs 119, 4 and 95, 3	195
54.	Dalfi d'Alvergne 119, 5 and Bertran de la Tor 92, 1	196
	Songs 119, 5 and 92, 1	196
55.	Dalfi d'Alvergne 119, 1 and Peire Pelisier 353, 1	197
	Songs 119, 1 and 353, 1	198
56.	Dalfi d'Alvergne 119, 8 and Richard-the-Lionhearted 420, 1	199
	Song 420, 1	200
	Song 119, 8	202
57.	Pons de Capdoill 375: 14, 18 and 20	204
	Song 375, 18	206
	Song 375, 20	207
58.	Guillem de Balaun 208, 1	209
	Song 208, 1	213
59.	Peire Vidal 364: 2, 36, 37 and 48	215
	Song 364, 2	217
	Song 364, 36	223
	Song 364, 37	225
	Song 364, 48	227
60.	Peire Vidal 364: 2, 36, 37, 48	217
	Song 364, 2	219
	Song 364, 36	223
	Song 364, 37	225
	Song 364, 48	227
61.	Peire Vidal 364, 16	229
	Song 364, 16	231
62./ 72.	Peire Vidal 364, 47	233
	Song 364, 47	284

63./ 65.	Peire Vidal 364, 21 and Raimon de Miraval 406: 4, 27, 38	247
	Song 364, 21	255
	Song 406, 4	251
	Song 406, 27	253
	Song 406, 38	243
64.	Raimon de Miraval 406: 12, 15, 28 and 38 and Uc de Mataplana 454, 1	234
	Song 406, 12	236
	Song 406, 15	239
	Song 406, 28	241
	Song 406, 38	243
	Song 454, 1	245
65./ 63.	Raimon de Miraval 406: 4, 27, 38 and Peire Vidal	247
	Song 406, 4	251
	Song 406, 27	253
	Song 406, 38	243
	Song 364, 21	255
66.	Raimon de Miraval 406: 8, 28 and 15	257
	Song 406, 8	261
	Song 406, 28	241
	Song 406, 15	239
67.	Raimon de Miraval 406, 12	263
	Song 406, 12	236
68.	Lombarda 288, 1 and Bernart d'Arnaut 54,1	265
	Song 54, 1 and 288, 1	265
69.	Almuc de Castelnou 20, 2 and Iseut de Capio 253, 1	267
	Song 20, 2 and 253, 1	268
70.	Raimbaut de Vaqueiras 392, 20 and 24	269
	Song 392, 20	271
	Song 392, 24	275
71.	Raimbaut de Vaqueiras 392, 2	279
	Song 392, 2	281
72./62.	Raimbaut de Vaqueiras / Peire Vidal 364, 47	283
	Song 364, 47	284
73.	Raimbaut de Vaqueiras 392, 9	286
	Song 392, 9	288
74./ 79.	Raimbaut de Vaqueiras 392, 31	291
	Song 392, 31	306

75.	Folquet de Marseille 155, 23	291
	Song 155, 23	293
76.	Folquet de Marseille 155, 27	295
	Song 155, 27	296
77.	Folquet de Marseille 155, 20	298
	Song 155, 20	298
78.	Folquet de Marseille 155, 15	301
	Song 155, 15	302
79./ 74.	Guillem del Baus and Raimbaut de Vaqueiras 392, 31	304
	Song 392, 31	306
80a.	Guillem de Cabestaing 213, 5	307
	Song 213, 5	318
80b./ 3.	Guillem de Cabestaing 213, 5 and Bernart de Ventadorn 70, 1	310
	Song 213, 5	318
	Song 70, 1	315
81.	Lanfranc Cigala 282, 14 and Guillelma de Rosers 200, 1	321
	Song 282, 14 and 200, 1	322

Acknowledgments

I would like to thank everyone who has helped me in completing this project. This includes, first and foremost, all those scholars who spent years preparing critical editions, translations, and studies of the troubadour poets. They are all mentioned under the works of the individual poets in staid print, when in fact they deserve flashing lights. I could never have undertaken this project without access to all they accomplished before me.

I would next like to mention the help I received in conducting research at the Bibliothèque Nationale and the Institut de Recherche et d'Histoire des Textes in Paris, at Stanford University, and at the University of Hawaii. I thank the Whiting Foundation for a 1986-87 grant which allowed me to get started on this work and the Graduate Division and Department of French and Italian at Stanford University for a summer travel grant in the summer of 1987 that kept me going. I am grateful to the College of Language, Linguistics and Literature at the University of Hawaii for granting me a course reduction in the Fall of 1989 so that I could complete the project.

Finally, I thank all who offered advice and friendship, especially Bruce Bruschi for his clear-sighted intelligence and day-to-day support and encouragement, Larry R. Riggs for his careful reading and critical insight, Patricia de Castres for her generous help with the computer, James J. Wilhelm and the editorial staff of Garland Publishing, and, above all, Brigitte Cazelles, for serving as my mentor and inspiration.

Introduction

The usage of the Occitan word *razo* within the body of thirteenth- and fourteenth-century texts collected in this volume reveals how fully medieval authors came to exploit the semantic richness of the word's Latin model, *ratione(m)*. The most generalized and reductive definition, and the one which came in time to define a literary genre, is this: introduction, explanation, reasoned commentary, subject matter, background, gloss. Indeed, we do find that all the short prose texts collected here clearly serve in one way or another an introductory function in relation to the songs with which they are paired. Referring to, and citing, specific lyric texts composed by the troubadours of Southern France, Northern Italy and Spain, the author claims to provide an explanation for why a particular poet composed a particular song or songs at the moment that he or she did. At the same time, he does not treat the song in a vacuum; rather, by adopting a uniform rhetorical practice and vocabulary, he relates the song to a larger social and literary phenomenon: the composition and exchange of vernacular songs of praise in the Southern French courts.

Further subtleties in the meaning of the word 'razo,' as used within the texts that now go by that name, both limit and expand this introductory function. Sometimes the word is used in the sense of 'justice,' as in 'the right thing to do,' or 'rights, rightful claim,' i.e. with the intent of justifying or claiming a right. In other instances, any one of those meanings can be supplemented with an oral component, as in 'speech,' 'argument,' 'defense.' Thus these razos must be seen as simultaneously explaining and supplementing the poetic texts, even to the point of providing them with subject matter that is not necessarily present in the original text. Then, to this supplementary gloss is added the intimation of a specific rhetorical task with a clear ideological bent: to defend the song, justify it, provide it with 'reason,' make it comprehensible and monologic, in the Bakhtinian sense. The potentially aggressive role of this second function should be noted. These texts were composed so as to ensure the survival of the songs and of the cultural practices they document, even as they deformed them.

Authors and Texts

Many questions regarding the function of these texts in the performance arena and their manuscript tradition remain unanswered. It has generally been assumed that they were first written down, beginning in the early thirteenth century, by poets and *joglars* who had for some time been using the material in oral performance to explain ambiguous and topical references in the songs they were performing. As the need for such explanations became more acute, due to spatial and temporal distance from the original composition, more of the introductory texts were composed by later authors to fill in the gaps (Boutière/Schutz, 1973: viii. Henceforth referred to as B/S). While this may be true, the extant prose texts give no clear indication as to whether they were actually used in performance or whether they were first written to be read rather than heard. Some textual evidence, particularly in the closing sentences of the texts, points to their complicity in systems of both oral and written transmission (see, for example, the common closing: "...which is *written* here, as you shall *hear*" [razo 4]). If they were, in fact, originally composed for oral presentation by traveling poets who had learned their lore and geography first-hand (Schutz, 1937-38, 1939), then these are not the versions that have survived. Most of those reproduced here show signs of having been composed or adapted to manuscript use by one or several scribe/poets who had been trained in practices of textual commentary and who viewed these commentaries as participating in a system subject to rhetorical and ideological constraints.

Within the larger field of 'prose introductions' to the poets, there exist two distinct genres, known today as the *vidas* and the razos, though in the manuscripts both are referred to as razos (see, e.g. razo 64 to the songs of Raimon de Miraval). The vidas are principally biographical texts that present a stylized view of an individual author's career rather than an explanation of any one of his works. The earliest *chansonniers*, the mid-to-late-thirteenth century Italian manuscripts I and K, are also those that contain the largest number of vidas, numbering eighty-five. Both genres probably existed in some oral form well before that time and many critics agree that they may have been gathered and reworked, or even in some cases composed on the spot, as early as the 1220s, in the area around Venice (Meneghetti, 245, note 28). As Margarita Egan (1984) and Maria Luisa Meneghetti (1984) have shown, both types of texts were composed or adapted by authors familiar with the Latin *Accessus ad auctores*, the introductions to the classical poet's lives, that were composed as part of a student's training in literary commentary in the schools. The razos offer additional evidence that their authors had adapted the *ethologiae* (character sketches) portion of *enarratio poetarum* commentaries to suit the needs of contemporary, vernacular, and secular songs (Murphy, 1974: 25). Neither genre, however, follows the format of its model to the letter. While the *accessi* are fairly rigidly structured, following either an Aristotelian or Boetian model (author's intention or *causa efficiens* / subject matter / form or utility; see Egan, xxvi and Meneghetti, 292), each of these two Occitan genres evolved (or was given, through the collecting and organizing skills of one author) a rhetorical pattern unto itself. In the case of the vidas this pattern involves some, though not necessarily all, of the following information: name of poet / "and he was ("si fo...")"/ place and circumstances of origin / talent/ protectors or love affair/ adventures, success or failure/ death (Egan, xvii; Meneghetti, 308). In addition, the placement of the vida in the manuscript quite logically precedes the poetic texts and is often illustrated with an image representing the poet.

The razos, on the other hand, to the extent that they follow any sort of pattern, tend to incorporate some of the following information and stylistic detail: a reference to a prior vida / a story-line beginning with the words: "And so it happened that one day..."/ a phrase connecting that story with the song that follows, as in: "And for that reason he composed..."/ a citation of between a line and several stanzas from the song / and a closing formula of the type: "And here you will hear (or find written) the song which you will now hear (or read)" (Meneghetti, 308). Some of the texts that are considered vidas by virtue of their adherence to the rhetorical patterns outlined above could, however, be considered razos in that they cite lines from specific poetic compositions. Since these hybrid texts were included in Margarita Egan's 1984 volume on the vidas, they have not been included here (see, for example, in Egan 1984, vidas 14B, 15B, 35, 67). Others consist of one single text which contains elements of one genre within the other. Such cases usually involve a razo that has been included within the frame of a vida and which can easily be excerpted to function as an independent text. The very first razo included in this collection (see Bertran de Ventadorn, razo 1), is an example of this phenomenon. All other known prose introductions to the troubadour songs are included here, including three razos taken from manuscript fragments found since the 1973 revision of the Boutière/Schutz critical edition (see Crespo, 1983).

In general, in discussing the razo texts, we cannot assume the same degree of uniformity of function and treatment that we find in the vidas. The earliest known razos, from the same thirteenth-century manuscripts I and K in which the earliest vidas are found, are by an Italian hand and were likely composed in the Lombardian/Venetian/Emilian region of Northern Italy. This does not, of course, mean that these are necessarily the earliest composed; simply that they are the first written versions that we know of. Manuscripts I and K are obviously linked, having been copied from the same source or having served one as the model for the other. They are noteworthy both for their treatment of the prose texts and for the early date of their composition, and these two factors may argue for their essential difference from other manuscripts in the razo tradition (i.e. they may have been composed entirely by one author who 'invented' the genre or may respond to the interests of a very specific audience). Each contains nineteen razos: 17 for Bertran de Born, one for his son, Bertran de Born lo fils, and one for Raimon Jordan (see Poe, 1989). The sheer number of texts dedicated to the works of this one poet implies that this project may have been undertaken specifically to explicate his works alone. Bertran's songs are, after all, infamous for their references to the intricacies of regional political alliances under the reign of Henry II of England and his warring sons, Henry, Richard, Geoffrey, and John. All of the songs by Bertran that are explicated are *sirventes*, i.e. topical, political, satirical or critical songs, and it has been suggested that these Italian collections or their source may have served as the impetus and model for the later razo collections that followed in the fourteenth century. This hypothesis is corroborated by the fact that later manuscripts done in Italy, such as manuscript H, also include razos only for *tensos* and *coblas* rather than for more well-known *cansos*. It has further been suggested that these early razos indicate that the entire reason for composing prose commentaries may have been to explicate just such political songs. Such a contention is nonetheless difficult to prove given the variety of manuscripts, their places of origin (from Italy, Languedoc and Catalogne), and the number of texts which have been lost. Manuscript F, a fourteenth-century Italian collection, also includes only the razos for Bertran de Born and his son and presents them in the same order as IK, thus clearly linking this manuscript with the IK tradition. In F, however, the razos precede the songs they explicate and in IK they follow. Such seemingly minor differences in presentation are nonetheless significant, for they emphasize that even nearly contemporary scribes were divided as to how to transmit the razos textually. Were they to be collected as separate texts, as they would be in the fourteenth-century manuscripts E, P and R? Were they meant to introduce a song before it is heard, or explain it after it has been sung? Are they principally to be read or listened to, as part of a performance or in a private reading?

Aside from the IKF affinity, there is little evidence to establish any clear patterns of transmission or to formulate any textual solutions to these questions. One thing seems certain: in the fourteenth century the razo texts were not considered subject to the rules of any one strict rhetorical classification. Rather, throughout the century, the manuscripts show that these prose texts were constantly evolving in one of two directions. In manuscripts P and R, the texts grow longer and more independent of their source poem and the percentage of razos to vidas increases (Poe, 1984: 110, note 1). Other manuscripts show signs of having been composed for a particular patron and tailored to the taste of that collector. Manuscript H, for example, of late-fourteenth-century Italian production, is characterized by very short texts that do extensive citations, and by a marked interest in the production of the women troubadours, the *trobairitz* (in fact, the only illuminations of troubadours in this manuscript are of trobairitz). The texts of manuscript H also stand out from among those of other manuscripts in that two-thirds of them (numbering 14) are found only in that one manuscript. As for the Italian manuscript P, dated 1310, and the sixteenth-century paper copy of an earlier manuscript, also done in Italy and known as N^2, they tend to include longer and more elaborate versions of the razo tales. These texts have rightly been linked with the emergence of independent prose tales in Italy during the fourteenth century (the *Novellino*) and with Dante's project of framing the poetry of his youth within a unified prose narrative in the *Vita Nuova* (Poe, 1984: 83-97).

The fourteenth-century manuscript R, produced in Languedoc, shares P's tendency to elaborate upon incidents but does so in such a way that even when recounting a tale found in other manuscripts, its version is sometimes so idiosyncratic that its full text is reproduced as a separate and independent version of a tale in Boutière/Schutz rather than as a set of variations on an original that can be cited in footnotes. One explanation for some of the variety found in the razo texts may lie in the question of patronage. Laura Kendrick and Maria Luisa Meneghetti have recently looked into the correlation between the treatment of certain themes in the biographical texts and the site of their production. In the case of manuscripts I, K, and F, there reigns a uniformity of treatment, both pictorial and textual, which suggests that these manuscripts were created for a patron whose interests in Occitan literary production dictated a carefully stylized portrait of this literary phenomenon. The preponderance of vida texts in I and K, with their uniform use of the historical past and firm grounding in geography, creates a static view of production that celebrates decidedly past achievements. At the same time that it glorifies the localities and social system that allowed for this extraordinary outpouring of poetry, it captures it and limits it, creating a sort of textual museum to a dead art. And that is, to some extent, an accurate assessment of the situation. The Albigensian Crusade had decimated many of the courts at which these songs were produced and sung and had upset the political balance that had kept the South of France an entity quite separate from, and resistant to, the royalist pretensions of the Ile de France. There were, nonetheless, poets still composing and courts still offering patronage even up to and beyond the period during which these manuscripts were compiled. Along the same lines, Meneghetti notes that the slant of the Venetian manuscripts D, I, and K occasionally extends even to customized versions of the songs. Bernart de Ventadorn's song: "La dousa votz ai auzida" (70, 23), for example, is presented in a version which eliminates references that seem out of line with a rather narrowly conceived idea of *fin'amors* as a secular system of ethics and ideals (Meneghetti, 1984: 51-52). Meneghetti then links this phenomenon with the idea of medieval 'mouvance', i.e. fluidity, susceptibility to change and adaptation through transmission (Zumthor, 1972: 66), thus suggesting that songs may have been deliberately adapted to suit the styles and tastes of particular court patrons.

Manuscript R is anomalous in one other regard. In it can be found a razo (#46 in this collection) for Savaric de Malleo's song: "Savaric, ie·us deman..." (432, 3) in which there is made the following statement:

> E sapias per ver que ieu, Uc de San Sirc, que ay escrichas estas razos, fuy lo mesatge que lay aniey e.l portey totz los mans e·ls escrisz.
>
> (And let it be known for a fact that I, Uc de Saint Circ, who have written these razos, was the courier who went there and delivered these messages and letters to him.)

Uc de Saint Circ is, of course, himself a poet for whom we have a vida and three razos. Does this admission mean that Uc "wrote" the razos as in "composed" them, or as in "acted as scribe"? Does it mean that he "wrote" only those razos (conspicuously plural) that pertain to Savaric or does he mean, in the broader sense, that he "wrote" all of the razos contained in manuscript R? The fact that this particular razo exists only in this one manuscript and that in manuscript R all razos and vidas are clumped together at the beginning of the collection (folios 1-3v) at least allows us to conjecture that Uc did, in fact, compose all of these razo texts (eighteen in all) and perhaps many others.

He did sign one other text, the vida to Bernart de Ventadorn that appears in manuscripts A, B, E, I, K, R and Sg. There are also indications within his own biographical account (or autobiographical, as some would maintain [Meneghetti, 269; Panvini, 89; Folena, 518]) that Uc was considered somewhat exceptional. His vida tells us that he was the youngest son of a poor vavassor (one ranking just below a baron or peer) from Quercy. He was sent to school in Montpellier to become a cleric but while his family thought he was studying 'letras,' i.e. biblical and rhetorical studies in Latin, he was, in fact, learning "...love songs, verses, sirventes, tensos, couplets, and the facts and deeds of the valiant men and ladies who were then, or had ever been, in the world; and with this knowledge he became a joglar (B/S, 239)." Such a description, with its emphasis on the various genres of the troubadour tradition and Uc's interest in literary/historical data, strongly suggests that the author believes Uc to have been instrumental in preserving this cultural heritage. The vida goes on to chronicle Uc's patrons the count of Rodez (coms de Rodes), the viscount of Turenne (Torena), the Dauphin of Auvergne (Dalfi d'Alvernhe), the countess of Benauges (Benaujas), Savaric de Malleo, King Alphonse of Aragon (Amfos), King Alphonse of Léon (Lion), King Peter of Aragon (Peire), i.e. among the most influential and supportive of the troubadour patrons, several of whom were themselves poets. His travels took him from Gascony to the Poitou, through Catalogne and into Spain, "...then into Provence, with all the barons, and then into Lombardy and La Marche" (B/S, 240). Uc, in other words, had a full and varied career which took him throughout the entire area of Occitan production (thus allowing him to acquaint himself with the geography, folklore and courtly protocol). It is also significant that during this time he was forced to earn his own living through the practice of his poetic and musical skills. The vida author says that Uc spent a long time in Gascony as a poor singer and that he owed all he had to the generosity of his patrons. He also says that Uc did not write many love songs (adding, however, that the ones he wrote were excellent) because he was not ever in love, but that with his fine rhetorical skills he was quite capable of feigning love. The essential facts of the vida establish that its author (once again, perhaps Uc himself) chose to emphasize factors in Uc's career that would explain his ability to assess others' biographies, production, and especially their successes and failures in attracting and retaining loyal patrons.

In the Italian manuscripts A and B, the version of Uc's vida is even clearer on one important point. After chronicling his travels and patrons, as in the passage cited above, the quotation ends: "...then into Lombardy and the *marca Trevisana*. He took a wife and had children" (B/S, 240). This more specific citation establishes even more clearly that Uc ended his career in Italy, where he settled in as court poet to the Da Romano family at Treviso. As noted above, most scholars agree that there are numerous signs within the vidas and razos that point to their having been composed for the most part in the Venetian area. Uc's documented presence in that area during a considerable portion of his mature life adds credence to that hypothesis (Meneghetti, 243). Meneghetti has asserted that one of the motivations for composing these prose introductions may have been the need to transform the ideals and aspirations of the lower Occitan nobility into terms that could be understood in a very different courtly setting in Northern Italy. The transplantation of troubadour poetry from its original setting in Southwestern France, and the loss of its frame of reference following the Albigensian Crusade, may have incited Uc to compose a series of biographical sketches which would memorialize the region's poetic production through a close identification of the poetry with the land. Much of the information for these vidas could have been gleaned from public performances and regional compilations gathered throughout his extensive travels. At the same time, or perhaps shortly thereafter, Uc may have found it necessary (or been commissioned) to compose explanatory texts to accompany the individual songs. Where in the past these texts would have been required only to explicate the politically involved sirventes of Bertran de Born, the new conditions and audience for Troubadour song now required that the allusive and ambiguous referents that played such a role in the elaboration of the lyric be grounded in an apparent historical reality. Love was no longer a satisfactory topic, love stories were now required; and the curious turns of the misogynistic love song, what Jeanroy called the "sirventes déguisé," had to be explained in terms of incidents of betrayal, exile, and reconciliation. What many critics have always objected to in the vidas and razos, i.e. their stylistic deficiencies, their deformation of the historical record, and their 'soap-opera mentality' might actually be better explained in terms of the needs of the audience for whom they were composed.

Topoi of Love and Patronage

Maria Luisa Meneghetti points out in her book, *Il pubblico dei trovatori*, that the earliest known chansonnier, the central section of manuscript D (known as D[a]), is a collection of songs chosen by Alberico da Romano, one of the two brother/lords of Marca Trevisana. The collection pre-dates the manuscript's table of contents, which is dated 1254; and this entire section is introduced by the sentence: "Hec sunt inceptiones cantionum de libro qui fuit domini Alberici et nomina repertorum earundem cantionum." If this collection was assembled for Alberico just prior to the date indicated, then Meneghetti quite rightly surmises that it was likely Uc de Saint Circ who undertook the project. Jeanroy (1934, xiv) dated Uc's stay in Italy from 1220 to 1253, during the end of which time he would have been permanently established at Alberico's court. If this is true, it would implicate Uc at the very inception of a written tradition of lyric transmission and suggest very practical reasons why he might have undertaken to compile a collection of vidas and razos as well. A 1974 article by François Zufferey disclosed that a recently discovered document from the Biblioteca Capitolare in Treviso mentioned Uc de Saint Circ, saying that in 1257 the ecclesiastical authority of the city had charged the poet with usury and heresy and that the accused had confessed his guilt. Meneghetti notes with reason that manuscript P's version of Uc's vida, also composed in Northern Italy at some time prior to 1310, adds weight to this isolated piece of evidence in the form of a phrase not found in the other five manuscript versions: "...e fort fo escars d'aver" (...and he was very tight with his money).

The reason I stress this otherwise minor incident during a supposed discussion of love and patronage is that if there is any one thing within the razo texts which sets them apart from subsequent readers' interpretations of the troubadour lyrics, it is precisely the emphasis they lay on money, contractual obligations, and exchange. It is not an exaggeration to say that the razos portray a world in which all value is perceived in economic metaphors. "Give so as to receive"; "reciprocity doesn't pay"; "a good ally is like a silver coin"; "value is a matter of speculation": all of these ideas find play in the razo texts and in ways that undermine much of the inherited critical lore concerning the troubadours. If Uc de Saint Circ is indeed the author of many of these texts and was also found to have been "escars d'aver" and guilty of usury, we have perhaps reached a happy convergence of history and literary practice.

The razos have often been criticized for having invented love stories through the arbitrary assignment of *senhals* (code names) to actual ladies and the willful deformation of historical information to fit a preconceived notion of the normal course of *fin'amors*. These same critics have then quite often gone on to construct their own *romans d'amour*, identifying each senhal with a new lady, and each song with a new heartbreak. A poet's career was charted according to periods of happiness when in love with lady X, grief after their break-up, a new patron, a new lady, etc.. The songs are not, of course, chronicles of love affairs. Nor can they always be so conveniently shown to address a lady. If the razos, for their part, are guilty of having invented many a love affair (and many a lady, for that matter), we might explain this by saying either that the author was just no more successful at fixing the meaning of the songs than we have been, or that he was simply responding to the requirements of his audience. I lean toward the latter explanation, given that the razos are built around the uneasy alliance of love and recompense mentioned above. If the author constructed a story that conformed to the horizon of expectations of those used to hearing idealized tales of love, he did not do so at the expense of censoring his own and fellow troubadours' experience in making their fortunes in the fickle and highly mimetic courts where the praise song reigned. On the contrary, he has given us a first-hand view of the system of patronage within which he had to work, then added to it a veneer of romantic fiction in the form of an eventual love-tie between lady and her singer, all the while letting the final conditions (the gift of sex, land, power) of their arrangement remain as ambiguous as possible.

In the razos, as will be clear from the numerous textual notes, ladies seek troubadours at least as much as troubadours seek ladies. The author is very forthright in his assessment of their motivations: ladies want praise because it increases their renown. Thus they seek out poets. As for the poets, they come to ladies wishing to be recognized as official singers of a court, i.e. expecting compensation that involves, among other things, the public recognition that comes from singing of a highly placed patron. Contrary to much of what has been written about the level of secrecy required in the practice of 'courtly love,' both parties have everything to gain from 'going public.' The reputation of each party is initially enhanced by such an arrangement, and the liaison attracts rivals and imitators; but any expectation of a long-term business or intimate relationship is actually doomed once it hits the public arena. Such a mutually enhancing and reciprocal relation can survive only as long as the true power-brokers, the courtly public, maintain their interest. To continue to prosper in such a market, one or the other of the parties must eventually move on, or at least pretend to move on, to another target. Nothing is so fatal to prestige as inaction. The troubadour must continually renew his standing by expanding his repertoire to new fields, new ladies, new patrons; and the lady/patron must also turn her attentions to whatever new figure blazes upon the cultural scene. The poems are thus replete with references to other ladies to whom the poet almost, but not quite, succumbed; or to whom he did succumb, but for which he must now repent. The razo author, in turn, explains the poet's very necessary forays into enemy (i.e. rival) terrority as merely unfortunate incidents, failings toward the one true lady; and he raises these crises to the level of melodrama by providing us with the names of each of these rivals, the names of their powerful husbands, and their standing at court. Thus he explains the poets' ambiguous references to crimes and scandal-mongers, indecision and masochism, as the literal consequences of straying from one's lady/lover at the same time that he exposes the poet's lady as but another interested patron.

This scenario is not very convincing, especially when applied to poets who are themselves very powerful lords who nonetheless compose their songs using terms that are identical to those used by 'bourgeois' poets or knights of the lower orders. Bernart de Ventadorn, Folquet de Marseille, Peire Vidal, Raimbaut de Vaqueiras, Gaucelm Faidit, Guillem de Saint Leidier, Gui d'Uisel: these are poets whose incomes, at least in the early portion of their careers, almost certainly depended upon their maintaining good relations with a patron and renewing periodically their appeal to that patron by demonstrating their appeal to others. But what of Savaric de Malleo, Dalfi d'Alvergne, and, to some extent, even Bertran de Born? These were powerful and influential men, capable of patronizing their own poets and singers, who nonetheless composed songs in the same style as their less well-off fellow poets. They were surely not in need of renewing their credentials or praising a patron in the same way or for the same reasons that a less-noble poet might.

There are two possible explanations for this paradox, both of which are suggested by the razo author but never really proffered as full explanations. The first is that much of what remains closed to our understanding in troubadour lyrics involves the degree to which these songs are coded messages that address one or several people mentioned only in veiled references. These codes can be broken once the references are understood, but they have for so long been so badly explained that they continue to resist clarification. Take for example the senhals by which the poets address an unnamed figure in the final stanzas (*tornadas*) of the song. Stanislaw Stronski showed in his 1910 edition of the songs of Folquet de Marseille that all of the senhals used in Folquet's songs are code names for other male troubadours (e.g. Bernart de Ventadorn, Bertran de Born and Pons de Capdoill), not code names for his various lovers. Stronski presented the convincing argument that many, even most, of the troubadour songs are missives exchanged between men, on the theme of love, rather than on any specific occasion of its practice. Thus a poet could adopt a collection of tropes about love and praise, set them to certain well-known rhythmic patterns, rework this material into an original composition, and direct it to the person to whom he wished to appeal. The song could then be personalized with a final address to a patron (male or female), friend, or lady, someone who is being praised in the conventional terms of a discourse on love; or it could be just a love song that is 'dedicated' to that patron, i.e. composed in his/her honor. In addition, one can find songs, and especially sirventes, that are addressed to another poet, identified only by a senhal ('My-Magnet,' 'My-Entire-Joy,' 'Better-than-a-Lady'), and to which that other poet responds, using the same melody and/or rhyme scheme as the original. The razo author several times refers to these arrangements without ever saying that what is really at stake is a sort of literary correspondence or competition. In keeping with his desire to render the songs comprehensible and attractive to a foreign audience eager for courtly fictions, he will only state, in enigmatic terms, that a certain poet and lord called each other by the same name (e.g. Peire Vidal and Sir Baraill, the lord of Marseille, who called one another 'Rainer', razo 59), or that a certain poet, his friend, and his lover all called each other by the name 'Bertran' (Guillem de Saint Leidier, razo 51). The ramifications of such arrangements are titillating and certainly pique interest in the story, but what is often at stake is no more than poetic muscle-flexing, a game of one-upmanship in which two poets of whatever social rank match their skills at versifying and in which the subject matter is of only secondary importance.

The other explanation for wealthy lords' dabbling in poetic themes about economics and advancement through love is that the troubadour's classic techniques for ensuring his usefulness, poetic praise and public censure, are equally applicable to issues of political alliance. In Bertran de Born's calls for an active gift economy, in his condemnation of hoarding and consumption, in his public announcements of the rising and falling fortunes of the barons of Aquitaine as they switch their allegiance from one Plantagenet to another, we see the potential for the conflation of amorous and political metaphors fully exploited. Bertran's lord is his lover, and he trumpets his own usefulness as public relations expert in much the same way that Raimon de Miraval does when he tells his lady/patrons that he can make them or break them. When lords/patrons/allies disappoint him by retiring from the marketplace (i.e. the practices of gift-giving and waging war), Bertran decries their cowardice. His own well-being, both material and moral, depends upon the symbiotic relation of patron and poet, master and slave, in which he holds them. Lest any of them forget, he goads them with love songs that turn poisonous and critiques that end with a kiss. Love, he has discovered, is stronger as metaphor than as reality, and is stronger still when paired with a blade. Are we really to believe, in razo 12, that the most powerful lords of Europe (Richard-the-Lionhearted, Geoffrey of Brittany, Raimon V of Toulouse, and King Alphonse of Aragon) are all vying for the attentions of Bertran's imaginary lover, Maeuz of Montaingnac, as the razo author pretends? How much more satisfying to accept the song (80,37) on its original allegorical level rather than follow the razo author's lead. Where Bertran tells us that his lady wants neither "...Poitiers nor Toulouse, Brittany nor Saragossa" and goes on from there to castigate lazy and inactive lords, the razo author sees each of these regions as representing a potential suitor. In fact, Bertran has constructed a series of synecdoches that do indeed refer to each region's principal lord, but with political implications that allow for the literal and allegorical to apply simultaneously: "she" (being Bertran or his castle, Autafort) has no desire for the man or pretensions to his land. Bertran is only demanding that a lord exercise his function in the public sphere and keep the economy moving through gift exchange and war. The courts of Northern Italy may have had ideological reasons for insisting on reducing love to a simple battle between the sexes, and so, for that matter, might the romantic critics who popularized the courtly lyric in the nineteenth century; but should we follow them in their biased readings, even when the razos so clearly deconstruct that fiction in other, more subtle ways?

Style

In her excellent study *From Poetry to Prose in Old Provençal*, Elizabeth Wilson Poe examined the ways in which verse was transformed into prose in the razos. She showed how one can follow the literal construction of certain razos by reading the poetic text and comparing it, stanza to sentence, to the razo's prose version. It is easy to imagine an author working in this way, especially in the case of razos that were composed specifically for a particular manuscript rather than having been inherited from prior oral versions. What, however, would have been an author's precedent for doing so? Assuming that he still expected these introductions to be performed (and one need only peruse the closing formulae of many of the texts to see that), what could have led him to compose in prose rather than in verse? Prose was surely an anomaly at this time; the vidas and razos are actually among the earliest vernacular examples of extended prose writing. Some of the impetus for such a decision may, once again, have been provided by the conditions under which Uc de Saint Circ and his followers were composing.

Wlad Godzich and Jeffrey Kittay have studied the emergence of prose in the thirteenth century and the tensions inherent in the act of translating from verse. Referring to prose as to a new 'signifying practice,' they illustrate how, in the first stages, the prose text was seen merely as a supplement to the older, versified text; how it retained many of the characteristics of the verse text and often contained the verse within it (Godzich and Kittay, 1987: 7). The impetus was often to break with a tradition that accorded to verse and oral performance hegemony in the dissemination of culture. Breaking with verse and, by extension, with performance, implies a break with the institutions that guaranteed the absolute authority of those utterances. Thus, these authors found that in the thirteenth century verse itself begins to come under attack, even from within verse, for being full of lies (Godzich and Kittay, xvi). In keeping with this idea, Gabrielle Spiegel has shown that the earliest prose translations of the versified *Pseudo-Turpin* cycle, translations which initiated the practice of vernacular, prose historiography in France, were all produced within the lands of, and with the patronage of, the French-speaking Flemish aristocracy, whose autonomy was being threatened by the pretensions of the French king, Philippe Auguste (1986: 207-224). Thus, at its very inception, prose can be seen to be ideologically motivated, its role being to appropriate a body of culturally canonized founding texts from the exclusive dominion of another supposedly privileged signifying practice, namely verse, that is too closely associated with the dominant political order. In a similar way, Godzich and Kittay liken the thirteenth-century *chantefable*, *Aucassin et Nicolette*, with its alternation between prose and verse sections, to a "...cultural revolution in which these [courtly] codes are forced to acknowledge their limitations of extension, thus losing their claim to universality, and to effect internal distinctions that reveal their constructed nature and deny their claim of organicity (p. 101)."

The razos are contemporary with the texts studied by Godzich and Kittay, and as Poe and Meneghetti had already shown, participate in many of the same strategies. Stylistically, the razos give evidence of having been conceived as translations. The sentences are often long and unwieldy, made up of chains of phrases (corresponding to verses) and lists (condensed information from the songs) joined by conjunctions. Pronominal referents are often unclear, as the switch from first to third person, dictated by the use of indirect discourse, multiplies the possibilities of referents for the accumulating 'he's' and 'she's.' On the other hand, some of the difficulties encountered in other prose translations are less apt to be found in the razos since the 'stories' they are retelling are often not stories at all in the songs, but rather disjointed reminiscences, maxims, and impressions to which a story line must be added. As Poe has noted, sirventes and tensos lend themselves particularly well to prose adaptation with their format of accusation and explanation, or issue and array of opinions (1984: 50). Not surprisingly, many more of the razos treat these latter genres rather than the more well-known *canso*. The function of the razos was indeed, first and foremost, to supplement the verse texts. Only in the later manuscripts were they adapted to the point where they could be considered independent tales capable of standing on their own. Thus they mark an intermediary stage in the development of prose rather than an outright revolutionary stance. They do, nonetheless, interpret the lyrics by framing them, and once a line of verse that has been heard as part of a razo presentation is read or heard within the song, it carries a semantic charge that is difficult to shake. In this respect, the razos are successful glosses. Some editors of critical editions (see, for example, Paden et al., 72) have, in fact, refused to include them with the songs, rightly assuming that once they have been read it will be difficult to view the songs on their own merits, or to read or hear them as the enigmas they were very likely meant to be. Paradoxically, this very defect in the razos is what makes of them such an important and fascinating body of texts today. Allowing a voice from outside the lyric to circulate within it, choosing which details to accentuate, explaining references, creating connections with historical events, both monumentalizes and destroys the pretensions of the songs. On the one hand, the prose commentaries valorize the songs, elevating their prestige to the rank of 'classic' and their language to the status of 'literary.' The songs are treated as important cultural and historical artifacts, the equivalents of other cultures' foundation myths, the guarantors of the nobility of a system of courtly patronage and political autonomy that made of the Hispano-Catalan-Italiano-Provençal region a privileged locus for the elaboration of a unique system of art and ethics. On the other hand, the prose texts are inevitably disruptive, challenging by their presence the songs' pretensions to truth as records of experience. The destruction of the Southern courts and the new cultural reality of the Venetian-area courts demanded a reinterpretation of the lyric that would eliminate much of the deliberate ambiguity of the originals. The coded messages of praise and threat that characterize the lyrics were referentialized; the gender confluence in the person of the lady or patron was dissipated or ignored; and the "self-fashioning" techniques of the troubadour anxious to create from textual elements in circulation a unique persona which would bring him material or political success were reduced to the plaints of an unsatisfied lover. Uc de Saint Circ and his like managed to retain some signs of the economic base on which the whole system rested. The nature of prose itself, demanding logic through antecedence, managed nonetheless to deny the play of meaning within the song and the mutability of its form as it circulated among the courts. Understandably, this more limited view of social practice, based on stable power structures, devoted lovers, and sound economic practice must have seemed a mirror to the burgeoning Italian court, a mirror in which they may have been able to glimpse the highly attractive image of their own becoming.

Editorial Policy for this Edition

The coupling of the razos and songs in this edition is based on the conviction that though the lyrics can and should first be read on their own, it is highly instructive to read the two together, as the razo authors intended. This allows us to attempt to read as a thirteenth-century contemporary might have. It also alerts us to re-read the lyrics' amazingly complex renditions of erotic experience in terms of the razo author's deliberate dilution of that complexity; and then to re-read the lyric in terms of the razo author's perspicacious analysis of the economic ambition that underlies the whole system of fin'amors.

The presentation of the texts is based upon the Jean Boutière and A. H. Schutz 1973 critical edition of the biographies of the troubadours. Within the category of biography, Boutière and Schutz (referred to throughout the text as B/S) included both vidas (biographies) and razos (commentaries). Margarita Egan published in 1984, in this same series, a translation and introduction to the vidas. This volume is thus limited to the razos, and excludes any texts which may have fallen into the cracks between the two pseudo-genres but are included in Egan's collection. I have followed the B/S edition even as to the order of presentation so as to facilitate the reading of the texts in their original Occitan or modern

French versions. I would, moreover, encourage readers to use this volume in just that way, reading the original text and then the English translation included here. The only exceptions to this policy are found among the razos to Bertran de Born. I have included three texts not known to B/S and made other minor adjustments in order based on the grouping of Bertran's songs in Paden, Sankovitch and Stäblein's 1986 edition. The razos are all identified according to the number of the song they explicate (as given in Pillet/Carstens' *Bibliographie der Troubadors*), just as they are in B/S. In addition, I have numbered the razos according to the order in which they appear in this text. All references in the notes and commentary will be to that number.

The songs, too, are identified according to the Pillet/Carstens classification, since that is the one commonly accepted bibliography to which almost all critical editions refer. Thus, in referring to songs in notes, I give the number of the razo that accompanies them and their Pillet/Carstens number. In addition to listing at the head of the song the source from which I have worked in translating, I have also included a listing of the manuscripts in which the various versions of the song can be found. I have done so both to indicate the 'popularity' of the song (for those wishing to examine why some songs and not others may have been accorded a razo in a given manuscript) and to provide a listing for those wishing to go directly to the manuscript sources to work on the original Occitan text. I regret that the original text is not included and expect that this archival information will facilitate the task of finding edited or unedited versions of the songs to read along with these translations. I have included only those manuscripts which contain at least two full stanzas of a song, as anything less would be of little use. More complete lists may be found in Pillet/Carstens and in any of the critical editions for the individual poets.

In general, I have translated all known stanzas of the song that is mentioned in the razo. In some rare cases where it is clear that the razo author did not have before him some of the stanzas included in the critical edition, I have dropped those stanzas and indicated in notes where they could be found. The main focus of this edition is to compare what the razo author may reasonably have known about a song, based presumably upon the version from which he was working, and what he then said about it. In the case of variant texts, I have generally followed the critical editors' texts, except in cases where I could see that a version of the song contained in a manuscript that also contains the razo gave a different reading for the line. In those cases, I have indicated in notes that I was

xxxiii

diverging from the critical edition and why. It is, unfortunately, extremely difficult to trace the passage of songs and razos from one manuscript to another or to find clear links between manuscripts. In comparing the manuscripts in which the razo text is found with the manuscripts in which the song is found, one is immediately struck by the fact that it often happens that a razo for a particular song is included in a manuscript which does not contain that song. Take, for example, Pons de Capdoill's song 375, 18. The razo is contained in four manuscripts: E, P, R and Sg. The song is contained in none of those manuscripts. The same thing can be noted for songs corresponding to many of the razos in manuscripts N^2, P, and R. This proves that those compiling these manuscripts (including most probably Uc de Saint Circ, see above) were either writing extended variations on a previously known razo and recognized that the story would now be able to stand on its own, independent of the song (as in manuscripts P and R); or that they were simply compiling every known version of a razo even if they did not have access to the song. Equally puzzling is the fact that the placement of the razo in the manuscript sometimes belies its stated relation to the vida or the song, whether or not the song is included. Razo 64, for example, which accompanies Raimon de Miraval's songs 406: 4, 27, 38 and Peire Vidal's song 364, 21, tells us: "You have certainly heard about Raimon de Miraval, who he was and where he came from, in the razo that is written before his songs..." In fact, in manuscripts E, P and R, the only ones that contain this razo, the vida (here called a razo) to which the razo refers does not precede the songs but is grouped with all other razos in a separate section of the manuscript. Again, this would imply that the scribe is copying from another document from which he has culled the razo texts and then reproduced them together.

I have left all proper names within the razo texts in the form in which they were given in the original Old Occitan in the B/S critical edition and changed only commonly known place names to their modern equivalents. I have also modernized names of places and people in the songs when that makes it clearer to whom they refer. I have tried to keep footnotes to a minimum yet still point out the more interesting features of each razo, offer alternate translations, relate the texts to others within the collection, and identify the references when possible. In cases where a reference to a person or site that is not explained within the text is also left unexplained in the notes it is because neither the editor of the critical edition nor I have been able to shed any light on the identification.

The Translations

The first thing that must be stressed about the translations is that there has been no attempt here to do 'literary' translations. These could more appropriately be termed 'working' translations whose purpose is not to beautify or simplify. I have tried to stay very close to the phrasing of the original text, even when that means that the phrasing in English sounds odd or convoluted. The original texts *are*, in many ways, odd and convoluted, and I see no reason to mask that with a smooth and colloquial English translation. It should therefore be understood that these translations are not intended in any way to replace the many fine translations of the songs that already exist. On the contrary, I would urge readers to seek out other translations listed in the introductory segment to each individual song. As for the razos, this is the only available English translation of the collection.

One could reasonably question the utility of translating those songs in the collection for which there exist published translations. My reasons can be summarized as follows: first, I wanted to provide a version of each song in numbered verse so as to facilitate the task of future scholars, unable to work exclusively in Old Occitan or French, who wish to compare my translations to the original text; second, I wanted to give some uniformity to the translations so that those which were done more with English poetics in mind would not stand out from among my more unadorned versions; and third, I wanted to do translations based on having first read the razo so as to stress elements in the songs that seemed significant enough to the razo author to mention them in his prose text. I therefore tend to translate more literally than many before me the economic language and metaphors that underlie much of the poets' dealings with the lady/patron. This was done consciously, even at the risk of destroying some of the more ethereal and idealistic passages, so as to open to examination the question of economics and poetry and to explain the razos' emphasis on ladies' and poets' quests for that elusive goal, fame.

I would therefore urge interested readers to return to other editors' work and the excellent anthologies that exist, especially those of Paul Blackburn, Meg Bogin, Anthony Bonner, Frederick Goldin, Alan Press, and James J. Wilhelm. In the case of individual editors, I am highly indebted to all of them for their editorial and investigative skills, and especially to James J. Wilhelm, Ruth Verity Sharman, and Joseph Linskill. I must mention, in particular, the model edition of the songs of

Bertran de Born published in 1986 by William D. Paden, Jr., Tilde Sankovitch and Patricia Harris Stäblein. The clarity and comprehensiveness of this edition, as well as its wonderfully literal translations, were of enormous help to me in dealing with the large section on Bertran de Born, and in innumerable other instances relating to other poets. I hope that the abundant notes referring the reader to their edition give some idea of the esteem in which I hold this invaluable contribution to troubadour studies.

Within the titles and footnotes I have standardized proper names, following the B/S critical edition, and have done the same for place names within the texts that are better known and recognized under an English equivalent. Within the razo texts I have followed the B/S edition in reproducing the myriad forms used, sometimes within the same text, to represent the spelling of proper names.

Glossary of Old Provençal terms:

cantar - to sing or perform.
canso - a lyric composition dealing with love.
caras rimas - complicated and unusual rhyme schemes and vocabulary.
cobla - a stanza. In the plural it refers to stanzas that taken together do not constitute an oeuvre by one author on one theme.
dire - to recite or sing or begin to sing a song.
entendre - to turn one's attentions to, keep in one's thoughts, aspire towards, court, or understand and explicate a song.
escondich - a lyric composition offering a defense of, or excuse for, one's actions.
estampida - a lyric composition set to dance music.
fin'amor - fine, true or pure love; also a code of behavior for the fictional lover/narrator and a frame within which a court poet was expected to compose.
gelos - a term that usually applies to a jealous husband. It is little used in the razos and songs in this volume. A term of ridicule or contempt (see razo 80a and b to Guillem de Cabestaing for an example).
joc partit - a lyric composition in which one speaker presents a point of view on an issue and another poet, or several others, respond with alternating stanzas.
joglar - one who performs lyric compositions before groups.
koïne - the literary language in which the troubadour songs were composed (See Zufferey, 312).
mala canso - a song in which a lady or patron is castigated for unseemly behavior.
merce - pity, forgiveness, or perhaps a token or sign of affection.
midons - I have translated this term of address as My-Lord throughout the text, treating it as a senhal. In doing so, I retain its feudal connotations so as to emphasize the gender conflation.

partimen - see above under: joc partit.
pastorela - a type of lyric composition which chronicles the attempted seduction of a young shepherdess by a man of higher social rank who comes upon her in a bucolic setting.
planh - a song of mourning in which a poet decries the death of public figure and chronicles his own grief.
pro - benefit, good, profit, usefulness, what the poet seeks from the lady/patron.
razo - a short prose text which introduces a song.
salutz - a song of greeting, addressed to a lady.
senhal - a code name by which a poet refers to other poets, patrons and ladies. Serves as a sort of poetic signature.
sirventes - a song which treats a subject other than love, such as satire, ridicule, criticism, or encitement to war.
tenso - a lyric dialogue in which one poet responds to another, either on a particular subject or more generally in order to comment on the the other's reputation, problems etc.
tornada - the final stanza or stanzas of a song in which a poet addresses his song to someone, praises someone, evaluates his song, or comments on the message of the song.
trobador - a male poet and, perhaps, (though not necessarily) a singer.
trobairitz - a female poet.
vers - a line of verse or an early type of lyric composition that is said to have been replaced by the canso.
vida - a short prose introductory text that gives biographical data on a poet.

Manuscripts cited

A: Biblioteca Apostolica Vaticana, lat. 5232.
B: Paris, Bibliothèque Nationale, fr. 1592.
C: Paris, Bibliothèque Nationale, fr. 856.
D: Modena, Biblioteca Nazionale Estense, R, 4, 4.
D^a: *Ibid.*, ff. 153-211.
D^c: *Ibid.*, ff. 243-60.
E: Paris, Bibliothèque Nationale, fr. 1749.
F: Rome, Biblioteca Apostolica Vaticana, Chigiani, L. IV. 106.
F^a: Florence, Biblioteca Riccardiana, 2981.
Frammento Romegialli: See Pio Rajna, "Bertran de Born nelle bricciche di un canzoniere provenzale," *Romania* 50 (1924): 233-46.
G: Milan, Biblioteca Ambrosiana, R. 71 sup.
H: Rome, Biblioteca Apostolica Vaticana, lat. 3207.
I: Paris, Bibliothèque Nationale, fr. 854.
J: Florence, Biblioteca Nazionale Centrale, Conventi Soppressi, F. IV, 776.
K: Paris, Bibliothèque Nationale, fr. 12473.
L: Rome, Biblioteca Apostolica Vaticana, lat. 3206.
M: Paris, Bibliothèque Nationale, fr. 12474.
Mh: See: Silvio Pellegrini, "Frammento inedito di canzoniere provenzale," *Studi Mediolatini e Volgari* 15-16 (1968): 89-99.
N: New York, Pierpont Morgan Library, M 819.
N^2: Berlin, Kgl. Staatsbibl., cod. Phillipps 1910.
O: Rome, Biblioteca Apostolica Vaticana, lat. 3208.
P: Florence, Biblioteca Mediceo-Laurenziana, Plut. XLI, cod. 42.
Q: Florence, Biblioteca Riccardiana, 2909.
R: Paris, Bibliothèque Nationale, fr. 22543.
Sg: Barcelona, Biblioteca Central de la Diputación Provincial de Barcelona, 146.

T: Paris, Bibliothèque Nationale, fr. 15211.
U: Florence, Biblioteca Mediceo-laurenziana, Plut. XLI, cod. 43.
V: Venice, Biblioteca Nazionale Marciana, app. cod. XI.
Ve. Ag.: Barcelona, Biblioteca de l'Institut d'Estudis Catalans.
W: Paris, Bibliothèque Nationale, fr. 844.
X: Paris, Bibliothèque Nationale, fr. 20050.

a: Florence, Biblioteca Riccardiana, 2814 (listed as "a" in Jeanroy).
a^1: Modena, Biblioteca Nazionale Estense, Càmpori, y. N. 8.4; 11, 112, 13 (listed as a^2 in Jeanroy).
b^1: Rome, Biblioteca Apostolica Vaticana, Barberiniani lat. 4087, folios 1-6.
b^2: *Ibid.*, folios 9-53.
c: Florence, Biblioteca Mediceo-laurenziana, Plut. XC inf. cod. 26.
d: Modena, Biblioteca Nazionale Estense, appendix to D, ff. 262-346.
e: Rome, Biblioteca Apostolica Vaticana, Barberiani lat. 3965.
f: Paris, Bibliothèque Nationale, fr. 12472.
m*: The Hague, Bibl. Roy., 135 F 28.
p: Perpignan, Bibliothèque Municipale, 128.
v: Barcelona, Biblioteca de Catalunya, 7.

*Crespo fragments for Bertran de Born: The Hague, Koninklijke Bibliotheek, 135 F 28, fragments 1-8.

Note the following differences under François Zufferey's classification:

The Romegialli fragment (Frammento Romegialli) is listed as y (under "Fragments"): / y: Sondrio, Arch. St., Romegialli.

N^2 is listed as d (under "Copies en papier de chansonniers perdus"): / d: Berlin, Staatsbibliotek, Phillipps 1910.

Sg is listed as Z (under "Chansonniers en parchemin"): / Z: Barcelona, Bibl. Cat., 146.

Select Bibliography

I. Major Editions

Arnaut de Mareuil, *Les poésies lyriques du troubadour A. de M.* Ed. R.C. Johnston. Paris: Droz, 1935.

Arnaut Daniel. *The Poetry of A. D.* Ed., trans. James J. Wilhelm. Garland Library of Medieval Literature, vol. 3, series A. New York: Garland, 1981.

Bernart de Ventadorn. *The Songs of B. de V.* Eds. Stephen G. Nichols, Jr. and John A. Galm. Chapel Hill: University of North Carolina Press, 1962.

_____. *B. de V., seine lieder mit einleitung und glossar.* Ed. Carl Appel. Halle: Niemeyer, 1915.

_____, *Troubadour du XIIe siècle: chansons d'amour.* Ed. Moshé Lazar. Paris: Klincksieck, 1966.

Bertran de Born. *B. de B., sein leben und seine werke.* Ed. Albert Stimming. Halle: Niemeyer, 1913. Rpt. Geneva: Slatkine, 1975.

_____. *Bertran de Born. L'amour et la guerre.* Ed., trans. Gérard Gouiran. Aix-en-Provence: Publications de l'Université d'Aix-en-Provence, 1985.

_____. *The Poems of the Troubadour B. de B.* Eds. William D. Paden, Jr., Tilde Sankovitch, Patricia H. Stäblein. Berkeley, Los Angeles, London: University of California Press, 1986.

Boutière, Jean and Schutz, A.H. *Biographies des troubadours: textes provençaux des XIIIe et XIVe siècles.* 2nd ed., with I. M. Cluzel. Paris: Nizet, 1973.

B/S. See above: Boutiere/Schutz.

Cercamon and Jaufré Rudel. *The Poetry of C. and J. R.* Ed., trans. G. Wolf and R. Rosenstein. Garland Library of Medieval Literature, Series A, vol. 5. New York: Garland, 1983.

Chabaneau, Camille. *Les biographies des troubadours en langue provençale.* Toulouse: 1885.

Crespo, Roberto. "Bertrand de Born nei frammenti di un canzoniere provenzale." *Studi Medievali* 3rd series, 24 (1983): 749-790.

Dalfi d'Alvergne. *A Critical Edition of the Poems of Dalfin d'Alvernhe.* Ed. Emmert M. Brackney. Dissertation, University of Minnesota, 1937.

_____. *La cour littéraire de Dalfi d'Alvernhe des XIIe et XIIIe siècles.* François de Labareyre. Clermond-Ferrand: Imp. G. Delaunay, 1976.

Favati, Guido. *Le biografie trovadoriche, testi provenzali dei secc. XIIIe et XIVe.* Bologna: Palmaverde, 1961.

Folquet de Marseille. *Le troubadour F. de M.* Ed. S. Stronski. Cracovie: Edition du Fonds Oslawski, 1910.

Gaucelm Faidit, *Les poèmes de G. F.* Ed. Jean Mouzat. Paris: Nizet, 1965.

Gui d'Uisel. *Les poésies des quatre troubadours d'Ussel.* Ed. Jean Audiau. Paris: Delagrave, 1922.

Guillem de Balaun. "Le Troubadour G. de B." Ed. Jean Boutière. *Annales du Midi* 48: 228.

Guillem de Cabestanh. *Les chansons de G. de C.* Ed. Arthur Långfors. Paris: Champion, 1924.

Guillem de Saint Leidier. *Les poésies de G. de S.-L.* Ed. Aimo Sakari. Helsinki: Société Philologique, 1956.

Guiraut de Borneilh, *Sämtliche lieder des trobadors G. de B.* Ed. Adolf Kolsten. 2 vols. Halle: Niemeyer, 1910-1935.

_____. *The Cansos and Sirventes of the Troubadour Giraut de B.: A Critical Edition.* Ed. Ruth Verity Sharman. Cambridge: Cambridge University Press, 1989.

Lanfranc Cigala, *Il canzoniere di L.C.* Ed. Francesco Branciforti. Biblioteca dell' Archivum Romanicum, 37. Florence: 1954.

Peire Vidal. *Poesie.* Ed. D'Arco Silvio Avalle. 2 vols. Milano: Riccardo Ricciardi, 1960.

_____. *Les poésies de.* Ed. Joseph Anglade. Paris: Champion, 1923.

Pons de Capdoill. *Leben und werke des trobadors P. de C.* Ed. Max von Napolski. Halle: Niemeyer, 1879.

Raimbaut de Vaqueiras. *The Poems of the Troubadour R. de V.* Ed. Joseph Linskill. the Hague: Mouton & Co., 1964.

Raimon Jordan, *Le troubadour R. J., vicomte de Saint-Antonin.* Ed. Hilding Kjellman. Upsala: Almquist & Wiksells, 1922.

Raimon de Miraval. *La vie et l'oeuvre du troubadour R. de M.: étude sur la littérature et la société méridionales à la veille de la guerre des Albigeois.* Ed. Paul Andraud. Paris: E. Bouillon, 1902.

_____. *Les poésies du troubadour R. de M.* Ed. Leslie L. Topsfield. Paris: Nizet, 1971.

_____. *The Cansos of R. de M.* Ed. Margaret Louise Switten. Cambridge, Ma.: The Medieval Academy of America, 1985.

Richart de Berbezill. *Rigaut de Berbezilh, Le canzoni.* Ed. Mauro Braccini. Firenze: Leo S. Olschki, 1960.

_____, *R. de B., Liriche.* Ed. A. Varvaro. Bari: Biblioteca di Filologia Romana, 1960.

Savaric de Malleo, *S. de Mauléon, Baron et Troubadour.* Ed. H. J. Chaytor. Cambridge, England: 1939.

Schultz-Gora, Oskar. *Die provenzalischen Dichterinnen, Biographieen und Texte.* Leipzig: G. Fock, 1888.

Uc de Saint Circ. *Les poésies de U. de S.C.* Eds. A. Jeanroy and J.J. Salverda de Grave. Toulouse: Edouard Privat, 1913.

II. English Translations and Anthologies

Anglade, Joseph. *Anthologie des troubadours.* Paris: E. Boccard, 1953.

Audiau, Jean and Lavaud, René. *Nouvelle anthologie des troubadours.* Paris: Delagrave, 1928.

Bartholomeis, Vincenzo de. *Poesie provenzale storiche relative all'Italia.* 2 vols. Rome: Tipografia del Senato, 1931.

Bec, Pierre. *Nouvelle anthologie de la lyrique occitane du moyen-âge.* 2nd ed. Avignon: Editions Aubanel, 1970.

_____. *Burlesque et obscenité chez les troubadours.* Paris: Stock/Moyen-Age, 1984.

Bergin, Thomas G., and Hill, R., et al. *Anthology of the Provençal troubadours.* 2 vols. 2nd. rev. ed. New Haven: Yale University Press, 1973.

Bertoni, G. *I trovatori d'Italia.* Modena: U. Orlandini, 1915.

Blackburn, Paul. *Proensa, Anthology of Troubadour Verse.* Berkeley, Los Angeles and London: University of California Press, 1978.

Bogin, Meg. *The Women Troubadours*. New York, London: Paddington Press, Ltd., 1976.

Bonner, Anthony. *Songs of the Troubadours*. New York: Shocken, 1972.

Goldin, Frederick. *Lyrics of the Troubadours and Trouvères*. New York: Doubleday, 1973.

Hamlin, Frank R.; Ricketts, Peter T.; and Hathaway, John. *Introduction à l'étude de l'ancien provençal*. Geneva: Droz, 1967.

Jeanroy, Alfred. *Anthologie des troubadours*, XII-XIIIe siècles. Paris: Renaissance du livre, 1927.

Kolsen, A. *Dichtungen der trobadors*. Halle: Niemeyer, 1916-1919. Rpt. Geneva: Slatkine Reprints, 1980.

Lindsay, Jack. *The Troubadours and Their World of the Twelth and Thirteenth Centuries*. London: Frederick Müller, 1976.

Nelli, René and Lavaud, René. *Les troubadours*. Paris: Bibliothèque Européenne, Desclée de Brouwer, 1966.

Press, Alan. *Anthology of Troubadour Lyric Poetry*. Edinburgh: Edinburgh University Press, 1971.

Raynouard, François-Just-Marie. *Choix des poésies originales des troubadours*. 6 vols. Paris: F. Didot, 1816-1821. Rpt. Geneva: Slatkine Reprints, 1982.

Riquier, Martín de. *Los trovadores. Historia literaria y textos*. 2 vols. Barcelona: Editorial Planeta, 1975.

Rochegude, Henri-Pascal. *Le parnasse occitanien*. Toulouse: Benichet Cadet, 1819. rpt. Geneva: Slatkine Reprints, 1977.

Smythe, Barbara. *Trobador Poets, Selections from the Poems of Eight Trobadors*. London: Chatto & Windus, 1929.

Topsfield, Leslie. *Troubadours and Love*. Cambridge: Cambridge University Press, 1975.

Wilhelm, James J. *Seven Troubadours, the Creators of Modern Verse*. University Park: Pennsylvania State University Press, 1970.

III. Critical Writings and Related Works

Akehurst, F. R. P. "The Troubadours as Intellectuals." *Mosaic* 8 (2), (1975): 120-134.

Andraud, Paul. See Major Editions above, under: Raimon de Miraval.

Andreas Capellanus. *The Art of Courtly Love by André le Chapelain*. Intro., trans. J.J. Parry. New York: Columbia University Press, 1941.

Anglade, Joseph. *Las leys d'amor*. 4 vols. Toulouse: Privat, 1919-1920.

_____. "Les Miniatures des chansonniers Provençaux." *Romania* 50 (1924): 593-604.

_____. *Grammaire de l'ancien provençal*. Paris: C. Klincksieck, 1921.

Appel, Carl. See Major Editions above, under: Bernart de Ventadorn.

Audiau, Jean. See Major Editions above, under: Gui d'Uissel.

Auerbach, Erich. *Literary Language and Its Public in Late Antiquity and in the Middle Ages*. Trans. Ralph Manheim. New York: Pantheon Books, 1965.

Avalle, D'Arco Silvio. *La letteratura medievale in lingua d'oc nella sua tradizione manoscritta*. Torino: Einaudi, 1961.

_____. See Major Editions above, under: Peire Vidal.

Bakhtin, M.M. *The Dialogic Imagination*. Ed. Michael Holquist. Trans. M. Holquist and Caryl Emerson. Austin: University of Texas Press, 1981.

Bloch, R. Howard. *Medieval French Literature and Law*. Berkeley, Los Angeles and London: University of California Press, 1977.

_____. "Medieval Misogyny."*Representations* 20, (Fall 1987):1-24.

Boase, Roger. *The Origin and Meaning of Courtly Love: A Critical Study of European Scholarship*. Manchester: Manchester University Press, 1977.

Boccaccio, Giovanni. *Il decamerone. Tutte le opere de G. Boccaccio*, IV. Ed. Vittore Branca. Milano: Mondadori, 1967.

Boswell, John. *Christianity, Social Tolerance and Homosexuality*. Chicago: University of Chicago Press, 1980.

Boutière, Jean. "Les 3e personnes du singulier en -a des 'Biographies' des Troubadours." *Actes et Mémoires du IIIe Congrès International de Langue et Littérature d'Oc*. Bordeaux: 1961: 1-11.

_____. "Les italianismes des 'Biographies' des troubadours." *Mélanges de littérature comparée et de philologie offerts à M. Brahmer*. Eds. C.V. Aubrun et al. Warsaw: PWN-Editions Scientifiques de Pologne, 1967: 93-107.

_____. "Quelques observations sur le texte des vidas et des razos dans les chansonniers provençaux AB et IK." *French and Provençal Lexicography: Essays Presented to Honor A.H. Schutz*. Eds. Urban T. Holmes and K.R. Scholberg. Columbus: Ohio State University Press, 1964: 125-139.

_____. See Major Editions above, under: Guillem de Balaun.

Braccini, Mauro. See Major Editions above, under: Riguat de Berbezilh.

Brackney, Emmert. See Major Editions above, under: Dalfin d'Alvernhe.

Branciforti, Francesco. See Major Editions above, under: Lanfranc Cigala.

Briffault, Robert. *The Troubadours*. Bloomington: University of Indiana Press, 1965.

_____. *Les troubadours et le sentiment romanesque.* Paris: Les Editions du Chêne, 1945.

Brundage, James A. *Richard Lion Heart.* New York: Scribner's, 1974.

Brunel, Clovis. *Bibliographie des manuscrits littéraires en ancien provençal.* Paris: Droz, 1935.

_____. "Almois de Châteauneuf et Iseut de Chapieu."*Annales du Midi, revue archéologique, historique* 28 (1916): 462-471.

Burgwinkle, William E. "From Commentary to Tale: Biography, Boccaccio and Beyond." *Literary History, Narrative, and Culture. Literary Studies East and West,* vol. 2. Honolulu: University of Hawaii Press, 1989.

Burns, E. Jane. "The Man Behind the Lady in Troubadour Lyric." *Romance Notes* 25 (1985): 254-270.

Camproux, Charles. *Le joy d'amor des troubadours.* Montpellier: Causse et Castelnau, 1965.

Cazelles, Brigitte. "Mots à vendre, corps à prendre, et les troubadours d'Aquitaine." *Stanford French Review* 7 (1983): 27-36.

_____. "Souvenez-vous." *Poétique* 60 (Nov. 1984): 395-410.

Chambers, Frank. "Imitation of Form in the Old Provençal Lyric." *Romance Philology* 6 (1952-53): 104-120.

_____. *Proper Names in the Lyrics of the Troubadours.* University of North Carolina Studies in the Romance Languages and Literatures, no. 113. Chapel Hill: University of North Carolina Press, 1971.

Chaytor, H. J. *From Script to Print.* Cambridge: Cambridge University Press, 1945; Rpt. 1977.

_____. See Major Editions above, under: Savaric de Mauléon.

Chickering, Howell and Switten, Margaret. *The Medieval Lyric.* 3 vols. South Hadley, Mass.: Mount Holyoke College, 1988.

Cluzel, Irenée. "La culture genérale d'un troubadour du XIIIe siècle." *Mélanges de linguistique romane et de philologie médiévale offerts à Maurice Delbouille*. 2 vols. Gembloux: J. Duculot: 91-104.

Crescini, Vincenzo. "Le *razos* provenzali e le prose della *Vita nuova*." *Giornale storico della letteratura italiana* 32 (1898): 463-64.

Cropp, Glynnis M. *Le vocabulaire courtois des troubadours de l'époque classique*. Geneve: Droz, 1975.

Dante [Alighieri]. *The Divine Comedy*. Trans., Commentary by Charles S. Singleton. 3 vols. Princeton: Princeton University Press, 1970-75.

_____. *Literary Criticism of*. Ed., trans. Robert Haller. Lincoln, Nebraska: University of Nebraska Press, 1973.

_____. *Dante in Hell: the Volgare Eloquentia*. Intro., trans. Warman Welliver. Ravenna: Longo Editore, 1981.

_____. *La vita nuova*. Intro., trans. Barbara Reynolds. New York: Penguin Books, 1969.

Delbouille, Maurice. *Le roman du Châtelain de Coucy et de la Dame de Fayel*. Paris: Anciens Textes Français, 1936.

Del Monte, A. Ed. *Conti di antichi cavalieri*. Milano: Cisalpino, 1972.

D'Herde-Heiliger, Marcelle. *Répertoire des traductions des oeuvres lyriques des troubadours des XIe au XIIIe siècles*. Béziers: CIDO and Liège: IPERB, 1985.

Dragonetti, Roger. *Le gai savoir dans la rhétorique courtoise*. Paris: Seuil, 1982.

Dronke, Peter. *Medieval Latin and the Rise of European Love Lyric*. 2 vols. Oxford: The Clarendon Press, 1965.

Duby, Georges. "Au XIIe siècle: les 'jeunes' dans la société aristocratique." *Annales* 19 (1964): 835-846.

_____. *Les trois ordres: ou, l'imaginaire du féodalisme.* Paris: Gallimard, 1978.

_____. *The Early Growth of the European Economy.* Trans. H. B. Clarke. Ithaca: Cornell University Press, 1978.

_____. *Guillaume le Maréchal ou le meilleur chevalier du monde.* Paris: Fayard, 1984.

Egan, Margarita. *The Vidas of the Troubadours.* Garland Library of Medieval Literature, Series B, vol. 6. New York: Garland, 1984.

_____. "'Razo' and 'Novella': A Case Study in Narrative Forms." *Medioevo Romanzo* 6 (1979): 302-314.

_____. "Commentary, Vitae Poetae and Vida: Latin and Old Provençal 'Lives of Poets.'" *Romance Philology* 37 (1983-84): 36-48.

Ehnert, Rolf. "Les amours politiques de Bertran de Born." *Neuphilologische Mitteilungen* 77 (1976): 128-43.

Faral, E. *Les arts poétiques du XIIe et du XIIIe siècles.* Paris: Champion, 1958.

_____. "La Pastourelle." *Romania*, 49 (1923): 204-259.

Folena, G. "Tradizione e cultura trobadorica nelle corti e nelle città venete." in *Storia della cultura veneta*, I. Vicenza: N. Pozza, 1976: 453-562.

Foucault, Michel. *La volonté de savoir. Histoire de la sexualite* 1. Paris: Gallimard, 1976.

_____. "On the Geneology of Ethics." *Foucault Reader.* Ed. Paul Rabinow. New York: Pantheon Books, 1984.

Frank, István. *Répertoire métrique de la poésie des troubadours.* 2 vols. Paris: Champion, 1953-57.

Gégou, Fabienne, "*Trobairitz* et amorces romanesques dans les 'Biographies' des troubadours." *Studia Occitanica in memoriam Paul*

Remy. Vol. 2. Kalamazoo, Michigan: Medieval Institute Publications, 1986: 43-51.

Girard, René. *Mensonge romantique et verité romanesque.* Paris: Editions Bernard Grasset, 1961.

Godzich, Wlad and Kittay, Jeffrey. *The Emergence of Prose: an essay in prosaics.* Minneapolis: University of Minnesota Press, 1987.

Goldin, Frederick. *The Mirror of Narcissus in the Courtly Love Lyric.* Ithaca: Cornell University Press, 1967.

_____. "The Array of Perspectives in the Early Courtly Love Lyric." *In Pursuit of Perfection.* Eds. J. Ferrante and G. Economou. Port Washington, N.Y.: Kennikat Press, 1975.

Gravdal, Kathryn. "Camouflaging Rape: The Rhetoric of Sexual Violence in the Medieval Pastourelle." *Romanic Review* 76 (1985): 361-373.

Greenblatt, Stephen. *Renaissance Self-Fashioning. From More to Shakespeare.* Chicago: Univ. Chicago Press, 1980.

Guiette, Robert. "D'une poésie formelle en France au Moyen Age." *Revue des sciences humaines* (1949): 61-68.

Guillaume de Tudèle. *La chanson de la croisade contre les Albigeois.* Ed. Paul Meyer. Publications de la société de l'histoire de France. Paris: Renouard, 1875-1879.

Hauvette, Henri. "La 39ème nouvelle du décameron et la légende du coeur mangé." *Romania* 16 (1912): 184-205.

Hodgett, Gerald A. J. *A Social and Economic History of Medieval Europe.* London: Methuen, 1972.

Huchet, Jean-Charles. *L'amour discourtois.* Toulouse: Editions Privat, 1987.

Huygens, R. B. C. *Accessus ad auctores. Bernard d'Utrecht. Conrad d'Hirsau: dialogus super auctores.* Leiden: 1970.

Jacquart, Danielle and Thomasset, Claude. *Sexualité et savoir médical au moyen-âge*. Paris: Presses Universitaires de France, 1985.

Jaussens, Jan. "Sur l'origine des qualifications dépréciatives dans les Vidas."*Cultura Neolatina* 44 (1988): 49-83.

Jauss, Hans-Robert. "Genres and Medieval Literature." *Toward an Aesthetic of Reception*. Trans. T. Bahti., intro. Paul de Man. Theory and History of Literature 2. Minneapolis: Univ. of Minnesota Press, 1982.

_____. "The Alterity and Modernity of Medieval Literature." *New Literary History* 10 (1979): 185.

Jeanroy, Alfred. *Bibliographie sommaire des chansonniers provençaux*. Paris: Champion, 1966.

_____. *La poésie lyrique des troubadours*. 2 vols. Toulouse: Edouard Privat, Editeur, 1934.

_____. See Major Editions above, under: Uc de Saint-Circ.

Jensen, Frede. "Provençal *Cor* and *Cors*: A Flexional Dilemma." *Romance Philology* 28 (1974): 27-31.

Johnston, R. C. see Major Editions above, under: Arnaut de Mareuil.

Kendrick, Laura. *The Game of Love: Troubadour Wordplay*. Berkeley, Los Angeles, London: University of California Press, 1988.

Kjellman, Hilding. See Major Editions above, under: Raimon Jordan.

Köhler, Erich. "Observations historiques et sociologiques sur la poésie des troubadours."*Cahiers de civilisation médiévale* 7 (1964): 27-47.

_____. *Sociologia della fin'amor. Saggi trobadorici*. Padoua: Mario Mancini, 1976.

Kolsen, Adolph. See Major Editions above, under: Guiraut de Borneilh.

Kristeva, Julia. *Histoires d'amour*. Paris: Editions Denoël, 1983.

Labareyre, François de. See Major Editions above, under: Dalfi d'Alvernhe.

Lacan, Jacques. *Feminine Sexuality. Jacques Lacan et l'école Freudienne*. Ed. Juliette Mitchell and Jacqueline Rose. Trans. Jacqueline Rose. London: McMillan, 1982.

Längfors, Arthur. See Major Editions above, under: Guillem de Cabestanh.

Lazar, Moshe. *Amour courtois et "fin'amors" dans la littérature du XIIe.* Paris: Klincksieck, 1964.

LeGoff, Jacques and Nora, Pierre. *Faire de l'histoire*. 3 vols. Paris: Gallimard, 1974.

Lejeune, Rita. "Ce qu'il faut croire des 'Biographies' provençales: La Louve de Pennautier." *Le Moyen Age*, 69 (1939): 233-249.

_____. "Le Personnage d'Ignaure dans la poésie des troubadours." *Bulletin de l'Académie Royale de langue et de littérature françaises de Belgique*. Brussels: 1939.

_____. *Littérature et société occitane au moyen-âge*. Liège: 1979.

Levy, Emil. *Petit dictionnaire provençal-français*. 5th ed. Heidelberg: C. Winter, 1973.

Levy, Emil and Carl Appel. *Provenzalisches Supplement-Wörterbuch*. 8 vols. Leipzig: Reisland, 1894-1924.

Lewent, Kurt. "The Troubadours and the Romance of Jaufre." *Modern Philology* XLIII, (1946): 153-169.

Linskill, Joseph. See Major Editions above, under: Raimbaut de Vaqueiras.

Longnon, Auguste. *Atlas historique de la France*. Paris: Hachette, 1885.

Makin, Peter. *Provence and Pound*. Berkeley, Los Angeles, London: University of California Press, 1987.

Marchello-Nizia, Christiane. "Amour courtois, société masculine et figures du pouvoir." *Annales* 36 (2) (1981): 969-982.

Marrou, Henri I. *Les troubadours*. Paris: Seuil, 1971.

Matzke, J.E. "The Legend of the Eaten Heart." *Modern Language Notes* 26 (1911): 1-8.

McPeek, Glynn S. "Kalenda Maia: A Study in Form." *Medieval Studies in Honor of R. W. Linker*. Eds. B. Dutton et al. Valencia: Castalia, 1973.

Méjean, Suzanne. *La Chanson satirique provençale au moyen-âge: choix de textes*. Paris: Nizet, 1971.

Meneghetti, Maria Luisa. *Il pubblico dei trovatori*. Modena: Mucchi, 1984.

Menocal, Maria Rosa. *The Arabic Role in Medieval Literary History: A Forgotten Heritage*. Philadelphia: University of Pennsylvania Press, 1987.

Mermier, Guy. "Interplay in the Love Poetry of the Troubadours, Its Aspects and Possible Meaning: A Socio-Sexological Interpretation." *Studies in Medieval Culture* 8 (1976): 31-48.

Monteverdi, Angelo. "Che cosa è il 'Novellino'?" *Studi e saggi sulla letteratura italiana dei primi secoli*. Milan-Naples: 1954.

Mouzat, Jean. See Major Editions above, under: Gaucelm Faidit.

Murphy, James J. *Rhetoric in the Middle Ages*. Berkeley, Los Angeles: University of California Press, 1974.

_____. *Three Medieval Rhetorical Arts*. Berkeley, Los Angeles: University of California Press, 1971.

Napolski, Max Von. See Major Editions above, under : Pons de Capdoill.

Nelli, René. *L'érotique des troubadours*. Toulouse: Edouard Privat, 1963.

_____. *Les cathares*. Paris: Marabout/culture, art, loisirs, 1972.

_____. *Le roman du troubadour Raimon de Miraval*. Paris: Albin Michel, 1986.

Nichols, Stephen G. "Toward an Aesthetic of the Provençal Canso." *Disciplines of Criticism*. Eds. P. Demetz, T. Greene, L. Nelson, Jr. New Haven: Yale Univ. Press, 1968.

_____. "Canso-Conso: Structures of Parodic Humor in Three Songs of Guilhem IX." *L'Esprit Créateur* 16 (1976): 16-29.

_____. See Major Editions above, under: Bernart de Ventadorn.

Il Novellino. Ed. Guido Favati. Genova: Fratelli Bozzi, 1970.

Nykl, A. R. *Hispano-Arabic Poetry and its Relations with the Old Provençal Troubadours*. Baltimore: J. H. Furst, 1946.

O'Donoghue, Bernard. *The Courtly Love Tradition*. Manchester: Manchester University Press, 1982; Barnes and Noble, 1982.

Ong, Walter. *Orality and Literacy: The Technologizing of the Word*. London: Methuen, 1982.

Ovid. *The Erotic Poems*. Trans., intro. Peter Green. New York: Penguin Books, 1982.

Paden, William D., Jr. "The Troubadour's Lady: Her Marital Status and Social Rank." *Studies in Philology* 72 (1975): 28-50.

_____. "Utrum Copularentur: Of Cors." *L'Esprit Créateur* 19 (Winter 1979): 71-83.

_____. *The Medieval Pastourelle*. 2 vols. Garland Library of Medieval Literature, Series A, vols. 34-35. New York: Garland, 1987.

_____, Ed. *Voice of the Trobairitz: Perspectives on the Women Troubadours*. Philadelphia: University of Pennsylvania Press, 1989.

_____. "Rape in the Pastourelle." *Romanic Review* 53 (1989): 332-349.

Paden et al. See Major Editions above, under: Bertran de Born.

Panvini, Bruno. *Le biografie provenzali: valore e attendibilità.* Firenze: Leo S. Olschki, 1952.

Paterson, Linda. *Troubadours and Eloquence.* Oxford: Oxford University Press, 1975.

Petrarca, Francesco. *Rime, trionfi e poesie latine.* Ed. F. Neri et al. Milano: Ricardo Ricciardi, 1951.

_____. *Petrarch's Lyric Poems: The Rime Sparse and Other Lyrics.* Ed. Robert Durling. Cambridge, Ma.: Harvard University Press, 1976.

Pillet, A. and Carstens, H. *Bibliographie der troubadours.* Halle: Niemeyer, 1933. Rpt. New York: Burt Franklin, Bibliography and Reference Series, no. 166, 1968.

Pirenne, Henri. *Histoire économique et social du moyen-âge.* Paris: Presses Universitaires de France, 1969.

Pirot, François. "L'idéologie des troubadours: examen de travaux récents." *Le Moyen âge* 74 (2) (1968): 301-331.

_____. *Recherches sur les connaissances littéraires des troubadours occitans et catalans des XIIe et XIIIe siècles: Les "sirventes-ensenhamens" de Guerau de Cabrera, Guiraut de Calanson et Bertrand de Paris.* Memorias de la Real Academia de Buenas Letras de Barcelona, 14. Barcelona: Real Academia de Buenas Letras, 1972.

(Poe) Wilson, Elizabeth R. "The Lyrics of Old Provençal Prose: Generic Movements of Space and Time in the Vidas and Razos." Diss. Princeton University, 1977.

_____. "The Meeting of Fact and Fiction in an Old Provençal Razo." *L'Esprit Créateur* (Winter 1979): 84-94.

_____. "Old Provençal Vidas as Literary Commentary." *Romance Philology* 33 (1980): 510-518.

_____. *From Poetry to Prose in Old Provençal.* Birmingham, Alabama: Summa Publications, 1984.

_____. "At the Boundary between Vida and Razo: The Biography of Raimon Jordan." *Neophilologous* 72 (1988): 316-319.

Pound, Ezra. *The Spirit of Romance.* New York: New Directions, 1952.

_____. *Translations.* Intro. Hugh Kenner. New York: New Directions, 1963.

Przychochki, G., ed.. *Accessus ovidiani, edidit, prolegomenis, epilegomenis instruxit G. P..* Krakow: 1911.

Quain, E.A. "The Medieval Accessus ad Auctores." *Traditio* 3 (1945): 215-264.

Raimon Vidal. *Abrils issia.* Ed. W. H. W. Field. Chapel Hill: University of North Carolina Press, Studies in the Romance Languages and Literatures, no. 110, 1971.

Raynouard, François J. M. *Lexique roman ou Dictionnaire de la langue des troubadours comparée avec les autres langues de l'Europe latine.* 6 vols. Heidelberg: Carl Winter, 1836-45.

Rey-Flaud, Henri. *La Névrose courtoise.* Paris: Navarin, 1983.

Riquer, Martín de. "Il significato politico del sirventese provenzale." In *Concetto, storia, miti, e immagini del medio evo,* edited by Vittore Branca. Venice: Sansoni, 1973: 287-309.

_____. *Historia de la literatura catalana,* I. Barcelona: 1964.

_____. "El Trovador Huguet de Mataplana" in *Studia hispanica in honorem R. Lapesa.* Madrid, I: 455-94.

Rougemont, Denis de. *L'amour et l'occident.* 3rd ed. Paris: Librairie Plon, 1972.

Rowland, Beryl. *Animals with Human Faces: A Guide to Animal Symbolism.* Knoxville, Tennessee: University of Tennessee Press, 1973.

Sakari, Aimo. See Major Editions above, under: Guillem de Saint-Leidier.

Sankovitch, Tilde. "Lombarda's Reluctant Mirror: Speculum of Another Poet." *Voice of the Trobairitz: Perspectives on the Women Troubadours.* Ed. William D. Paden. Philadelphia: University of Pennsylvania Press, 1989.

Schutz, Alexander H. "Preliminary Study on *Trobar e Entendre*: An Expression in Medieval Aesthetics." *Romanic Review* 23 (1932): 129-138.

———. "More on *Trobar e Entendre.*"*Romanic Review* 26 (1935): 29-31.

———. "Where were the Provençal *vidas* and *razos* Written?"*Modern Philology* 35 (1937-38): 225-232.

———. "Were the *vidas* and *razos* Recited?" *Studies in Philology* 36 (1939): 565-570.

———. "The Provençal Expression *Pretz e Valor.*" *Speculum* 19 (1944): 493.

———. "Prose Style in the Provençal Biographies." *Philological Quarterly* 30 (1951): 179-185.

———. "Joglar, borges, cavallier dans les biographies provençales: Essai d'évaluation sémantique." *Mélanges de linguistique et de littérature romanes à la mémoire d'Istavan Frank.* Saarbrücken: 1957: 672-677.

Serres, Michel. *Le parasite.* Paris: Bernard Grasset, 1980.

Shapiro, Marianne. "The Provençal *Trobairitz* and the Limits of Courtly Love." *Signs* 3 (1978): 560-571.

_____. "The Fictionalization of Bertran de Born (Inferno XXVIII)." *Dante Studies* 92 (1974): 107-116.

Sharman, Ruth Verity. See Major Editions above, under: Guiraut de Borneilh.

Shell, Marc. *The Economy of Literature.* Baltimore and London: The Johns Hopkins Press, 1978.

Spiegel, Gabrielle. "Pseudo-Turpin, The Crisis of Authority and the Beginning of Vernacular Historiography in France." *Journal of Medieval History* (Sept. 1986): 207-224.

Stanton, Donna C., Ed. and Trans. *The Defiant Muse: French Feminist Poems from the Middle Ages to the Present.* New York: The Feminist Press, 1986.

Stimming, Albert. See Major Editions above, under: Bertran de Born.

Stock, Brian. *The Implications of Literacy.* Princeton: Princeton University Press, 1983.

Strayer, Joseph. *The Albigensian Crusade. Crosscurrents in World History,* Ed. Norman F. Cantor. New York: Dial Press, 1971.

Stronski, Stanislaw. *La poésie et la réalité au temps des troubadours.* Oxford: the Clarendon Press, 1943.

_____. *La légende amoureuse de Bertran de Born.* Paris: Honoré Champion, 1914. Rpt. Geneva: Slatkine Reprints, 1973.

_____. "Recherches historiques sur quelques protecteurs des troubadours." *Annales du Midi* 19: 40-56.

_____. See Major Editions above, under: Folquet de Marseille.

Sumption, Jonathan. *The Albigensian Crusade.* London, Boston: Faber, 1978.

Sutherland, D. R. "Flexions and Categories in Old Provençal." *Transactions of the Philological Society* (1950): 25-70.

Switten, Margaret Louise. See Major Editions above, under: Raimon de Miraval.

Taylor, Robert A. *La littérature occitane du moyen-âge: bibliographie sélective et critique.* Toronto: University of Toronto Press, 1977.

Topsfield, Leslie. See Major Editions above, under: Raimon de Miraval.

Tristan et Yseut. Ed. J. C. Payen. Paris: Garnier, 1974.

Van der Werf, Hendrik. *The Chansons of the Troubadours and Trouvères: A Study of the Melodies and their Relation to the Poems.* Utrecht: A. Oosthoek's Uitgeversmaatschappij, NV, 1972.

Vance, Eugene. "Love's Concordance: The Poetics of Desire and the Joy of the Text." *Diacritics* 5 (1975): 40-52.

Varvaro, A. See Major Editions above, under: Richart de Berbezilh.

Wakefield, W. L. *Heresy, Crusade, and Inquisition in Southern France, 1100-1250.* Berkeley: University of California Press, 1974.

Warren, W. L. *Henry II.* Berkeley and Los Angeles: University of California Press, 1973.

Wartburg, Walter von. *Französisches etymologisches wörterbuch.* Bonn: Klopp, etc., 1928-.

Wiacek, Wilhelmina M. *Lexique des noms géographiques et ethniques dans les poésies des troubadours des XIIe et XIIIe siècles.* Paris: Nizet, 1968.

Wilhelm, J.J. *The Cruelest Month: Spring, Nature and Love in Classical and Medieval Lyrics.* New Haven: Yale University Press, 1965.

_____. See Major Editions above, under: Arnaut Daniel.

Zanders, Josef. *Die Altprovenzalische Prosanovelle. Eine litterarhistorische kritik der Trobador-Biographieen.* Halle: 1913.

Zufferey, François. "Un document relatif à Uc de Saint-Circ à la Bibliothèque Capitulaire de Trévise."*Cultura Neolatina* 34: 9-14.

_____. *Recherches linguistiques sur les chansonniers provençaux.* Geneva: Droz, 1987.

Zumthor, Paul. *Essai de poétique médiévale.* Paris: Seuil, 1972.

_____. *La Poésie et la voix dans la civilisation médiévale.* Essais et Conférénces, College de France. Paris: Presses Universitaires de France, 1984.

_____. *La Lettre et la voix de la "littérature" médiévale.* Paris:1987.

Razos and Troubadour Songs

1. Bernart de Ventadorn 70, 43 (B/S, 29)
   Base text: Sg 178

...And B(ernart) called her "Lark" because of her love of a knight who loved her, and she called him "Ray".[1] And one day the knight came to the duchess and entered the bedroom. The lady, who saw him, lifted up the side of her coat and put it around his neck and let herself fall onto the bed. And B(ernart) saw all this, for one of the lady's young servant girls had secretly shown it to him; and it is for this reason[2] that he composed the song which says:

When I see the lark move...[3]

[1] In the sense of a ray of light.

[2] "Razo" in the original text, meaning 'pretext' or 'reason' as well as being a reference to the prose text itself.

[3] Most commentators agree that this is one of the oddest of the razos. Pierre Bec includes it in his collection of humorous and obscene troubadour texts (Bec, 1984). See also Kendrick, 202, note 1 for her discussion of this razo as an example of "sentenssa follatina", i.e. parodic explanation.

Uc de Saint Circ is identified as the author of one version of the vida text for Bernart (MSS E and R; see B/S, p. 25 note 8, and p. 29; Egan, 11).

Song 70, 43   Bernart de Ventadorn: "Can vei la lauzeta mover..."
              MSS: A 90, C 47, D 16, E 102, F 22, G 10, I 28, K 16, L 19, M 39, N 139, P 16, Q 25, R 56, S 53, U 89, V 55, a 91, W 190 (attributed to Peire Vidal); anonymous in O 60, X 148.
              Source: Appel, 249.
              Other English translations: Bonner, 91; Goldin, 145; Lindsay, 101; Nichols, 166; O'Donoghue, 116; Press, 76; Smythe, 34.

1. When I see the lark move its wings
   With joy against a ray of sun,
   Then forget itself and let itself plunge
   With the sweetness that invades its heart;
   Oh, such great envy do I feel   5
   For the one I see in such ecstacy
   That it is a wonder that right then and there
   My heart doesn't melt with desire.

2. Alas, I thought I knew so much about love
   And how little I really know.   10
   For I cannot prevent myself from loving
   One from whom I shall reap no benefits.
   She has it all: my heart, all my being,
   Herself and all the world;
   And when she took herself from me, she left me nothing 15
   But my own desiring and a wanting heart.

3. Never have I had power over myself
   Or belonged to myself from the moment
   That she let me look into a mirror
   In her eyes that greatly pleased me.   20
   Mirror, ever since I saw myself in you
   Deep sighs have been killing me
   And I have lost myself like the beautiful Narcissus
   who lost himself in the fountain.

4. Of ladies I despair.   25
   Never again shall I trust them.
   For just as I used to defend them,
   I shall now tear down their defenses.
   Since I see that not one of them will come to help me
   Against she who destroys and confounds me,   30
   I suspect them all and mistrust them;
   For I know well that they are all alike.

5. In this way my lady shows herself to be a true
   Woman and it is for this that I expose her:
   For she doesn't want what one should want   35
   And whatever she has been forbidden to do, she does.
   I have fallen into ill favor
   And have really acted like the madman on the bridge;

4

And I don't know why this is happening to me
Other than that I climbed too high above me.   40

6. Mercy is now truly lost,
And I never even knew it;
For she who should have the most
Has none at all, and where else shall I seek it?
Oh, how awful it must seem to an onlooker   45
That she leaves this poor man to die, longing with desire,
Who will never have any good without her,
Without coming to his aid.

7. Since neither prayers nor mercy nor the justice
Of my appeal have done me any good before My-Lord,   50
And since the fact that I love her
Brings her no pleasure, I won't tell her anymore.
Thus I leave her and retire from her service.
She has left me dead and with death I will answer her.
Since she does not wish to retain me, I am going off,   55
Miserable, into exile, I know not where.

8. Tristan, you will have no more of me,[1]
For I am going away, miserable, I know not where.
I give up singing and renounce it,
And take refuge from joy and love.   60

[1] The senhal, "Tristan" is used by other troubadours, including Bertran de Born and Raimbaut d'Aurenga. Many troubadour songs were written to respond to other songs, and were often constructed using the rhyme scheme of the original song. Maria-Luisa Meneghetti sees this song as an answer to two others: Raimbaut d'Aurenga's song: "Non chant per auzel" (389, 32) and a northern French song by Chrétien de Troyes: "D'Amors qui m'a tolu." Tristan, in this case, would be a reference to Raimbaut d'Aurenga. (Meneghetti, 139)

2. Bernart de Ventadorn 70, 6 (B/S, 30)
   Base Text: N² 21

   Bernart de Ventadorn loved a noble and beautiful lady and he so served and honored her that she did what he wanted in word and in deed. And their joy went on for a long time in loyalty and in pleasure. But then the lady's desire changed and she wanted another lover. Bernart knew this and was sad and mournful and he thought of leaving her, for the company of the other lover was painful for him. Then, like a man conquered by love, he realized that it would be better to have half of her than to lose all of her. Later, when he was before her, along with the other lover and other people, it seemed to him that she looked at him more than at all the others. And often he gave up believing what he had believed, as should all fine lovers, for they should not believe what they see with their eyes if it works to the disadvantage of their lady. Thus Bernart de Ventadorn composed this song which says:

   Counsel me now, Lord...

Song 70, 6   Bernart de Ventadorn: "Era·m cosselhatz, senhor..."
           Source: Appel, 30.
           MSS: A 92, B 58, C 57, D 20, E 105, G 13, I 27, K 16,
               M 48, Q 26, R 57, S 48, V 62, a 96, f 63;
               anonymous in O 62.
           Other English translations: Goldin, 141; Nichols, 56.

1. Counsel me now, Lord,
   You who have wisdom and good sense.
   A lady I have loved for some time
   Has granted me her love
   But I know for a fact   5
   That she has another secret friend;
   And never has the companionship
   Of any other companion been so hard to bear.

2. There is one thing that distresses me
   And I think about it constantly.   10

If I consent to this arrangement,
I prolong my pain;
And if I tell her what I think,
I will see my losses doubled.
Regardless of what I do or don't do   15
Nothing works to my benefit.

3. If I love her in dishonor,
I will be a laughingstock
And they will all say I am
Cuckolded and permissive.   20
But if I lose her friendship on account of this,
I am truly dispossessed
Of love; and may God never again allow me
To make verse or song.

4. Since I am driven to madness,   25
I shall truly be mad if I do not take
The lesser of these two evils.
For, as I see it, it is better
To have half of her
Than to lose all of her through madness;   30
For I have never seen any spiteful lover
Get from love what is good for him.

5. Since my lady wants
Another lover, I do not forbid it.
I let myself go along with it more out of fear 35
Than out of choice.
If ever a man were to be thanked
For involuntary service,
It is I who should be given a reward
For pardoning such a great wrong!   40

6. Her beautiful and treacherous eyes
Which used to gaze on me so graciously
Are committing a serious offense
If they now gaze elsewhere in the same manner.
On the other hand, they have also honored me greatly: 45
For amidst a thousand people gathered together
They gaze more toward the spot where I stand
Than at all the others who surround me.

7

7. With the water that pours from my eyes
   I write more than a hundred greetings[1]   50
   That I send to the most gracious
   And attractive of ladies.
   Many times since then have I remembered
   What she did to me at our parting,
   When I saw her cover her face   55
   So that she couldn't tell me yes or no.

8. Lady, love openly
   The other, and love me in secret;
   So that I get all the benefits
   And he gets the beautiful words.[2]   60

9. Garsio, sing me now my song
   And bring it for me
   To my Messenger, who was there.
   Tell him I am asking for any advice he can give me.

[1] "Salutz," meaning also a specific type of poetic text in which a poet sends his greetings to a Lady.
[2] "Razo" in the original text, signifying talk, explanation, reasoning etc.

3./80b. Bernart de Ventadorn 70, 1 and Guillem de Cabestaing 213, 5.

Song 70, 1 is included under razo number 80b.

4. Arnaut de Mareuil 30, 19 (B/S, 36)
MSS: E 191, P 42, R 2
Base text: E

You have heard who Arnaut de Mareuil was[1] and how he fell in love with the Countess of Béziers, who was the daughter of the good Count Raimon de Toulouse[2], and mother of the Viscount of Béziers, whom the French killed after taking him at Carcassonne.[3] This same Viscountess was called the Countess of Burlatz because she was born in the castle of Burlatz. Arnaut greatly loved her[4] and composed many good songs for her and beseeched her with great fear and she loved him very much.

King Anfos, who was courting the countess[5], realized that she loved Arnaut de Mareuil and he was very jealous about this and mournful when he saw the loving glances she gave Arnaut and heard the good songs that he composed about her. And so he reproached her over Arnaut and said so much to her and made her say so much that she sent Arnaut away, admonishing him that he should never again appear before her or ever write songs about her; and that he should leave and give up his love for her and all his beseeching.

Arnaut de Mareuil, when he heard that he was exiled in this way, was mournful beyond all mourning and he left her and her court like a man in despair and went to Sir Guilem de Montpellier, who was his friend and his lord. And he stayed with him for a long time and there he moaned and cried and composed this song which says:

Very sweet were my thoughts...

and which is written here, as you shall hear.[6]

---

[1] This is one of many razos in which the opening strongly suggests that it was composed to be read or heard directly after the vida, the presumed source of the information referred to. It does, in fact, appear in that position in the three manuscripts in which it can be found: E 190, 191; P 42; and R 2.

[2] The genealogical information on the lady is characteristic of some of the razos. The poet's own genealogy, when given, is usually confined to the vidas. This lady has been identified as

Azalaïs of Toulouse, daughter of Raimon V. In 1171 she married the viscount of Béziers and Carcassonne, Roger II, known as Taillefer. She is linked with Anfos of Aragon in another song by G. de Berguedan (210, 17); (see B/S, 35 and 38).

[3] One of the few mentions within the vida or razo texts of the tragic events of the Albigensian Crusade. The Southern courts mentioned here had been largely decimated by the time that this razo would have been composed. Whether or not the countess' son, Raimon-Rogier, was killed during this battle is disputed. In the *Chanson de Croisade*, Guillem de Tudèle says that he was taken prisoner by Simon de Montfort and that he died in prison. See Johnston, xiv, and razo 67 to Raimon de Miraval's song: Bel m'es q'ieu chant e coindei (406, 12).

[4] "Loved" is the preferred translation for the Provençal expression "li volia ben" which corresponds to the very similar modern Italian and Spanish expressions.

[5] "Courting, turning one's attention to" are translations for the Provençal term "entender" and terms formed from this word such as "entendimen." It may refer to the fact that the poet would begin to compose about a lady or patron, thus applying his skills to that subject. It also seems to be able to refer in some cases to his ability to explain the references in his song, i.e. compose razos. A more apt translation might include the idea that the lady allowed him to sing his love songs with her as the subject before a group, thus proclaiming her merit publicly. See: Schutz, 1935, and Kendrick, 1988, for differing interpretations of this word.

[6] Once again the reference to writing and hearing in the same phrase, suggesting that the razo and the song were to be performed, or at least read aloud, and from a written text.

Song 30,19   Arnaut de Mareuil: "Mout eron doutz miei cossir..."
              Source: Johnston, 146.
              MSS: A 106, B 67, C 108, D 37, D^c (stanzas II, III, IV) 253, E 66, G 33, I 47, K 34, M 129, N 67, Q 65, R 80, S (Stanzas I, II, III, IV) 125, c 31.

1. Very sweet were my thoughts,
   And without any sadness,

When the beautiful one with the noble body,
Humble, honest and debonaire,
Told me to renounce her love, 5
A love from which I cannot part.
Because she will not retain me,
And I dare not beg for her mercy,
All pleasures are foreign to me;
Since from her all joy is lacking. 10

2. Lady, if only you would allow,
   At your discretion,
   That I, with sweet and precious prayers,
   Humbly imploring like a fine lover,
   Should dare expose to you my heart 15
   Instead of seeking pleasure elsewhere.
   It would cost you nothing
   And would do me so much good;
   For when a sick man complains
   It offers him relief, even if it doesn't cure him. 20

3. Sweet lady of my desire,
   In all your wisdom,
   Do not deny me the warm welcome
   That you used to grant me.
   I am too frightened and hardly dare 25
   Ask for any more,
   For you are so highly placed.
   But Ovid explained
   That between true lovers at heart
   Wealth and position mean nothing.[1] 30

4. Your rich and precious reputation
   Is everywhere so highly considered
   That I fear my praise can't be of much worth;
   Nonetheless I know for sure
   That no matter how full the scale is, 35
   If one should put more on one side,
   Even if it be but a grain, the weight will
   Shift to that side.
   Your honor grows in the same way
   Each time that a man praises you. 40

5. Learning and beauty,
   Honesty and noble speech,
   A warm welcome and the giving of honor,
   Courtly and with a gay appearance:
   These bring you honor above all others.   45
   This is why joy and pleasure
   Revive through you and are born
   In every direction,
   And it isn't Love which makes me say this;
   It is truth and your worth.   50

6. Genovese, you know this:
   Just as April and May
   Are gayer than other seasons,
   So do the resplendent colors
   Of your noble reputation shine above all others.   55

7. Frenchman, whoever else may turn away
   Or give up on excellence,
   In you there is merit and worth,
   Joy, amusement and love.

[1] These particular lines, and several other references in this song, support Erich Köhler's thesis that the phenomenon of fin'amors was at least partially created or appropriated by knights from the lower nobility anxious to rise in the social order through gifts of property and goods from the wealthy patrons for whom they sang.

5. Guiraut de Borneill 242, 69 (B/S, 43)
   MSS: N^2 22; Sg 91.
   Base text: N^2

Giraut de Borneil loved a lady from Gascogne whose name was Lady Alamanda d'Estanc.[1] This lady was highly esteemed for her wit, worth and beauty; and she permitted the beseechments and courting of Sir Giraut because of the way he furthered her reputation for merit and honor, and because of the good songs he composed about her, songs in which she found great delight, for she knew how to interpret them.

For a long time he beseeched her; and she, with fine words and fine rewards[2] and fine promises, fended him off most courteously, for never did she make love or give him any sign of joy except for one of her gloves. Because of that glove he lived for a long time in a state of joy and happiness and then, after he had lost it, in a state of great sorrow; for my lady Alamanda, seeing how insistently he was begging her to give him some pleasure in love[3] and knowing that he had lost the glove, reproached him on account of that glove, saying that he had guarded it badly and that she would never give him any gift or any pleasure in love. And that which she had promised him she revoked, for she saw that he had strayed far from her command.[4]

When Giraut learned of the new accusation and the exile that the lady was imposing, he was very sad and mournful and he went to one of her servant girls, whose name was Alamanda, the same as the lady's. This young girl was wise and courteous and she knew how to compose songs as well as perform and interpret them.[5] Giraut then told her all that the lady had said and asked for her advice about what he should do, saying:

If I ask for your advice, lovely friend, Alamanda...

[1] Ruth Verity Sharman considers this identification to be unfounded, especially given that the Alamanda referred to in the song is the lady's handmaiden rather than the lady herself (Sharman, 18).

[2] "Onors, onramens" can refer to gifts of property and goods as well as to abstract "honor."

[3] "Plaser d'amor" is a term that comes up repeatedly in the razos to refer to physical manifestations of love. It is what poets often demand after lengthy service and would seem to carry a sexual connotation, though the degree of intimacy remains veiled and seems to vary from one razo to another.

[4] That the lady would accuse Guiraut of straying from her command suggests either that he left her court, addressed a song to a lady from another court, or is demanding more from her than was

agreed upon. It is clear in the razo that her attachment to Guiraut is based on his skill in public relations ("...because of the way he furthered her reputation for merit and honor") and that this straying may be a literal foray into a competitor's camp.
⁵ Alamanda is thus one of the few women troubadours, *trobairitz*, referred to in the razos. See other mentions in razos to Guiraut de Borneilh (# 5), Gaucelm Faidit (#41), Maria de Ventadorn (#45), Raimon de Miraval (#66), Lombarda (#68), Almuc de Castenlnou and Iseut de Capio (#69), Lanfranc Cigala and Guillelma de Rosers (#80), and studies by Bogin, 1976, and Paden, 1989.

Song 242, 69 Guiraut de Borneill: "Si.us quer conselh, bel'ami'Alamanda..."
Source: Sharman, 384.
MSS: A 18, B 18, C 8, D 11, G 70, H 37, I 23, K 12, N 181, Q 87, R 8, Sg 65, V 74, a 41.
Other English translations: Bogin, 102; Sharman, 384.

1. If I ask your advice, lovely friend, Alamanda,
Don't refuse me; it's a desperate man who appeals to you.
For now your deceitful lady has told me
That I have strayed far from her command   4
And that what she gave me she now takes back and revokes.
   What do you think I should do?
For the heart within me is about to burst into flame, from the anguish,
So deeply am I enraged.

2. For God's sake, Giraut, a lover's desire is never
Completely fulfilled or satisfied just like that;   10
For if one partner fails, the other must continue to offer service
So that their problem doesn't become known, and worsen.
If she tells you that some high peak is a low plain,
   Believe her.
Be happy with both the good and the bad that she orders   15
   For in this way you will be loved.

3. I can't stop myself from speaking out against arrogance
   Even if you are, Young Girl, blond and beautiful.
   A little bit of sorrow hurts you and a little bit of joy
       overwhelms you
   And still you're not even first or second in this affair.   20
   And I, who fear that this anger will kill me,
       You advise me
   That if I feel myself dying I should pull myself closer to the
       wave!
   I don't think much of the way you guide me!

4. When you come asking about such profound matters   25
   My God, Giraut, I don't know how to answer you.
   You may think that I was satisfied with little
   But I'd rather shave my field than have someone else mow it.[1]
   For if today what you are seeking is to make her want
       To reconcile with you,   30
   When she's withholding and hiding from you her beautiful
       body,
   It is apparent that you are a confused man.

5. Young lady, don't be so talkative from now on.
   If she lied to me over a hundred times right from the
       beginning,
   Do you really think that I could put up with it forever?   35
   It would look like I do it out of lack[2]
   Of any other friendship; and now I feel like hitting you
       If you don't be quiet.
   Lady Berengeira gave better advice
       Than what you are giving me!   40

6. I see now that she is changing things on you
   Because you call her fickle and frivolous.
   And you think that this will make her reconcile?
   I don't think she's that docile.
   No, from now on, her promise will be far behind her,   45
       Regardless of what you say,
   If ever she should even give in so much as to offer
       Truce, faith or peace.

15

7. Listen, lovely, for God's sake, let me not lose your help,
   For you know perfectly well what was promised to me.   50
   If I have failed because of the sorrow I've felt
   Don't hold it against me, my friend, if ever you have felt how easily
   The heart of a lover can change. And if ever you were a lover yourself
   Think about resolving this affair.
   For I tell you truly: I am dead if I have lost her.   55
   But don't tell her that!

8. Lord Sir Giraut, I would have wanted to see an end to this
   But she told me that she was right to have gotten angry;
   For, like a madman, you were courting another right in the open;
   One who is not her equal, dressed or nude.   60
   Won't she just be acting like a conquered woman if she doesn't dispose of you
   When you're courting someone else?
   I will still help you, even though I have been defending her,
   If you'll never again get yourself in this trouble.[3]

9. My lovely, if in the name of God she believes you,   65
   Assure her of that for me.

10. I will do it; but once her love has been returned to you,
    Don't you ever leave her.[4]

---

[1] These lines have not yet been adequately explained. Coming straight after Guiraut's accusation that this young girl hasn't ever felt the full range of emotions (i.e. any little thing gets you all upset...), her retort seems to mean that at least she takes things into her own hands and doesn't wait around until things fester and explode as he does. It has obvious sexual connotations as well and could have been meant for humor.

[2] Sharman notes that "o faire" ("to do it") has a sexual connotation and could be used here in that sense.

[3] "Mesclar" (to get mixed up in trouble) also has a sexual connotation and could be the continuation of an erotic subtext.

[4] Bertran de Born responded to this tenso using the same rhyme scheme. He refers to it in line 26 of song 80, 13: "D'un sirventes

no·m cal far loignor ganda", saying that he is composing a song "...to the melody of lady Alamanda" (see razo 23).

6a. Guiraut de Borneill 242, 36 (B/S, 247)
MSS: N^2 20 and 22

Version from manuscript N^2:

Giraut de Borneil had been in love with a lady from Gascogne whose name was Lady Alamanda d'Estancs and she had accorded him pleasures.[1] And it so happened that she began to think that her worth had gone down too much, for all that she desired was desired by someone else.[2] So she sent Giraut away and took away her love, and all for someone because of whom she was highly criticized, for he was an unstable and wicked man.[3] Giraut de Borneil remained sad and mournful for a long time over this fact, over his own loss, and over the criticism that the lady had received, for it was not right that she should have taken such a man as her lover.

And so he composed this song, expressing bitterness over the treatment that she had accorded him and over the fact that joy, amusement and pleasant company no longer appealed to him:

I am not just totally giving up...

[1] This razo uses the same term as the previous one to indicate signs of love ("plaser") but the sense is much more suggestive of sexual relations than in the previous razo (#5).
[2] This curious expression indicating reciprocity in the love relation is indicative of a dynamic at work in many of the songs. This lady sees her reputation suffer from having taken part in a reciprocal love relation. Treating her reputation as something of a public commodity, the poet uses the language of the marketplace to indicate that value increases when one is seen as desired but not

desiring. Reciprocity implies retirement from the active market, an apparently disastrous state for the lady avid for praise and great renown. (Girard, 1961)

[3] Criticism of the lady plays a major role in the songs as well as in several of the razos. The adoration of the lady quickly turns to castigation when her behavior is seen as other than favoring the further renown of herself, her court, or her poet; and the poet is himself the instigator of this castigation in many of the purported love songs. Many such songs begin as cansos and end as sirventes (topical or satirical songs).

6b. Guiraut de Borneilh 242, 36 (B/S, 49)

version from manuscript Sg 91:

There was nothing Sir Giraut could do or say to get back into the graces of my Lady Alamanda, for she was wicked to him and wanted to break off with him and to this end had used the reproach about the glove. And so Giraut, though it caused him much grief, left her. Let it be known then that my Lady Alamanda did not send Giraut away solely because of the glove, even though she used that as a reproach. She had done this because she had taken as her lover[1] a man because of whom she was highly criticized, for he was an evil, wicked man. All of this left Giraut de Borneyl sad and mournful for a long time over his own loss and the criticism of the lady, for she had made someone her lover who was unsuitable for her ...and because conversation, amusement and laughter no longer appealed to her lady; the song in question is written in this book.[2]

[1] The use of the two terms, "drut" and "amador" in the same razo implies that, at least for this author, the terms are interchangeable. Usually "drut" is thought to have a more sensual overtone than other terms indicating lover, such as *amador*, *aman*, *entendedor*. This is in line with the generally more frank tone of

this version of the razo (taken from a fourteenth-century Catalan manuscript as opposed to the preceding sixteenth-century Italian version). Note how the author demasks the lady's ploy of using the glove as a pretext to take on a new lover from the beginning, without bothering to discuss the issue of reciprocity.

[2] There is a lacuna in the text that is not indicated in the manuscript but which Boutière/Schutz indicate in their edition. The reference at the end of the razo shows that at least this portion of it was composed to be written in a specific manuscript. This also implies that this particular fourteenth-century Catalan manuscript contains razos that were composed or adapted specifically for it, even if they were taken from some other source.

Song 242, 36 Guiraut de Borneill: "Ges aissi del tot no.m lais..."
Source: Sharman, 264.
MSS: A 12, B 7, C 19, D 11, G 72, I 21, K 10, M 10, N 166, P 2, Q 103, R 10, Sg 71, U 18, V 72, a 18, c 6.
Other English translations: Sharman, 268.

1. I am not just totally giving up
On singing, amusement and laughter
Even though I am not doing much of it right now.
But since encouragement and amusement
Are no longer appreciated   5
I don't feel like spending my fine and precious words
On myself alone.
So instead I clench my teeth
Just as soon as I begin
My lovely songs   10
For I dare not recite them.
I see almost no one
Who takes any pleasure in joy;
Nor do I see anyone who would emulate me
When I rejoice and feel happiness.   15

2. And yet what really hurts me the most,
More than I like to admit,

Is my wicked friend who betrays me;
And it seems like madness to me
For I have proved myself on that score   20
Since I cannot resist her.
I did behave badly,
And for this I will be patient,
Even if her joy and good graces
Are slow in coming.[1]   25
For never has any lover
Who easily loses his temper
Known anything about love;
Love commands   29
That one be respectful of and thankful for the other's failings.

3. It is true that it is she who withdrew her love from me,
And this she cannot hide.
But since it is force which feeds the field,
What good does truthfulness do me?
It would be much better for me   35
If, while waiting, I turned my heart
In another direction;
For since it is force that conquers,
Justice is worth nothing.
But the little sense   40
Which guides me
Leads me to the conclusion
That I only debase myself
In denouncing her,
For it is in her power to raise me up or bring me to ruin. 45

4. But if someone were to be my true friend
And rejoice over my good fortunes,
Someone noble and honest, without evil intentions
Who could keep a secret with me
Without having to be begged,   50
He could still bring joy back to me.
I am not so far removed from it!
But the suspicious heart
Fights back and so do reason
And thirdly, fear.   55
Never has any fearful thief
Broken into a secure

dwelling alone
   Without his body and all three fears,
   One worse than the next, assaulting him. 60

5. Now she can relax and feast,
   For she knew just how to kill me.
   I have never again been happy or gay
   Since a madman spread it about
   That I brought sin upon myself. 65
   He got my trust and made me believe
   Great lies, and since then
   Fortune has not been with me as much
   As the state of worry
   In which my memory keeps me. 70
   And no courter of ladies,
   Even if he were an emperor,
   Would be envied
   With this excessively heavy load, 74
   For love does not wish that one should be lord over others.

6. Never has a man who has shown the proper attitude,
   Allowed himself to be conquered, and been patient,
   Even if he has been vile in some other area,
   Not been paid,
   Like someone who has gone beyond reason 80
   And threatens to break all bonds.
   For humility
   Is valuable to those in the know.
   Don't you learn, therefore,
   That pride will get you nowhere? 85
   And that it is the good and patient man,
   Provided he keeps quiet about it,
   Who conquers the one who kisses
   And holds him and stays with him?
   But I'm not saying that it's a good place to be. 90

7. Nobility which has been corrupted by money,[2]
   With the aim of allowing agreeable commen men to be seated,
   Can never come close to attaining perfection.
   Nor should a base rich man[3]
   Or one who is ill-mannered 95
   Ever aspire to higher position.

If such a thing were ever considered to be just
It would be for nil--Do you understand me?--
Yes--Then do you admit
That when a base man 100
Dares to approach a
Gracious and well-bred lady
There arises a situation
In which he could make a fool of himself?
But as for anyone who doesn't care about this, let him
   renounce love. 105

[1] The good graces, "bens", he mentions can also mean "the goods" in economic terms.

[2] The translation of this passage depends on the sense of "pretz" as money or payment rather than reputation or merit (though of course in the troubadour world reputation and merit are both considered payments, conferred by the poet on the patrons in return for goods.)

[3] A base rich man can refer either to cheap rich men, those who don't come through with the expected gifts, or rich, though not noble, merchants.

7. Guiraut de Borneill 242, 51 (B/S, 51)
   MSS: N^2 23; Sg 92
   Base Text: N^2

Giraut de Borneil once went overseas with King Richard[1] and with the Viscount of Limoges, whose name was Lord Aimar, and he was present at the siege of Acre. When the city had been taken and all the barons returned, Guiraut de Borneil went off to the court of the good Prince of Antioch, who was a very noble man. Giraut was greatly honored and served there by the Prince and he spent an entire winter with him waiting for the return passage that was to arrive at Easter. And while he was there he dreamt a dream, which you will hear about in this song, which says:

I cannot prevent that to the pain...

[1] This is a reference to King Richard-the-Lionhearted, one of the three eminent leaders of the Third Crusade, along with Philip Augustus and Frederick Barbarossa. Sharman says that Guiraut did go on the Third Crusade but not with King Richard.

Song 242, 51   Guiraut de Borneill: "No posc sofrir c'a la dolor..."
Source: Sharman, 216.
MSS: A 21, B 6, C 22, D 13, G 72, I 19, K 8, M 5, N 165, Q 96 (anonymous), R 82, Sg 83, V 73, a 9, D^c 244 (line 1 and stanzas 5, 6).
Other English translations: Sharman, 219.

1. I cannot prevent my tongue
From moving to the pain in my tooth
Or my heart to the new flower
When I see the branches blossom.
The songs of birds in love   5
Are heard through the woods
And though I am troubled
And look unhappy,
When I see songs and gardens and fields
I am refreshed and take some comfort.   10

2. I don't bother to undertake any labor
But that of singing and making joy.
For one night in the springtime I dreamed
Such a dream that I was ecstatic.
It was about a feathered sparrowhawk   15
Who was seated on my fist;
And though he seemed to me quite tame
I have never seen one more wild.

But later he became familiar and submissive
   And was fastened securely by a cord at his feet.   20

3. I told my lord about the dream
   As a man should tell his friend;
   And he interpreted it in terms of love
   And told me that I cannot fail
   To have someone beyond my rank   25
   As my lady friend, and without any problems,
   If only I work at it diligently.
   For never has a man of my background
   Or even anyone way beyond my rank
   Loved or been loved in quite this way.   30

4. Now I am ashamed of all that and am afraid.
   I wake up over it, moaning and sighing,
   I consider the dream just a mad episode
   And do not believe that it could ever come true.
   However, a noble thought   35
   Cannot be ousted from a foolish heart,
   No matter how overweening and boastful it seems.
   So after our crossing
   I know that the dream will come true
   In exactly the way it was explained to me.   40

5. And then you will hear a singer,
   And songs both coming and going.
   For now, when I know nothing more than where he is,
   I want to become a bit more daring
   And send forth my messenger   45
   To carry news of our friendship for us.
   I do know that we are half-way there,
   But I have no proof of her love
   And I can't imagine how a thing can be finished
   Until after it has started.   50

6. For I have seen how one begins to build a tower
   With just one stone
   And how with each one it grows taller
   Until finally one can prepare it for occupation.
   This is why I maintain chivalrous conduct   55
   So carefully, just as you advise me to,

And once my song is put to music
I shall send it on its way
If I can find someone to carry it there quickly for me
So that she can enjoy it and take delight in it.   60

7. And if ever I go to see an emperor
Or a king, and he wants to reward me
In the same way that he would his traitor
Who doesn't know how and isn't able to protect
Or support him,   65
May he send me away as a hostage to a foreign kingdom.
Likewise, I will be punished
And will suffer great harm
If her lovely white and highly-prized body
Is kept away from me or if she is angry with me.   70

8. So you see and understand,
You to whom my language is familiar,
That where I once used closed and covered words
I now make them good and clear.

9. And toward this end I have made a real effort   75
That you might understand every song that I compose.[1]

[1] Guiraut's ending is a reference to the fact that he previously wrote songs that were difficult to interpret (*trobar clus*). He might also mean that he used to compose songs that had multiple meanings and that encouraged alternate, often humorous and erotic readings (see Kendrick 1988). His declaration of clarity is nonetheless belied by the not altogether clear context in which it is found.

8. Guiraut de Borneill 242, 73 (B/S, 53)
   MSS: N^2 22; Sg 91
   Base Text: N^2

Due to the pain and sorrow that Sir Giraut de Borneil felt at the death of King Richard of England and to the trickery that his lady Alamanda had pulled on him, Giraut had retired from singing and composing and socializing. But Sir Ramon Bernart of Rovingna[1], who was a very noble man from Gascogne and his very good friend and with whom he shared the reciprocal name of "Above-All-Others," begged him and counseled him to be gay and so he composed this song which says:

If it were not for my Above-All-Others...

(Manuscript Sg adds at the end of this razo the statement):

...which song you will find written in this book.[2]

[1] Sharman does not believe that Ramon Bernart is truly the perrson represented under the senhal, Sobre-Totz.
[2] See note 2 to razo 6b.

Song 242, 73   Guiraut de Borneill: "Si per mo Sobre-Totz no fos..."
                Source: Sharman, 473.
                MSS: A 19, B 20, C 25, D 4, I 16, K 6, N 183, Q 88, R 9, Sg 77, a 46.
                Other English translations: Sharman, 477.

1. If it were not for my Above-All-Others
   Who tells me I should sing and be gay,
   Neither the lovely season when the grass grows,
   Nor the fields nor the branches nor the woods nor the flowers,
   Nor a cruel lord or a pointless love   5
   Could get me up and moving.
      But this is why I stay with him:
      For since joy is failing and fleeing,
      Renown and manly virtue have sunken low;
      And ever since the powerful   10
      Renounced such virtues,
      No matter what the worst of them has done
      He has not been praised by me.

    For this is what I have decided:
    Not to court any rich man   15
    Who abuses his power.

2. At one time the world was a good place,
   When joy was welcomed everywhere,
   And he who was most joyful was most honored,
   And good reputation went with wealth.   20
   But now they call the worst men worthy
   And the one who takes
       The most that he can from others
       Is even more courted
       Than the one who shows the worst temper.   25
   No wonder I feel violated
   When I see a man in a miserable and dishonorable
       situation
   Gathering praise as a good and true man
   For actions that should have earned him censure.
   And why do you not consider   30
   Whether it is right to praise someone
   Who has behaved abominably?

3. Reason has been sorely misguided
   Since the dishonorable have been found praiseworthy
   And the generous, courtly and honest men   35
   Have been judged to be their inferiors.
   And it was the fault of the people on top
   When the sense of justice cracked and shattered.
       For now I don't know for whom it is
       That they take way the land of a man[1]   40
       Who rightfully occupied it.
       And if you accuse them of this
       They will say that that's the way it should be
       Because the one whose name I won't mention
       Will be better armed.   45
       And then if you strive for
       Reputation and courtly service
       You have the equipment for the harvest.[2]

4. I have seen how men used to cherish songs
   And how they enjoyed dance music and stories in song. 50
   Now I see that ever since men's tastes have moved away

> From courtly amusement and tales of noble deeds
> And the adventures of fine lovers
> They have veered away from justice
>> And flee *en groupe* the call of righteousness.   55
>> For if a man deprives himself of
>> Meat, wine and wheat
>> And you accompany him like a fool,
>> I wouldn't consider that praiseworthy.
>> I wouldn't be believed if I did,   60
>> And I'd get no profit for saying so;
>> For wealth is worth little to a man
>> Who uses it badly and who in doing so
>> Follows neither law nor justice.

5. Now I hear about the King, who was more noble[3]   65
   And worthy in his affairs
   Than any man who feeds on food,
   For he overcame both the base and the high-born,
   Embellished his honor and reputation
   And never feared trouble and hard work.   70
   > But if two people are bemoaning his fate
   > A third will denounce him before them,
   > And this seems to me to be very ill-advised.
   > For I do not think there has ever been born,
   > From the time of Charlemagne on,   75
   > A King who has been so supported and praised
   > For so many fine endeavors.
   > But don't think for a moment
   > That you could get all three together to mourn him
   > No matter how bad the state of affairs!   80

6. So what good is a fine appearance
   Or great power which can fade like this?
   Never has any other name or reputation or terror
   Extended beyond Edessa
   Among the lying pagans   85
   That any one of them was able to drive them back any further
       than he.
   > This is why anyone who enjoys himself is wrong:
   > For what he most wants and loves
   > Can so quickly evade him.
   > This is why I maintain that those who are in a position

To do more here for the effort over there	91
And don't do it will be punished	
At the moment when their riches are transformed.	
Let them have some pleasure	
From their generosity	95
When they stand before that greatest of Kings.	

7. For this wicked and tiresome world
Gives merit only to the one who acquires the most,
Who thinks of nothing more than fattening himself,
Whose body does whatever he can get away with, 100
And loses his soul without receiving any help
From the one whose covenant he has broken.
   For never has any man taken sufficient refuge
Or locked and closed himself tightly enough
Behind beautiful fortified walls 105
When the moment comes at which he must pass over to
    that port
From which no one escapes,
No matter how secure he may seem.
This is why it is good advice
That a man should repent here 110
For his sins, rather than suffer for them over there.

8. I beg him, who alone is called
God and Trinity,
That he keep me from committing such folly
Here that I should suffer for it there. 115

9. May every man pay him court here
So that his faults not bring him grief over there.

---

[1] The word "onor" is clearly to be read in both senses here: as "honor" and as "land, goods."
  [2] The use of the word "correi/conroi" here seems to invite a bawdy oral reading as well: "...at least you have the cunt, King, to harvest." Given that Guiraut is criticizing the failure of the nobility to maintain ancient values, it seems reasonable to assume that he would suggest that courtship of ladies (domnei) has also been debased to a question of genitals. See razo 10 for an

illustration of what Guiraut is denouncing in stanza 3: a lord taking over another's property.

[3] The King is Richard-the-Lionhearted.

9. Guiraut de Borneill 242, 46 (B/S, 55)
   MS: N^2 23, Sg 92
   Base Text: N^2

   Giraut de Borneil had departed from the court of the good King Anfos of Castille. The King had given him a very fine gray saddle horse along with many other presents and all the barons of his court had given him great gifts. And Giraut was off to Gascogne and was to pass through the territory of the King of Navarre. Now that King knew all about how rich Giraut was and that he would be passing through his lands at the border of Castille and Aragon and Navarre and so he had him robbed. He took all his equipment, kept as his own the gray horse, and left the other riches to the robbers who had done the job. This is why Giraut composed this song which says:

   The sweet song of a bird...

Song 242, 46   Guiraut de Borneill: "Lo dolz chans d'un auzel..."
                 Source: Sharman, 377.
                 MSS: A 16, B 14, C 17, D 9, I 15, K 5, M 8, N 174, Q 105, R 82, Sg 81, a 35.
                 Other English translations: Sharman, 382; Smythe, 139.

1. The sweet song of a bird
   Who was singing in a hedge
   Diverted me the other day

From my path and drew me toward itself.
And just next to the enclosure 5
Where the little bird was,
Three young girls, in unison,
Were bemoaning in song
The harm and abuse
That joy and courtly pleasure have undergone. 10
I moved more quickly toward them
So as to better hear the song
And then I said to them:
"Girls, what are you singing about
Or what it is you denounce?" 15

2. The older one, who knew better,
Grabbed her coat,[1]
And said: "About a refusal to cooperate
On the part of some despicable noble men,
On account of whom youthfulness has fallen by the
    wayside. 20
For just as the noble man acts as a guide[2]
To good reputation and brings it along,
Augmenting and advancing it,
So have the worst of the wicked
Taken to insuring its ruin. 25
For if you are happy
And make that known by your appearance
They will arrange that
You never have any joy
If ever you are made part of their inner circle."[3] 30

3. "Young girl, they are not as eager now
To put themselves to the test
As the earlier lords were,
Back when joy abounded
And singing was welcomed. 35
I, myself, can find no one
Who calls for me, seeks me out
Or asks for me, and I am sorely vexed.
Quite the contrary. This year,
Between three esteemed kings, 40
I was taken for all I had and one of the kingdoms
Is still after me.

This is clear in the case of the gray horse
Who was given to me graciously
But presented to me to my misfortune."   45

4. "Lord, anyone who robs someone who works for him
And feeds and clothes himself on what he gets
Takes on a vile bundle
And a shameful load.
And any place where he is welcomed   50
Is greatly disgraced.
If any other powerful person
Should support such a despicable thief,
Full of evil and treachery,
Or treat him with favor,   55
It is very unlikely that he will ever be praised;
For it will quickly be said
By those who don't know the full story
That he himself is guilty of what the other has done
Or that half of the blame should fall on him."   60

5. "My friend, it used to be that in the new season
Men would be gay.
But now no one wants an orchard
Until he can get fat off the fruit,
And song and public display no longer please.   65
Everyone is depressed,
And the young men are the worst of all
For they don't even encourage one another.
I have seen a group of nobles skirmish
For an entire year   70
Over a glove
That had been sent to them.
Now they will hide
Their silly friendships from you
Once their reputation has been established."   75

6. "My Lord, fortified castles,
From which wickedness is born,
And walls of stone and ramparts,
Have wrongfully and unnaturally[4]
Cut off gift-giving and invitations to feasts.   80
Now no man is given what he needs

But those who man the war-machines
That sit atop the fortification,
From which point a wild townsman
Will go screaming   85
All night long: 'Get up,
I heard a noise!'
Then up they get,
And you, if you don't get up,
Will be blamed for it."   90

7. "What good will it do me, my friend,
   If I revolt or get angry about it?
   Do you think even the least of them
   Would take any action
   Based on such small blows?   95
   Or that some hardened youth,
   Once I have a hold of him[5]
   Would take a turn for the better
   Over such a little slap of the rod
   Or bestir himself?   100
   For even a truly esteemed and noble man
   Who treats you like a companion
   Will soon fear trouble
   And think himself sorely put upon
   If you ask him for the slightest little thing."   105

8. "My friend, if the lord of Bordeaux[6]
   Doesn't take up the burden
   And doesn't make it his concern
   That the entire world is going downhill
   Then let it perish.   110
   For once joy has failed
   I see nothing in all the others
   That is worthy of a good reputation.
   Nor will God or faith or peace
   Ever go to a place   115
   Where the lord rules in bad humor;
   For those who surround him
   Will imitate him,
   And once joy begins to please him
   All around him will be happy."   120

33

9. "Young girl, I am giving up
   On singing any more this year
   If it pleases my Above-All-Others
   That I am not to be rewarded."

10. "Lord, I am sure that the two Bertrans[7]   125
    Will tell you
    That giving up singing
    Is ill-advised."

11. "Young girl, one who loves but is unloved
    Is completely disgraced."   130

12. "Lord, be patient and put up with it
    For thus you will be loved."

[1] The older girl's grabbing her coat is likely a reference to the situation portrayed in the Old French and Provençal *pastourelle*, in which a nobleman comes upon a young girl in the countryside and seduction or rape ensues. On the pastourelle see Faral, 1923; Bec, 1970; Gravdal, 1985; and Paden, 1987 and 1989.

[2] "Pros" could also be translated "profit" here, implying that profit is what leads one to seek a good reputation.

[3] "Privatz" could mean part of the intimate circle or quite the opposite: "banished, solitary."

[4] "De tort et de biais" might also refer to ramparts twisting and turning on the hills (Smith) or the "criss-cross" of walls and earthworks (Sharman).

[5] An alternate erotic translation, based on the auditory word play of "pel" and "verjan" would be:
...Or that some hardened youth/ Once I have him by the balls ("tir a la pel")/ Would get any better/ With a little thrust of the prick? (colp de verjan").

[6] Identified by Kolsen as Henry II of England. If the poem was written after 1189 it would be a reference to Richard-the-Lionhearted (Sharman, 384).

[7] The "Bertrans" are referred to in razo 51 to Guillem de Saint Leidier's song 234, 16: "Pois tant mi forss'Amors que m'a faich." Kolsen had identified them as Bertran I del Baus and his son. Sakari, in his edition of Guillem's songs, says they should be looked on as

a sort of footnote referring one back to Guillem's song. Stronski's argument, that the senhals refer first and foremost to other poets seems to make good sense in this case, though to which two fellow poets Guiraut may be referring is unclear.

10. Guiraut de Borneill 242, 55 (B/S, 57)
MS: N^2 23, Sg 92
Base Text: N^2

After Gui, the Viscount of Limoges, had had Giraut de Borneil robbed of the books from his house and of all his equipment, Giraut realized that merit had fled, sociability had gone to rest, gallantry had died, prowess had faltered, courtesy was lost, good upbringing had fallen into decadence, and trickery had permeated everywhere among lovers of both sexes. This incited Guiraut to take it upon himself to revive gracious conversation, joy and merit and so he composed this song which says:

To revive courtly pleasure...

Song 242, 55   Guiraut de Borneill: "Per solatz revelhar..."
Source: Sharman, 467.
MSS: A 12, B 8, C 6, D 6, I 19, K 9, N 167, P (attributed to Blacasset), Q 103, R 35, Sg 81, U 21, V 75, c 5.
Other English translations: Bonner, 126; Goldin, 196; Press, 144; Sharman, 470.

1. To revive courtly pleasure
   Which has been asleep for too long
   And to bring back and give welcome to
   Good reputation, which has been in exile,

        I decided to put myself to work.   5
        But now I've given up on all that.
        This is the reason I failed at my task:
        Because it cannot be accomplished.
    For just when my will and desire are strongest
    There comes from there increasing disarray and damage. 10

2.   It is hard to put up with.
        I am only telling you for you heard
        How joy was rewarded
        With all its fine accompaniments.
        But now you can't swear   15
        That you haven't seen splindly mares
        And broken-down, old, riff-raff[1]
        Charging about on horseback against their will.
    It's a dirty business, cruel and inappropriate,
    In which man loses God and is left in misery.   20

3.   You saw tournaments proclaimed
        And well-equipped men attend them
        And how people would talk for a long time
        About those who struck the best blows.
        Now it is considered glorious to take sheep from the
            flock   25
        And run off with them.
        May he be disgraced, any knight
        Who turns to courting ladies
    After having laid a hand on bleating sheep
    Or robbed churches and travelers.   30

4.   Where have they fled to, those entertainers
        You saw so nobly welcomed?
        For he who used to serve as a guide
        Now needs one himself.
        And yet nowadays, without casting any blame,   35
        Ever since a good reputation has lost its appeal,
        They go about in a state of penury,
        Those who used to lead
    I don't know how many companions about,
    All beautiful, noble, well-bred and well-equipped.   40

5.   You saw well-accomplished joglars
      Going from court to court,
      Finely shod and dressed
      Just to give praise to ladies.
      Now we don't even dare talk about them,   45
      So far have their fortunes declined!
      Where did the evil practice start
      Of speaking badly of ladies?
   I don't know.--Who is to blame, the ladies or the lovers?
   I say both, for deceitfulness robbed them of their great
      renown.   50

6.   I, myself, whom every noble
      And distinguished man used to seek out,
      Am so bewildered
      That I don't know where to turn;
      For instead of refined conversation   55
      I now hear in the courts such a low level of talk
      That the story of Bretmar's goose
      Would be just as well received
   By them as a well-made song
   About the noble deeds of our times and of the past.   60

7.   But in order to soften a heart
      That has grown too hard
      Shouldn't a man commemorate
      The forgotten and ancient deeds?
      It is wrong to give up on   65
      A code of behavior after it has been sworn to
      And I don't need to take any medicine
      For the sickness of which I've been cured.
   But what a man sees, let him turn and twist and weigh it,
   Take it up and let it go and penetrate it from both sides![2] 70

8.   Of this much I can boast:
      That never was my little house
      Invaded by them;
      For I see it is feared by them all.
      They have never done me anything but honor,   75
      the cowardly and the brave.
      Thus should My-Lord in his mercy
      Give some thought to the fact

> That it brings him no glory, praise or pomp
> That I, who am praising others, should be complaining about
>   him.   80

9. No more now. Why? Don't ask me;
   For there will be mourning if this is how my song ends.

10. So says the Dauphin, who recognizes good songs.[3]

[1] An alternate to "fronitz" (broken-down) in seven manuscript versions is "formitz" which is a pun meaning both "ants" and "highly accomplished".
[2] These very ambiguous lines were explained by Goldin, 1973 (p. 200) through reference to Kolsen's notes: "Because one courageously reveals the abuses he witnesses, speaks in every direction and continually stigmatizes, he helps toward the removal of those abuses." The final portion, "forse d'ams los pans!" seems intended to convey the poet's desire to criticize what he sees through use of a sexual metaphor: "rape it from both sides."
[3] Dalfi d'Alvergne, himself a poet and patron of the troubadours. See razos 53-56.

11. Arnaut Daniel 29, 2 (B/S, 62)
    MS: R 2

And it happened that he was in the court of King Richard of England and, while at that court, another joglar[1] provoked him, saying that he composed in richer rhymes than he (Arnaut)[2]. Ar(naut) took offense at this and, with the King's power as guarantor, they made a bet, each betting his saddle horse that the other couldn't do as well as he could. The King locked each of them in a room. Sir Ar(naut), due to the indignation that he felt, was unable to link one word with another. The joglar composed his song quickly and with ease. They had been given only ten days, and in just five days they were to be judged by the King. The joglar asked Ar(naut) if he had composed his song and Ar(naut) said yes, that he had finished three days earlier, when in fact he had not even thought about it. The joglar sang his song all night so that he would be sure to know it well. Sir Ar(naut) thought of a way to pull a joke on him. One night while the joglar was singing, Sir Ar(naut) went and memorized the song and the melody. When they went before the King, Sir Ar(naut) said that he wanted to perform his song; and he began to sing beautifully the song that the joglar had composed. And the joglar, when he heard it, looked him in the face and said that it was he who had composed it. The King asked how that could be, and the joglar begged the King to find out the truth; so the King asked Ar(naut) how this had come about. Sir Ar(naut) told him what had happened and the King was greatly amused[3] and took it all as a great joke. The bets were called off and he had fine gifts given to each of them. And to Sir Arnaut Daniel was given the song which says:

"Never did I have her, but she keeps me..."

And here you will find some of his works.[4]

[1] The word *joglar* I have left untranslated as it does not correspond to any one word in English and can mean different things depending upon the context. Here it suggests a composing singer, i.e. a poet who performs his own works. In other settings, it can mean simply an entertainer who performs others' works.
[2] The reference to "rich rhymes," "caras rimas" is indicative of the importance that the technical construction of the song held for the audience and composers. Although the tale that serves as the base for this razo could just as easily apply to any singer as to Arnaut and was probably a tale in circulation into which his name was inserted, the reference to "rimas caras" does fit Arnaut's poetry. He was known even in his day as the finest fashioner of song and modern poets, such as Ezra Pound, have reiterated this craftsman's praise. Dante refers to Arnaut as the "miglior fabbro del parlar materno" (*Purgatorio* 26..117). See Wilhelm, 1982.
[3] The term used here is 'gaug' (joy) which is often contrasted with 'joi,' the other Provençal term for joy. Here the distinction is seen to be between laughter, on the one hand, and intellectual or sensual bliss on the other. In keeping with Arnaut's usage, "gaug"

has been interpreted as pertaining to the physical (bliss in sexual terms) and "joi" as ethereal, pure, religious or philosophical bliss.

[4] Again, the reference to the book itself, implying that someone will consult the manuscript for the purpose of finding songs. This would mean that in this collection of prefaces to songs the razos were not written down exactly as they were performed. Either the razo has had this last sentence added to it by the scribe or it was, in fact, composed expressly for the written manuscript. The paradox implicit in this razo is that the song that one is about to read or hear was supposedly not even composed by Arnaut, only attributed to him.

Song 29,2   Arnaut Daniel
             Source: Wilhelm, 26.
             MSS: A 40, C 204, D 52, E 59, G 74, I 67, K 51, L
                  109, N 191, N^2 3, Q 40, R 48, c 41.
             Other English translations: Smythe, 112; Wilhelm, 26.

1. Never did I have her, but she keeps me
    forever in her power, Love.
    And she makes me angry, happy, wise and crazy,
    Like someone who can never veer from his course.
    For a man who loves well cannot defend himself   5
    When love commands
    That he serve and court her.
    This is why I wait,
    Enduring what I must,
    For a good portion   10
    When it will be allotted to me.

2. If I say little, there is within my heart
    A fear which keeps me trembling;
    The tongue complains but the heart wants
    What it sorrowfully endures.   15
    And so it languishes, but does not speak out
    For within the entirety of all those people
    In the land that the sea embraces

   There is not one
   Present 20
   So gracious as the chosen one
   I have longed for.

3. So well do I know her fine and certain value
   That I cannot turn elsewhere.
   This is why I act like this, making my body (heart) ache, 25
   For, from daybreak to its closing,
   I dare not say who it is who sets me aflame.
   My heart (body) scorches me
   Yet my eyes have their food,
   For just 30
   Seeing
   Her brings relief.
   You see what is keeping me alive!

4. He who, through his talking, seeks to turn
   His joy to sorrow is mad; 35
   For the false flatterers (may God bring them to ruin!)
   Don't have a clever little tongue.
   One of them counsels and the other one rails.
   That is why love gives up altogether:
   What a great thing it might have been! 40
   But I defend myself,
   Pretending,
   Against their noise,
   And I love without failing.

5. Yet she keeps me safe and in rapture 45
   Through a pleasure with which she raised me.
   But never will it pass through my throat
   For fear that she might be displeased with me.
   I still feel the flame
   Of love, which commands 50
   That my heart (body) not divulge itself.[1]
   Still, I often do so,
   In fear,
   For I see that talk in public
   Destroys many a love. 55

6. I would have composed many more good, simple,
   And easy songs if she had helped me,
   She who gives me joy and takes it away.
   For now I am happy; then she turns things around on me.
   Because she binds me to her will.   60
   My heart (body) asks nothing
   Of her; nor does it stray from her.
   Rather, I give
   Myself to her openly.
   Thus, if she forgets me,   65
   Mercy is dead.

7. To Better-than-Good
   Deliver these songs
   (If she accepts you) and my thanks,
   For Arnaut does not forget.   70

[1] There is an erotic subtext here, which could be translated: "She keeps me healthy and in a state of rapture with a kind of pleasure that keeps me high, but it will never get through my neck for fear that it might upset her. I still feel the flame of love, which is telling me that my body shouldn't let it flow..." A passage such as this, read in conjunction with Jacquart and Thomasset's strange but often convincing interpretation of the troubadour lyric as a coded message on *coitus interruptus*, can obviously take on several different layers of meaning (Jacquart and Thomasset, 1985).

12. Bertran de Born 80, 37 (B/S, 72)
    MSS: F 90, I 183, K 168.
    Base Text: I

Bertran de Born and Jaufre de Bretagne, who was the brother of the Young King and of Sir Richard the Count of Poitiers, called each other "Rassa".[1] Sir Richard and Sir Jaufre were both courting Bertran de Born's lady, Maeuz of Montaingnac,[2] as were King Anfos of Aragon and Sir

Raimon, the Count of Toulouse. And she refused them all in favor of Sir Bertran de Born, whom she had taken as her admirer and instructor. In order to induce the others to cease addressing their pleas to her, Bertran decided to show Count Jaufre just what kind of Lady it was that he was courting; and so he praised her in such a way that it appeared that he had seen her and held her in the nude. He wanted it to be known that Maeuz was his lady, the same one who had refused Poiters--referring to Sir Richard, who was the Count of Poitiers-- and Sir Jaufre, who was the Count of Bretagne, and the King of Aragon who was the Lord of Saragossa, and Count Raimon, the Lord of Toulouse. And that is why Sir Bertran said this:

> Rassa, to the mighty she is haughty
> And she has good sense about her, being a girl
> Who wants neither Poitiers nor Toulouse,
> Brittany or Saragossa.
> She is, on the other hand, so desirous of good repute
> That she gives her love to the valiant poor...(80, 37: 12-17)

And so for the reason that I explained to you he composed his sirventes[3] and also to castigate the rich who hold back on their gifts, who speak and wish evil, who accuse when there is no wrong, who offer no pardon and do not reward service; as well as those who talk only about the flight of hawks and don't dare speak of love and arms amongst themselves. And he wanted Count Richard to go to war against the Viscount of Limoges and that the Viscount should defend himself with valor. And for these reasons he composed the sirventes which says:

> Rassa, she who is free of all trickery
> So grows, climbs and ascends...

[1] Bertran was implicated in the political struggles of the sons of Henry II, including Richard-the-Lionhearted, Geoffrey of Brittany, John Lackland, and Young Henry. He played an important role in the Young King's (Henry) attempts to assert his independence from his father, as can be seen in the following razos. This song is an exhortation to Geoffrey to consider "...the sources of personal worth in men and women" (Paden et al., 194), especially as his brother Henry is calling on him to act as his ally against brother Richard.

[2] Stronski (1914) showed that this lady is a fiction. The genealogy outlined in the following razo, 80, 12, is invented but given the veneer of truth by placing it among mention of some of the best known political figures of the day. Note also that the "frères ennemis", Richard and Geoffrey, rivals for political power and prestige, are here represented as rivals in love. In Bertan's world, one sphere acts as metaphor for the other.

[3] A song of satire, ridicule, criticism, or encouragement to war, or simply one which treats a political subject rather than a drama of love.

80,37   Bertran de Born: "Rassa, tan creis e mont'e poia..."
        Source: Paden et al., 194.
        MSS: A 190, C 144, D 122, D^c 257, E 98, F 90, I 183, K 168, M 231, R6.
        Other English translations: Bonner, 139; Blackburn, 154; Paden et al., 194.

1. Rassa, she who is free of all trickery
So grows, climbs and ascends
That her reputation irritates the other women.
There isn't one to whom she has to give up a thing.
For the sight of her beauty lures   5
Noble men into her service, regardless of who is hurt.
The wisest and best
Will always sound her praise
And consider her the most noble
For she knows so well how to give undivided honor: 10
She wants only one suitor.[1]

2. Rassa, to the mighty she is haughty
And she has good sense about her, being a girl
Who wants neither Poitiers nor Toulouse,
Brittany nor Saragossa.   15
She is, on the other hand, so desirous of good reputation
That she gives her love to the valiant poor.
Since she has taken me on as her mentor

  I beg her to be sparing with her love
  And love a noble vasassor   20
  More than a count or deceitful duke
  Who might hold her in dishonor.

3. Rassa, this lady is fine and fresh,
  Young, gracious and gay,
  Blond hair with ruby highlights,   25
  White skin and a neck like a hawthorn blossom,
  Soft elbows and firm little breasts,
  And from the back you'd think she was a rabbit;[2]
  And she has fine, fresh color,
  Good reputation and is widely praised.   30
  Those who really know me
  Can easily pick her out as the finest of all
  And figure in which direction I have turned my praise.[3]

4. Rassa, a rich man who gives nothing,
  Who neither entertains, spends or invites,   35
  Who accuses people for no reason,
  And who doesn't give pardon when he has been asked for mercy
  Irritates me, as does any person
  Who doesn't reward service.
  Rich hunters irritate me too;   40
  And so do those who hunt with hawks,
  And go on and on about the goosehawk's flight
  And never say a word amongst themselves
  About feats of arms or love.

5. So Rassa, I am asking you to admire   45
  A rich man who does not tire of war;
  Who does not give up when threatened
  Until the other gives up and does him no further harm.
  His time is better spent than in hunting and bird-chasing
  For he gathers and amasses praise for his name.   50
  Maurin and his lord, Sir Aigar
  Are considered to be aggressive fighters.
  Let the viscount defend his land
  And the count make his claim on it with force
  And let's see it happen now, in the spring.[3]   55

6. Mariner, you have your land
   And we have exchanged a lord
   Who was a good warrior for a tourney-goer.[4]
   And I pray that Golfier de la Tor
   Will not be frightened by my song.   60

7. Papiol, run through my song again
   In the court of my bad Fair Lord.[5]

[1] Identifications in the song include: Maurin e'n Agar, characters from the Provençal epic *Aigar et Maurin*; "the viscount", Aimar V of Limoges, who had joined young Henry and Geoffrey in defiance of Richard-the-Lionhearted; "the count," Richard-the-Lionhearted; "Mariner," possibly another code-name for Geoffrey; and Golfier de la Tor, Bertran's nephew, ancestor of the hero of the First Crusade. For more detailed information see Paden et al., 194-203 and 1-32.

[2] When spoken, this line can also take on the more erotic meaning: "and her little cunt, it looks utterly delicious" (i.e. when "e sembra conil de l'esquina" is pronounced so as to suggest: "e sembra con ilh delechina").

[3] The Viscount of Limoges, Aimar V, had joined with the Young King and Geoffrey in February 1183 against Richard (the count) (Paden et al., 201).

[4] The good warrior would be Richard; the tourney-goer, Henry, the Young King (Paden et al., 203).

[5] I have followed the stanza order used by Paden et al. in the critical edition although the razo manuscripts (F, I, K) do not contain the final three stanzas and reverse stanzas 2 and 3. Papiol is Bertran's singer. It is he, rather than a lord of Bertran's status, who would travel to the other courts to perform these compositions. He is mentioned in several of Bertran's other songs (80/ 37, 12, 21, 31, 36, 38).

13. Bertran de Born 80, 12 (B/S, 75)
    MSS: F 83, I 182, K 167.
    Base Text: I

Bertran de Born was the lover of a noble, young, highly esteemed lady whose name was Maeuz of Montaignac, the wife of Lord Talairan, who was the brother of the Count of Perigord; and she was the daughter of the Viscount of Turenne and the sister of Lady Maria of Ventadorn and of Lady Elis of Montfort.[1] And, according to what he says in his song, she broke off with him and sent him away, leaving him very sad and upset; and he reasoned[2] that he would never get her back or find another as beautiful, good, charming or learned. And since he would not find another the equal of his lady, he decided that he should make one through a system of borrowing from each of the other good and beautiful ladies one trait of beauty: an expression, a warm welcome, a lovely way of speaking, beautiful composure, perfect height or an ideal figure. And so he went around asking all the good ladies to give him one of the gifts that you have heard me name in order to bring back to him the lady he had lost. In the sirventes that he composed on this subject you will hear named all the ladies whom he visited seeking aid and abetment in his project of creating the borrowed lady. And the sirventes that he composed on this topic begins:

  Lady, since you do not care for me...

  [1] Stronski showed that Lady Maeuz is fictional, though all the rest of the facts in this family history are true.
  [2] Literally, "fez razo," or "made/composed a razo." The sense of this phrase is that he analyzed the situation and came up with a solution. In the same sense the author(s) of these texts analyzed the song before him and came up with the a possible explanation for the events outlined in the song. In the last two lines, the word "razo" is twice used to indicate subject matter and topic.

Song 80, 12 Bertran de Born: "Dompna, puois de mi no.us cal..."
      Source: Paden et al., 150.
      MSS: A 189, B 113, D 124, F 83, I 182, K 167.
      Other English translations: Bonner, 142; Goldin, 234;
        Paden et al., 150; Wilhelm, 166.

1. Lady, since you do not care for me
   And have sent me away
   For no good reason,
     I don't know where to look;
       For never again   5
   Will I find a joy so rich,
   And if I do not find a lady
   Whose appearance is to my liking
   And who is the equal of you, whom I have lost,
   Then I never want to have another lover.   10

2. Since I can find no one to equal you:
   Who is as beautiful and noble,
   Whose precious body is so full of joy,
     Who is of such lovely appearance
       And so gay,   15
   Or whose glorious reputation is so well-founded,
   I will go everywhere looking
   For one trait of beauty from each of the others
   To make up an imaginary lady
   Until you are returned to me.   20

3. Fresh, natural color,
   I will take from you, My-beautiful-Sable,
   As well as your sweet and loving glance;
     I am being presumptuous
       In leaving you anything,   25
   For there is nothing good that you lack.
   I ask My-Lord, Lady Elis,
   To give me her clever and bountiful talk
   To help me with My-Lord
   For that way she will be neither stupid nor mute.   30

4. I want the would-be viscountess of Chales[1]
   To give me at once
   Her throat and both her hands.
     Then, sticking to my route,
       Without veering off in either direction,   35
   I head straight for Rochechouard,
   For Lady Agnes' hair, so that she will give me some;
   For we know that not even Iseut, Tristan's lady,

Who was celebrated by one and all,
   Had hair so beautiful.   40

5. As for Lady Audiartz, although she wishes me ill,
   I want her to give me her face,
   For she looks so good when she fixes herself up;
      And because she is whole
         And her love doesn't break   45
   Or veer off in other directions,
   I ask my Better-than-Good
   For her celebrated young body
   Which, from just a glance, gives the impression
   That it would be a pleasure to hold her naked.   50

6. Likewise for Lady Faidida,
   I want from her her lovely teeth as a gift,
   And the welcome and fine conversation
      She offers to those
         In her home.   55
   I want My-Beautiful-Mirror to give me
   Her gaiety and good taste
   For she knows how to maintain her own well-being
   And doesn't change and isn't fickle:
   She is known for this.   60

7. Beautiful-Lord, I ask nothing more of you
   Than that I be as desirous of this lady
   As I am of you,
      For there is a lusty
         Love born   65
   That has my body lusting.
   I would rather be asking you for love
   Than making it with any other.
   Why then does My-Lord refuse me
   When she knows how much I have wanted her?   70

8. Papiol, you shall go to My-Magnet[2]
   And tell him in song
   That love is no longer recognized here
   And has fallen low from high above.

[1] "Viscountal lady from Chales" is identified by Paden et al. as the wife of Olivier, lord of Chalais, whose son and brother were viscounts. They see this as a case of Bertran gloating over their slightly less noble standing (Paden et al., 155).

[2] Stronski identified My-Magnet with the troubadour Folquet de Marseille, who also used this senhal, presumably to refer to Bertran (*Folquet*, 37-43). Stronski shows that many of the senhals, and especially reciprocal ones, actually refer to other troubadours, who were also, in some cases, political allies.

14. Bertran de Born 80, 1 and 15 (B/S, 78)

MSS: F 85, I 182, K 168.
Base Text: I
Other English translations of the song: Blackburn, 157; Paden et al., 130.

Bertran de Born was the lover of my lady Maeutz of Montaingnac, the wife of Tallairan, the same lady I told you about in the razo to the sirventes on the "borrowed lady."[1] And as I told you, she broke off with him and sent him away and made accusations about him and my lady Guiscarda, wife of the Viscount of Comborn, an esteemed lady from Burgundy, sister of Sir Guiscart de Beaujeu. She was a lovely and learned lady, replete with all the signs of beauty, and he highly praised her in speech and in song. On account of all the good things he had heard about her, Bertran was her friend even before he saw her and before her marriage to the Viscount of Comborn. And from the happiness he felt at her coming, he composed these verses which said:

> Ah, Limousin, free and courtly land,
> It delights me that such honor accrues to you;
> For joy and merit, amusement and gaiety,
> Courtliness, conversation and courting of ladies
> Become available to us; and may this spirit stay on forever!
> Anything who thinks of himself as a lover must note
> For what deeds a lady should be sought.[2]

Gifts and service, generosity and the granting of arms
Nourish love as does water a fish;
So do learning, valor and prowess,
Arms and assembled courts, wars and tournaments.
And anyone who is good or pretends to be
Will be in trouble if he doesn't show it
Now that Lady Guiscarda has been sent here to us.

And on account of this Lady Guiscarda, my Lady Maeuz sent him away from her, for she believed that he loved the other more than he loved her and that she was giving him her love. It was over this parting that he composed "the borrowed lady" and the sirventes which says:

"Lady, I defend myself; may no evil come to me..."

[1] See the previous razo and song 80, 12. It is clear that the "I" refers to the author of some, and perhaps all, of the other razos to Bertran's songs. These razos are unusual in that they are all found together in the thirteenth-century northern Italian manuscripts I and K and in the later fourteenth-century manuscript F. Their presence in the earlier manuscripts, as well as their number and uniformity in text and in order from one manuscript to the next, suggests a project that differs from the almost random explanatory function of many of the other razos.

[2] The ambiguity of this line points out the duality of the lady/lord, patron/poet relation and both senses must be retained in translation, as in:

"...for what deeds a lady should be sought" (i.e. what she does to deserve it)
"...by means of what deeds a lady should be sought" (i.e. what deeds performed make a knight worthy of her.)

It is clear that the deeds by which a lady makes herself desirable (gifts, tourneys etc.) are actions generally offered by the lord of castle. Hence it may frequently be the case that the poet is singing to the patron as if to a lady, regardless of the actual gender. If, on the other hand, we understand it to mean that these are the traits required of the lover, then the song is still a call to the lord/lady to provide him the framework within which he will be able to fulfill love's requirements. Lady Guiscarda's arrival provides the excuse for the lord's granting of that framework in the form of public celebrations.

Song 80, 1   Bertran de Born: "Ai Lemozis, francha terra cortesa..."
 MSS: F 85, I 182, K 168.
 Other English translations: Blackburn, 157; Paden et al., 130.

The full, extant text of the song is contained within razo 14, above.

Song 80, 15 Bertran de Born: "Eu m'escondisc, dompna, que mal non mier..."
 Source: Paden et al., 142.
 MSS: A 196, B 116, C 142, D 122, E 98, F 85, I 182, K 167, R 97, T 97 (attributed to Peire Cardenal).
 Other English translations: Blackburn, 158; Paden et al., 142; Wilhelm, 164.

1. Lady, I defend myself; may no evil come to me[1]
 Over what those false-flatterers have said about me.
 I beg you for mercy. Let no one be able to cause trouble
 Between me and your fine, true, loyal,
 Humble, pure, refined and pleasing body,   5
 By the telling of lies, my lady.

2. May I lose my sparrowhawk on the first throw
 Or let lanner falcons kill him on my fist
 And carry him away; and let me see him plucked by them
 If I don't prefer the thought of you   10
 To having my way with another
 Who would give me her love and hold me tight in bed.

3. I will make another more serious protestation of innocence
   And I cannot wish for a worse predicament:
   For if ever I fail you, even if only in thought,   15
   The next time we are alone in the bedroom or in the garden
   Let my powers fail me in front of my companion
   So badly that he cannot help me.[2]

4. If I sit down at the table to gamble
   May I never get a cent out of it   20
   Or, having sat at the table, ever be allowed to get into the game.
   Rather, may my throws always take me backwards
   If ever I approach or ask for any lady
   But you, whom I love and desire and cherish.

5. May I be the lord of a jointly-owned castle.   25
   Let there be four of us, equal owners of a tower,
   And let none of us like any of the others.
   Instead, let me forever need crossbowsmen,
   Doctors, mercenaries, guards and watchmen at the doors
   If ever I had the desire to love any other lady.   30

6. May I ride through a storm with my shield at my neck;
   Wear a hat I've put on backwards
   And too-small belts that can't be made any longer;
   Have long stirrups on a small trotting horse
   And find an ill-tempered innkeeper at the inn   35
   If ever I had the desire to seek another lady's love.

7. May my lady abandon me for another knight,
   And leave me not knowing whom to serve.
   May the wind fail me when I am out at sea
   And the watchmen beat me at the king's court;   40
   And may I be the first to flee in a time of need
   If the man who told you these things wasn't lying.

8. Lady, if I have a beautiful and moulted
   Duck hawk, good at the catch and yet tame,
   Who could overcome any other bird,   45
   Be it a swan, a crane, or an eagle, white or black;
   Would I want a badly-moulted chicken-chaser
   Who is fat, worn-out and can't even fly?

9. You false, envious, lying flatterers,
   Now that you've caused trouble between me and My-Lord   50
   I would advise you to leave me alone.

[1] This is the only extant song which conforms to the definition of the genre "escondich" ("I excuse myself") as given in the *Leys d'Amor*, a fourteenth-century codification and canonization of the troubadour songs of the previous two hundred years.

[2] Seeing that this incident occurs within a bedroom or garden, the traditional erotic sites, the narrator's failure obviously refers to sexual impotence as well as to a moral sense of failure to be true. The reference to the companion can thus be explained in several ways:
--he is referring to the lady and the male companion as one (as in"midonz", i.e. "May I be impotent and she [my companion] be unable to do anything about it);
--he is saying that if ever he failed her, it would then be right that he later fail his companion in a separate incident. In this case, the sexual sense of the first explanation is likened to a tryst: sex-as-skirmish;
--he is speaking of an incident of male performance anxiety in which two men compete and measure one another's prowess (sexual or otherwise) before a woman.

15.   Bertran de Born 80, 38 (B/S, 81)
      MSS: F 86, I 182, K 168.
      Base Text: I

Bertran de Born was sent away by his lady, Maeuz of Montaingnac, and nothing availed him; neither his oaths nor his protestations of innocence, in speech or in song, could make her believe that he did not love Lady Guiscarda.

And so he went off to Saintonge to see Lady Tibors of Montausier, who, in beauty, merit and learning, was one of the most esteemed women in the world.[1] And this lady was the wife of the lord of Chalais, of Berbezieux and of Montausier. And Sir Bertran complained to her about my Lady Maeutz, who had sent him away and who refused to believe that he did not love Lady Guiscarda despite his oaths and all he had said. He beseeched her to take him on as knight and servant. My Lady Tibors, like the wise lady that she was, answered him in this way: "Bertran, given your motive for coming here to see me, I am, on the one hand, very happy and gay and take it as a great honor and, on the other, displeased. I take it as an honor that you came to see me and ask to be taken on as a knight and servant. I am greatly displeased if you did and said this because my Lady Maeuz sent you away or is angry with you. But I am one of those who knows very well how quickly the hearts of lovers of both sexes can change. If you really did not fail my Lady Maeuz, I will soon know the truth and in that case you will presently be returning to her good graces. And if the failing was of your doing, neither I nor any other lady must ever again welcome you or take you on as knight or servant. But I will do my best and try to help you and restore peace between you and her." Bertran was very satisfied with my Lady Tibor's response[2] and he promised her that he would neither love nor serve any lady but her if it turned out that he was unable to regain the love of my Lady Maeuz. And my Lady Tibor promised Sir Bertran that if she were not able to get him back with my Lady Maeuz that she would take him on as knight and servant.[3]

It was not long before my Lady Maeuz found out that Sir Bertran had done no wrong and she listened to the pleas that were made on behalf of Bertran and allowed him back into her graces to the extent that she would see him and listen to his pleas. He told her about the support that my Lady Tibors had given him and the promise that she had made to him. My Lady Maeuz then told him to take leave of my Lady Tibors and to have the promises and oaths that they had made to one another dissolved. It is on this subject that Bertan de Born composed this sirventes:

If April, leaves and flowers... (80, 38: 1)

Manuscript F, just prior to the final sentence (It is on this subject...) adds the following:

He recalled the help he went and requested from my lady Tibors and the reception she gave him in her home in a verse that says:

Lady, if I sought help... (80, 38: 12)

In the other verses he castigated rich barons who, without giving gifts, wanted to be renowned out of fear, saying that one didn't dare list all the evil that they had done. Then there are those who, though sufficiently well-off, want to make it seem that they are rich men; others (he blamed) for having dogs and hawks; others for waging war and giving up on joy and youth and love; others for their grand gestures at tourneys where they stole from the poor knights and abandoned great deeds of honor.[4] And for all of these reasons he composed this sirventes:

[1] B/S notes that common errors concerning the Lady Tibor in the vida of the troubadour Jordan Bonel and in this razo suggest that the same author composed both texts (B/S, 85).

[2] The text reads "ben pagatz," well-paid. The expression is frequently used when referring to the troubadour's feeling of satisfaction at the conclusion of a transaction in which he has offered something and received something, usually love, in return. The term underscores the economic metaphor which governs the relation between patron and poet.

[3] We should note that the poet's offer of service to the lady is again in the form of a bargain. His service and 'love,' i.e. the composition of song on the subject of the lady, is given in return for protection.

[4] The addendum from manuscript F is considered by Boutière/Schutz to be a later addition that merely paraphrases the song itself. Though this may be true, its inclusion fits with the dominant economic language used to describe the relation of poet and lady. The razo author seems to want to show that there are some deals that Bertran approves of (Lady Tibors and his own) and some he does not approve of (Lords who withhold the gifts on which the system of courtly poetry depends).

Song 80, 38:   Bertran de Born: "S'abrils e fuoillas e flors..."
Source: Paden et al., 254.
MSS: A 192, B 114, C 136, D 119, F 88, I 182, K 168, N 246, R 6, U 141, V 49, a[1] 451.
Other English translations: Paden et al., 254.

1. If April, leaves and flowers,
   And the beautiful mornings and clear evenings
   Full of the rich joy I hope for
   Don't make me happy; and if love
   And the little nightingale I hear singing,   5
   And the new, green and lovely season
   Which brings us joy and sweetness,
   And the charming, flowering spring
   Don't boost My-Lord's courage
   And quiet her fear,   10
   It will be a long time before I have any enjoyment.

2. Lady, if I sought help
   Elsewhere, I didn't do it sincerely.
   Here I am now at your command,
   Me, my songs and my towers.   15
   I take my leave of the home
   In which I was so well received,
   Where joy, good sense and merit are born.
   He who helps the exiled
   For the sake of his own honor   20
   Completes his agreement
   When a good treaty is signed.

3. I find your accusation quite a mouthful,
   Rich man, for you think you're so worthy
   That you'd like to receive praise   25
   Just out of fear, without having given any gifts.
   And even if no one dared reproach you
   When you do something vile,
   It would seem to me as if it were out of fear
   If I covered it up,   30
   Whether you're a count, a viscount, a duke or a king.
   Just do what you do so nobly
   That good word of you will follow.

4. Some of them are warriors
   Who have all the time in the world to do evil   35
   And don't know how to get by
   For any time at all without their military engineers.[1]
   So much do they love hurling and firing
   That I see them perpetually in armor,

As if they lived on the run. 40
   That is why I am not very favorable to them:
   For a rich man never gains
   A good reputation if he hasn't had joy and youth
   And valor on his side.

5. Other rich men, 45
   For the sake of custom,
   Get themselves up to look like hunters
   Who dearly love dogs and goshawks,
   Horns, drums and barking.
   Their reputation is so weak, 50
   And they have so little real worth,
   And their power is so shaky,
   That nothing but beasts and fish
   Obey them
   Or follow their orders. 55

6. Others are builders,
   Rich men of great power
   Who know how to hold on to their land
   And build gates and turrets
   Out of limestone, sand and gravel, 60
   And vaulted towers with spiral staircases.
   I see those big eaters
   Who make their gifts ever smaller;
   Their reputations will never grow;
   For such behavior 65
   Is not esteemed by good people.

7. Rich tourneyers can never really
   Appeal to my heart
   For although they throw away their money
   I see them as such cheaters. 70
   A rich man who, in order to raise money,
   Announces tournaments
   Designed to take from his vassals
   Knows no honor or courage.
   But no strap can hold him back 75
   Provided that the money goes with him,
   Even if people later speak badly of him.

8. I want rich men to know how
   To attract knights with love
   And how to keep them 80
   Through good deeds and honors
   And that one find them doing no wrong:
   Honest and courtly and merciful,
   Generous and quick to give gifts.
   This is how good reputations were established 85
   In the days when men would battle in tournaments,
   And Lent and Advent
   Would make of mercenaries rich men.

9. Sir/Lady-Temperance, so much joy will be accorded me
   That from now on 90
   Gall mixed with absinthe will seem like
   It has turned for me to spiced wine.

10. Rassa, I am no renegade.
    Why my faith is so firm
    That even if I did once pull away a bit 95
    I am now a reformed man.

11. Papiol, I have been so bold!
    Take my song and go with it
    To Sir-Yes-and-No, for I offer him as a present
    These many running words.[2] 100

[1] Paden et al.'s notes to this song explain that Bertran is commenting on the social effects of contemporary technological advances. The reference in stanza four to engineers and in stanza six to building materials, reflect changes in warfare introduced by new weaponry and the construction of castles made of stone and masonry rather than wood. In stanza eight, Bertran is nostalgic for days of yore, before the institution of the Truce of God (1054), which forbade the waging of war during some 285 days of the year (Paden et al., 259, 261, 251).

[2] The identity of Sir or Lady Temperance is unknown. Rassa is Geoffrey of Brittany; Sir Yes-and-No is Richard-the-Lionhearted, and Papiol is Bertran's singer.

16. Bertran de Born 80, 19 (B/S, 86)
MSS: F 81, I 181, K 167.

Base Text: I

Bertran de Born had gone off to see a sister of King Richard, the mother of the Emperor Othon, whose name was my Lady Eleina and who was the wife of the Duke of Saxony.[1] She was a beautiful lady, very courtly and learned, and she bestowed great honor through her welcome and her noble speech. Sir Richard, who was then the Count of Poitiers, sat down beside his sister and and told her to talk to him (Bertran) and give him pleasure and honor. And she, because of the great desire she had for renown and honor and because she knew that Sir Bertran was such a highly esteemed and noble man and that he could greatly advance her reputation, paid him so great an honor that he felt fully satisfied.[2] He fell completely in love with her and so began to praise her and glorify her.

During the same time that he had gone to see her, he (Bertran) was in an army with Count Richard in the winter season and this army was suffering from a scarcity of food. And it happened that on one Sunday they had still had nothing to eat or drink by noontime. He was tormented by hunger and so he composed this sirventes which says:

From now on, morning should not be for eating...

---

[1] The second child of Henry II, the princess Maeut, did marry the Duke of Saxony, and her son, Othon IV, served as emperor of Germany from 1198-1218. The author of the razos here calls her Eleina because of a misunderstanding which caused him to take the senhal Lena to be her name. He then created a fictional woman, Maeuz of Montaingnac to fit the name Maeut (B/S, 87).

[2] As in the previous razo, Bertran's love resembles a transaction in which both sides see that they clearly have something to gain. Eleina will get good public relations and Bertran will be well connected. At the moment that their liaison is established, Bertran feels "ben pagatz" (fully satisfied).

Song 80, 19   Bertran de Born: "Ges de disnar non for'oimais
              maitis..."
              Source: Paden et al., 168.
              MSS: A 194, D 124, F 82, I 181, K 167.
              Other English translations: Paden et al. 168.

1. From now on, morning should not be for eating,
   Even if you have found good lodging
   And inside there be meat, bread and wine,
   And the fire be bright with beechwood.
   Today is the choicest day of the week   5
   And it should be pleasurable for me.
   Let Lady Lana and the lord of Poitou
   Bring me as much pleasure as they want!

2. I return to the land of the Limousins
   To bid adieu to their ladies of highest repute.   10
   Henceforth My-Beautiful-Lord and My-Beautiful-Sable
   Must seek someone else to praise them
   For I have found the noblest
   And most dependable lady yet sung of.
   It is because her love is so steady   15
   That I am harsh on the others.

3. Noble young body, pure, true and fine,
   Of high and royal birth,
   For you I will become a stranger to my own country
   And move beyond the Anjou.   20
   For you are sovereign over all others
   And this makes your worth even greater.
   The roman crown will be honored
   If it is your head that it encircles.

4. With the sweet glance she gave me and her clear face,   25
   Love made me her slave.
   My lord had placed next to her
   Her brown imperial cushion, for me.
   Her words were sweet and unpretentious
   And her conversation, noble and unhurried.   30
   She seemed a Catalan with her lovely manners,
   And a lady from Fanjeaux in the way she received me.[1]

5. She spoke to me so graciously and revealed her beautiful smile
And when I saw her teeth of crystal
And her slight body, so smooth, fresh and delicate,   35
Perfect within its tunic,
And how fresh and rosy was her color,
She locked up my heart within her.
I have had more joy than if someone were to give me
  Khorossan,[2]
Because it is at her perogative that I feel such joy.   40

6. Lady Maier is superior to all others
Surrounded by land and sea.

[1] Paden et al. note that this is a word play on "Fan Jau," i.e. "make joy" (173, n. 32).

[2] "Khorassan, in Persia, regarded by crusaders as the gateway to Baghdad; here symbolic of immense wealth" (Paden et al., 173, n. 39).

17. Bertran de Born 80, 44 (B/S, 88)
MSS: F 76, I 181, K 166.
Base Text: I

Bertran de Born, as I have told you in the other razos,[1] had a brother whose name was Constantine de Born, and he was a good knight of arms but not the type of man to concern himself much with nobility and honor; and he was always wishing evil upon Sir Bertran. One day he took over for himself the castle of Hautefort, which belonged to both of them jointly. Sir Bertran recovered it and cut off all his brother's power. Constantine then went off to the Viscount of Limoges, asking that he be supported in his struggle with his brother, and he gave him his support. King Richard also supported him against Sir Bertran.

Sir Richard was at war with Sir Aimar, the Viscount of Limoges; and Sir Richard and Sir Aimar were both at war with Sir Bertran, whose land they were destroying and burning. Bertran had previously arranged an oath of fidelity between the Viscount of Limousin and the Count of Perigord, whose name was Talleyrand, and from whom Sir Richard had already taken his city, Perigord. And the count never retaliated against Richard, for he was weak-willed, mediocre and indolent. Sir Richard had also taken Gourdon from Sir Guillem de Gourdon and he (Guillem) had promised to pledge his loyalty to the Visount, to Bertran de Born and to the other barons of Perigord, Limousin and Quercy, who were being dispossessed by Sir Richard. For such actions Bertran greatly blamed him and for all of these reasons he composed this sirventes which says:

> I have composed a sirventes in which no
> Word fails, and it didn't cost me a clove of garlic...

[1] This reference back to previous razos implies both that the same author is responsible for most or all of the collected razos to Bertran de Born's songs and that when he composed them he had intended the whole body of songs and commentaries to stand together, linked as a narrative whole, so as to recount a history of the life and times of the poet, much as in Dante's *Vita Nuova*. The differences between the two are many and important, but Dante's references to Bertran in the *Inferno* (canto 26) indicate that he was aware of the accusations of having planted discord between father and son that were directed against Bertran, and these accusations are found only in the vida text and in razos 18, 19, and 22. See Poe Wilson (1984: 83-97) for a discussion of the affinities between the razo texts and Dante's *Vita Nuova*, and Shapiro (1974) on Dante's use of Bertran in the *Commedia*.

Song 80, 44   Bertran de Born: "Un sirventes on motz non faill..."
Source: Paden et al., 120.
MSS: A 190, C 141, D 123, F 77, I 181, K 166, M 227, N 246 (anonymous).
Other English translations: Blackburn, 148; Bonner, 145; Paden et al., 120; Wilhelm, 150.

1. I have composed a sirventes in which no
   Word fails, and it didn't cost me a clove of garlic.
   And I have learned such art-ifice
   That if I have a brother, a cousin, or a second cousin
   With whom I split my egg or half-denier   5
   And who then wants my part
   I'll toss him out of that joint venture.[1]

2. Every day I struggle and fight,
   Fence, defend myself and vent my spleen,
   For they rip into my land and burn it,   10
   Turn my forested land into barren fields
   And mix my grain with straw.
   There isn't one under-handed, cowardly
   Enemy who doesn't attack me.

3. Talairan doesn't trot or jump   15
   Or budge from his fortress, Arenaill;
   He doesn't even fear lances or stinging remarks.
   No, he lives there like a coward,
   So full of indolence
   That it hurts me to see him yawning and stretching   20
   While other people are pitted against one another.

4. Guillem de Gordon, that's a useless clapper
   You've put in your little bell,
   And I love you, so help me God.
   But the two viscounts   25
   Think you're a fool and a dreamer
   With that treaty, and they think it's high time
   That you joined them in their battle.

5. I keep my opinions under lock and key
   Even though they have gotten me into big trouble   30
   With Sir Azemar and Sir Richard.
   It's a long time now that they've kept me worried.
   But now I'm starting such strife
   That if the king doesn't keep them apart
   The children will be getting their part in the guts. 35

6. Right to the wall of Perigeux I want to come,
   Astride Baiart,

And I'll strike as hard as I can, dressed in armor.
If I find there a pot-bellied Poitevin[2]
He'll learn how well my sword can slice,   40
For atop his head I'll make him a mortar
Of brains mixed with chain-links.

7. All day long I re-sole the barons, cut them down to size,
Melt them down and put them back together again.
I was thinking of clearing them all out,   45
So I'm a fool if I let them get to me;
For they're no better made
Than chains protected by Saint Leonard.[3]
That's why anybody who gets too worked up about them is a fool.

8. Barons, may God save you, watch over you,   50
Help you out and be with you to the end
Provided that you tell Sir Richard
What the peacock told the crow.[4]

[1] Much of this song echoes the first stanza's use of the word "part," which means alternately "portion, blow, dispute, strife."

[2] "Poitevins" is a reference to the followers of Richard, the Count of Poitiers.

[3] Saint Leonard was the patron of prisoners. Against his authority no chain was worth much (Paden et al., 127).

[4] "He warned him not to transgress the bounds of nature through vanity" (Wilhelm, 1970: 152).

18. Bertran de Born 80, 32 (B/S, 107)
MSS: F 73, I 180, K 166.
Base Text: I

King Henry of England had Sir Bertran de Born holed up within Hautefort and was attacking the castle with his war machines, for he really had it in for him. He believed that the whole war that his son, the Young King, had waged against him had occurred because Sir Bertran had made him do it. And so he he had come to Hautefort to see him dispossessed. The King of Aragon joined with King Henry's army before Hautefort. When Bertran found out, he was very happy to know that the King of Aragon was with the (English) army, for he was a special friend of his. The King of Aragon sent his messengers inside the castle to ask Bertran to send them bread and wine and meat and he sent it to them in abundance. And with the messenger by whom he sent the presents, he sent a message asking him to do what he could to have the war machines moved to another area of the castle for the wall before which they were stationed was weakened. And the other (the King of Aragon), avid for the riches of King Henry, told him everything that Bertran had told him. King Henry then put more of the machines before the portions of the castle that he knew were weak. Thus were the walls brought down and the castle captured.

Sir Bertran and all his followers were led before King Henry's pavilion and the King received him very badly, saying to him: "Bertran, Bertran, you said that you have never needed more than half your wits in any situation but now you must realize that you need every bit you have." "Lord," said Sir Bertran, "it is true that I said that and it was the absolute truth." And the King said: "It looks to me as if they have failed you this time." "Lord," said Sir Bertran, "they truly have failed me." "And how is that?" asked the King. "Lord," said Sir Bertran, "the day that the valiant Young King, your son, died, I lost all my wits, intelligence and learning." And the King, when he heard what Sir Bertran had said about his son and saw him crying, felt such sadness and pity in his heart and in his eyes that he could not hold back from fainting with sorrow. And when he came out of it, he cried out, saying through his tears: "Sir Bertran, Sir Bertran, you are so right; and it is understandable that you would lose your wits over my son, for he loved you more than any man in the world. And I, for love of him, absolve your person, your goods and your castle and give you back my love and grace. I also give you five hundred marks of silver for the damages you have suffered." Sir Bertran fell to the King's feet, giving him thanks and homage. The King then departed with all his army.

When Bertran learned of the great treason that the King of Aragon had perpetrated against him, he was furious with King Anfos. He learned how the king had come to offer his services as a paid mercenary and that the King of Aragon had come from a poor family from Carladais, from a castle named Carlat, which is under the jurisdiction of the Count of Rodez.[1] Sir Peire de Carlat, who was the lord of the castle, through his nobility and prowess, took as his wife the Countess d'Amillau, who had come into an inheritance. With her he had a son who was noble and valorous and who conquered the county of Provence. One of his sons was named Raimon Berrengier. It was he who conquered the county of Barcelona as well as the kingdom of Aragon and was the first ever to serve as king of Aragon. He went to Rome to be crowned but during his return trip, while in the city of Saint-Dolmas, he died. He left behind three sons: Anfos, he who was the king of Aragon and who did such harm to Sir Bertran de Born; another named Don Sancho; and another, Berrengier de Bezalu. Bertran learned how this same Anfos had betrayed the daughter of the emperor, Manuel, whom the emperor had sent to him to be his wife, along with great treasures, riches and much honored company; and how he robbed them of the riches that the lady and the Greek party had.[2] He learned how Alphonse had sent her away by ship, sad, worried and helpless; how his brother Sancho had taken all of Provence and how Alphonse had perjured himself for the riches that King Henry gave him in the struggle against the count of Toulouse. For all of these reasons Sir Bertran composed the sirventes which says:

Since the sweet, flowering season...(80, 32: 1)

[1] B/S note that most of this genealogy is incorrect. See Paden et al., notes to pages 269-273, for more information.

[2] Eudossia, the daughter of Manuel I, emperor of Constantinople, was sent by her father to marry Alphonse. When she arrived, he had already married, and she was subsequently married to Guillaume VIII of Montpellier. She is mentioned by other poets including Peire Vidal, Giraut de Borneilh and Folquet de Marseille (see Stronski, 1910: 153).

Song 80, 32   Bertran de Born.

This song is included after the following razo, number 19.

19. Bertran de Born 80, 20 and 32 (B/S, 91)
    MSS: F 94, I 184, K 169.
    Base Text: I

    As you have heard many times now, Sir Bertran de Born and his brother, Sir Constantine, were always at war with one another and held each other in the highest contempt, for each wished to be the lord of Hautefort, the castle which by rights they held in common.[1]

    And so it happened that after Sir Bertran had captured and taken control of Hautefort, and chased Constantine and his sons from the land, Sir Constantine went off to see Sir Aemar, the Viscount of Limoges and to Amblart, the Count of Périgord and to Sir Tallaran, the lord of Montaingnac, to ask for their mercy and their assistance in helping him against his brother, Sir Bertran, who was wrongfully in sole possession of Hautefort, which was half his, and who, because he did not wish to give up a single bit of it, had unlawfully dispossessed him. They aided and advised him against Sir Bertran and after a long war finally wrested from him the control of Hautefort. Sir Bertran escaped with his supporters and began to assail the castle with the help of all his friends and relatives. Finally, Sir Bertran sought peace with his brother. A peace agreement was reached and they became friends. But once Sir Bertran had gotten inside the castle of Hautefort with all his supporters, he failed to conform to the agreement, broke his promises and covenants, and in an act of treason to his brother, took over control of the castle. This all occurred on a Monday, at an hour and moment which did not bode well for the undertaking of any great affair, according to the omens and astrological calculations.[2] Sir Constantine set off to find the King of England and Sir Richard, the Count of Poitiers, to ask for their support against Sir Bertran.

King Henry had it in for Sir Bertran, for he had been the friend and counselor of the Young King, the son who had waged war against him, and the King believed that the blame for that affair belonged to Bertran; he therefore agreed to help him, as did his son, Richard. They raised a large army, attacked Hautefort, and finally took the castle, and Sir Bertran prisoner. When he was led before the King, he was greatly afraid. But due to the fact that he reminded King Henry of some words about his son, the Young King, Henry returned to him the castle of Hautefort and both he and Count Richard pardoned him for all his evil intentions, as you heard in the story which is written above this and concerns the sirventes which says:[3]

Since the sweet, flowering season... (80, 32: 1)

But as King Henry was returning Hautefort to him, he said to Bertran, in a joking manner: "Let it be yours. It is right that you should have it no matter how great the act of treason you committed against your brother." Sir Bertran knelt down before him and said: "Many thanks, my Lord. I am much pleased by such a judgement." Then Sir Bertran went into the castle and King Henry and Count Richard went back to their own lands with their men. When the other barons who had helped Constantine heard about this and saw that Sir Bertran was again in possession of the castle, they were saddened and upset and advised Constantine to plead his case before the King, who would surely hold him to be in the right. And so he did it. But Bertran showed the King the judgement that he had rendered, for he had had it written, and the King found this amusing and had a good laugh.[4] Sir Bertran went back to Hautefort and Constantine had no further rights to the land. But the barons who had helped Constantine waged war with Bertran for a long time and Bertran stayed continually at war with them.

So long as he lived, he did not want to give up the castle or make peace with his brother or consent to any cessation of hostilities. When he died, his sons made peace with their uncle Constantine and with their cousins, his sons. And for all of these reasons Sir Bertran composed this sirventes which says:

I never put off composing a sirventes
I just do it without any trouble at all... (80, 20: 1-2)

[1] The word "razo" comes up repeatedly in this account of Bertran's struggles with his brother:
"per razo" (used twice) means "by rights," "legitimately";
"mantener en razo" means "to hold someone to be in the right";
"no ac autra razo" means that he has no further claims; his legal options are exhaused;
"per aquesta razo" means "for this reason, on this subject matter."
The razo we are reading is then the subject matter and pretext of the song as well as the text that legitimizes in some sense the meaning of the song it is glossing.

[2] References in the razos can usually be traced directly to a statement in the song and generally represent an interpretation or misinterpretation of an ambiguous detail (Poe, 1984: 35-65). This reference to astrology is, however, a gratuitous and independent addition on the part of the razo author.

[3] This is a reference to the razo to song 80, 32, #18 in this collection. In all three manuscripts that razo precedes this one, though it follows in Boutière/Schutz' critical edition (1973).

[4] An interesting reference to the growing importance of the written record in mid-twelfth century.

Song 80, 32   Bertran de Born: "Pois lo gens terminis floritz..."
Source: Paden et al., 266.
MSS: A 195, B 115, C 139, D 123, E 100, F 75, I 180, K 165.
Other English translations: Bonner, 149; Paden et al., 266.

1. Since the sweet, flowering season
Spreads its seed, joyful and gay,
The idea has come to my heart to go to work
On composing a new sirventes
So that the Aragonese might know   5
That it was ill-fated,
Of that they can be sure,

That their king came here; for he is now disgraced
   And his men are paid mercenaries.

2. I know that his base but overweening 10
   Stock will end up like a *lai*,
   Going right back where they came from--
   Meillau and Carlades.¹
   When each of them has gotten his rightful share,
   Off he'll go to Tyre! 15
   It's hard to believe that the wind at sea won't make him puke,
   For he's so little suited to face danger--
   Soft, weak and lazy.

3. He is losing Provence, where he came from,
   Since they prefer his brother, Sancho. 20
   He doesn't care about anything but getting fat
   And drinking his way through the Roussillon,
   Where Geoffrey was disinherited.²
   In Vilamur,
   Around Toulouse, all those to whom he gave his word 25
   Now consider him a liar.
   For he abandonned them out of fear.

4. To the king who holds Castrojeriz
   And the palace of Toledo
   I advise him to show some initiative 30
   Here toward the son of Barcelona
   Since he is, by all rights, his pitiful liege man.³
   I have more esteem for the court and trappings
   Of the rascal king
   Than for the one who betrayed me 35
   The very day I began to serve him.⁴

5. When his life gave out, the good king Garcia Ramirez
   Was about to recover Aragon
   Which the monk had snatched from him;
   And the good king of Navarre, to whom it belongs by right,
   Will recover it with his men from Alava 41
   If only he puts his mind to it.
   For by as much as gold is worth more than lapis lazuli,
   His renown is more perfect and more esteemed
   Than that of the phony king.⁵ 45

6. For the sake of the one he married,
   The good queen, I shall stop here,
   Just as soon as she tells me what I need to know.
   I would go over once more the case of
   Berengier of Besaudun, if it pleased her,   50
   But I clean up
   His evil deeds, shameful as they are;
   For it was through his doing that he was murdered and betrayed
   And his lineage has been dishonored.[6]

7. How vilely he betrayed the emperess,   55
   Like a truly false, lying and wicked king,
   When he took away the money Manuel had sent him
   In piles and packages,
   And all her treasures and personal affairs.
   Then, with his hardened heart,   60
   After he had taken from her the green and the ripe.[7]
   He sent them off on the sorrowful sea,
   That lady and the Greeks he had betrayed.

---

[1] The song is a cutting history of the reign of Alphonse II of Aragon, who helped Henry II at the siege of Limoges and aided Richard in attacking Hautefort. The reference to the *lai* concerns its form: it ends as it begins. The family of Alphonse II of Castile had originally held only the relatively modest holdings of Millau and Carlat (Paden et al., 268).

[2] Alphonse had inherited the Roussillon from the son of Geoffrey, who had indeed been dispossessed for repudiating one wife and marrying another (Paden et al., 271).

[3] This king is Alphonse VIII of Castile. Alphonse of Aragon had been, but was no longer, his liege man (Paden et al., 271).

[4] Razo 18 tells how Alphonse betrayed Bertran during the siege of Hautefort by disclosing to the forces of King Henry private information that had been meant for him, as a supposed ally of Bertran.

[5] Sancho VI was the son and successor of Garcia Ramirez of Navarre. Alphonse of Aragon's grandfather had been a monk before becoming king, and had gained control of Aragon (Paden et al., 273).

[6] Ramon Berengar, Alphonse's brother, was killed by a partisan of Raimon of Toulouse. Alphonse invaded the county to Toulouse to avenge his murder. There is no evidence to show that Alphonse was responsible, as Bertran alleges (Paden et al., 273).

[7] There is a strong suggestion of rape in this passage as well. "La rauba" in line 59 can be taken to mean: "He robbed her" or "He raped/kidnapped her"; and the mention of the green and mature in line 61 could refer to the taking of her virginity and subsequent sexual attacks. "His hardened heart" in the previous line can also be read: "his hardened body" due to the frequent and deliberate confusion between the use of "cor" (heart) and "cors" (body) (see Jensen, 1974).

20. Bertran de Born 80, 20
MS: The Romegialli Fragment

When King Henry had given his forgiveness to Bertran de Born, let him out of prison, returned to him Hautefort and declared that it was he who should henceforth be the lord of the castle; and when King Richard, who was at that time the count of Poitiers, had pardoned his evil intentions, Bertran was very happy and gay and immediately began to wage war against Lord Aseimar, the viscount of Limoges, Sir Talairan, the lord of Monteignac, and Sir Amblart, the brother of the count of Perigord and all those who supported his brother Constantine, the one he had exiled from Hautefort. Count Richard came to his aid with all his men and ordered that all the castles be opened to him. And he composed this sirventes which says:

I never put off composing a sirventes....

Song 80, 20   Bertran de Born: "Ges de far sirventes no.m tartz..."
            Source: Paden et al., 248.
            MSS: A 190, C 139, D 119, E 100, F 96, I 183, K 169.
            Other English translations: Paden et al., 248.

1. I never put off composing a sirventes.
   So fine is my art and my skill that
   I just do it, without any trouble at all.
   I have worked myself into such a fine position,
       Plus I've so much good luck,   5
       That here I am, out on my own,
       With no count or king
       To push me around or give me grief.

2. Since the king and Count Richard
   Have gotten over their bad feelings for me,   10
   May Sir Aimar and Sir Amblart
   Never offer me peace, or Sir Talairan either.
       From Autafort I will never
       Let him have a single garden.
       Anyone who wants it, let him fight me   15
       Because I have to have it.

3. I am so strong on every side
   That out of that war I got the bread;
   And a stye in the eye to anyone who tries to take it from me!
   Even though I'm the one who started it,   20
       Peace doesn't really suit me;
       It's with war that I see eye-to-eye
       For I believe in and hold to
       No other law.[1]

4. I have no regard for Sunday or Monday,   25
   Or for weeks, months or years,
   And I don't stop in March or April either
   Scheming how to bring damage
       To those who have hurt me.
       But never under any condition   30
       Will those three conquer
       So much as a belt-buckle from me.

74

5. I have always gone to great trouble to insure
   That anyone who goes around laying low forests[2]
   Can get hold of good blades and arrows,   35
   Helmets and hauberks, horses and spears.
      For this is what I do
      For comfort and amusement:
      War and tournaments,
      The giving of gifts and the courting of ladies.   40

6. My coproprietor is so outrageous
   That he wants the land that belongs to my children
   And I am so subservient that I'm willing to give it to him!
   Then they can all call me: "Soft Sir Bertran."
      But all wrong-doing aside,   45
      I do think he'll come
      To a bad end, and of this I guarantee you,
      Before he ever makes his peace with me.

7. I don't care any more if what I do
   About Autafort is right or wrong,   50
   For I place my faith in the judgement of
   My lord, the king.

[1] Paden et al. (251) interpret this line and the following stanza as examples of Bertran's defiance of the Truce of God, which called upon warriors to refrain from battle during some 285 days of the year.

[2] This line makes more sense when read in conjunction with song 80, 44 under razo 17, where he used the clearing out of forests as a metaphor for warring.

21. Bertran de Born 80, 33 (B/S, 98)
    MSS: F 72, I 180, K 165.
    Base Text: I

As I have told you, during the time that Bertran de Born was at war with Count Richard, he arranged for the viscount of Ventadorn and the viscount of Comborn and the viscount of Segur--who was the viscount of Limoges--and the viscount of Turenne to all swear allegiance to a pact with the Count of Périgord, with the bourgeois of those lands, with the lord of Gourdon and with the lord of Montfort. They united together so as to defend themselves against Count Richard, who wished to rob them of their lands because of their love for his brother, the Young King, with whom he was at war and from whom he had taken all the revenues from carriage traffic. The Young King did have a certain stake in these carriages as his father had given them these rights; and Richard left the Young King no safe resting place anywhere in his own territory. And Bertran composed this sirventes on the topic of the oath that these men had taken to wage war against Sir Richard:

Since Ventadorn and Comborn with Ségur...

The sirventes was to reassure all the people of that land by mentioning the oath that all had sworn to uphold against Richard. He also blamed the Young King for not being more valorous in war, reminding him that Sir Richard had taken from him his revenues from the carriages and had had a castle built right in the middle of the land that his father had given him; and he praised the lords of Puy-Guillaume and of Clérens, Grignol and Saint-Astier, who were four great barons from Périgord, as well as praising himself and others from Turenne and Angoulême. And he suggested that the viscount of Béarn and of Gavardan,--who was at that time Gaston of Béarn, the head of all of Gascogne--and Sir Vivias of Lomagne and Sir Bernard of Armagnac and the viscount of Tartas join them, since they all had it in for Richard, for then he'd have plenty to do. And then if only the Lord of Mauléon, Sir Raoul of Mauléon, the father of Sir Savaric, and the the lord of Tonnay and the viscount of Civray and the lord of Taillebourg and the viscount of Thouars would come help them and join with them because of the harm that Sir Richard was inflicting upon them, for these were all great barons from Poitou! For all of these reasons Bertran composed this sirventes which begins:

Since Ventadorn and Comborn with Ségur
And Turenne and Monfort with Gourdon...(80, 33: 1-2)

Song 80, 33 Bertran de Born: "Pois Ventedorns e Comborns ab Segur..."
Source: Paden et al., 176.
MSS: A 191, C 142, D 124, F 73, I 180, K 165.
Other English translations: Blackburn, 151; Paden et al., 176.

1. Since Ventadorn and Comborn with Ségur
   And Turenne and Monfort with Gourdon
   Have made an agreement with Perigeux and sworn an oath
   And the townspeople are taking refuge all around them,
   It seems like a good time for me to sing and undertake 5
   A sirventes to reassure them.
   For I would never want to be part of Toledo
   Because I could never feel safe there.

2. Ha! Puy Guilhem and Clérans and Grignols
   And Saint-Astier, you have great honor, 10
   As I do myself; I want that to be recognized.
   Those from Angoulême have the most of all, more
   Than Sir Carter who abandoned his cart.
   He hasn't a cent nor does he take any without fear
   For I would rather have a tiny parcel of land in honor 15
   Than a great empire in dishonor.

3. If the mighty viscount who is head of the Gascons wants it,
   He to whom Béarn and Gavardan defer,
   And Sir Vezian and Sir Bernardo 19
   And the lord of Dax and the one who holds Marsan do too,
   Then the count will have his hands full down there;[1]
   And morever, since he is so valiant,
   With the great army he is amassing and putting together,
   Let him climb up here and get together with us!

4. If Sir Taillebourg and Sir Pons and Lusignan 25
   And Mauléon and Tonnay were up and ready,
   And there were a viscount alive and well in Civray,
   I will never believe they wouldn't help us.

> May the one from Thouars, whom the count is threatening,
> Stick with us and never go against us; 30
> And let's lay our claim, until such time as he does what is right,
> On the lands he has taken right out of our hands.

5. Between Poitou and l'Ile-Bouchard
   And Mirebeau and Loudon and Chinon
   They have arrogantly built a beautiful castle 35
   On a flat field in Clairvaux.
   But I don't want the Young King to hear about it
   Or see it, for he wouldn't like it;
   But I'm afraid that with its incredible whiteness
   He will surely see it from Mateflon. 40

6. We shall soon know whether King Philip takes after his father
   Or will follow the good example of Charlemagne
   In the affair of Sir Taillafer, for he has recognized him as lord
   Of Angoulême, of which territory Philip then made him a gift.

7. And it's not right that a king who grants something, 45
   Since he said yes, should ever say no.[2]

[1] The count is Richard, count of Poitiers. Most of the references are to historically verifiable rulers of the area and are mentioned in the razo. See Paden et al., 177-78 and 181-3 for specific identifications.
[2] This is simultaneously a reference to and comparison with Richard-the-Lionhearted, to whom Bertran elsewhere refers as "Sir Yes-and-No." See song 80, 38 under razo 15.

22. Bertran de Born 80,21 (B/S, 103)
    MSS: F 62, I 178, K 163.
    Base text: I

At the time that Sir Richard was the count of Poitiers, before he became king, Bertran de Born was his enemy because of his love for the Young King, who was at that time at war with his brother, Sir Richard. Sir Bertran had arranged for these men to sign a pact against Richard: the good viscount of Limoges, whose name was Sir Aimar; the viscount of Ventadorn; the viscount of Gimel; the count of Périgord and his brother; the count of Angoulême and his two brothers; count Raimon de Toulouse; the count de Flandres; the count de Barcelona; Sir Centule d'Astarac, a count from Gascony; Sir Gaston de Béarn, the count of Bigorre; and the count of Dijon. And they all abandoned him, making their peace without him and perjuring themselves in his regard. Even Lord Aimar, the viscount of Limoges, who was more closely attached to him through love and oaths, abandoned him and made his peace without him. Upon hearing that all had abandoned Bertran, Sir Richard came to Hautefort and set up camp with his army before the castle, saying and swearing that he would never leave until Bertran had given him Hautefort and surrendered to his command. Bertran, when he had heard what Richard had sworn to do, gave up his castle to him and surrendered to his command. And Count Richard received him, pardoning him and kissing him. From these two events[1] Sir Bertran composed this sirventes:

> I am not so discouraged
> Even though I have lost... (80, 21: 1-2)

And you should know that on account of one stanza that he included in the sirventes, the one which begins:

> If the count is kind to me
> And not stingy... (80, 21: 45-46)

Count Richard forgave him his harsh temper and returned his castle to him and they became steadfast friends.[2] Bertran left him then to begin a war with Aimar, the Viscount who had abandoned him, and with the Count of Périgord, from which war Bertran came out with a lot of damage and also did them a great deal of harm. Sir Richard, when he had become king, went overseas; and Sir Bertran went on waging war.

---

[1] Literally: "From these two razos..."
[2] "Fin amic coral" means literally "fine friends of the heart" which implies a close personal relationship rather than a strong political bond. The expression is interesting for its similarity to the

term, "fin'amans," "courtly" lover, and both seem to imply that the person acts out of a a deep respect and personal tie rather than through adherence to a standardized code of behavior that characterizes other social ties. Thus 'fine' lovers and friends 'of the heart' are distinguished from those who simply follow the etiquette required of lover or friend.

Song 80, 21   Bertran de Born: "Ges no me desconort..."
　　　　　　　　Source: Paden et al., 231.
　　　　　　　　MSS: A 189, D 121, D^c 257, F 63, G 108, I 177, K 163, M 230.
　　　　　　　　Other English translations: Paden et al., 231.

1. I am not so discouraged,
   Even though I have lost,
   That I don't sing or enjoy myself
   Or do what I can
   To recover Autafort,   5
   Which I lost
   To the lord of Monfort
   Because he wanted it.[1]
   And ever since I came before him
   Asking for forgiveness,   10
   And the count, granting me pardon,
   Received me with a kiss,
   I don't have to suffer any further damage,
   Regardless of what he did to me before,
   Or praise any scandal-monger.   15

2. They swore me a false oath,
   Two paladins,
   And all the viscounts
   of Limousin,
   And the two swells   20
   From Angoulême,
   And the three stupid counts
   From Périgueux

    And Sir Centol and Sir Gaston
    And Sir Raymond of Avignon   25
    And the count of Dijon
    With the Breton count,
    And many other barons
    Gave me their assurances
    And then didn't help me a bit.   30

3. When a friend doesn't help me
    I love him about as much
    As I do an enemy
    Who isn't hurting me.
    In an ancient abbey   35
    Dedicated to Saint Martial
    Many mighty men swore by me
    On top of a missal.
    One promised his faith,
    Saying that he would never make peace without me.   40
    From that moment on he never did a thing to help me
    And he made his own private peace accord.
    This I swear to you on my faith:
    They were wrong to do this
    For they did make their peace without me.   45

4. If the count is kind to me
    And not stingy,
    I will be of great service to him
    In his affairs,
    Fine as a coin of silver,   50
    Bright and friend-like.[2]
    May the count show good sense,
    Like the sea:
    For when something valuable falls in
    She wants to keep it;   55
    But when something is useless to her
    She throws it back out on the sand.
    This is what I want of a baron:
    That he honor his pardon
    And, if he takes something, that he return it.   60

5. I want to ask the count
   Who has my house
   To lend it to me for safekeeping
   Or just give it to me.
   For these barons   65
   Are so stingy with me
   That I can't be around them
   Without a fight starting.
   Now the count can take me back
   Without fear of retribution   70
   And I can return to him,
   To serve and honor him.
   But I didn't want to do this
   Until I came to be forsaken
   By Lord Aimar.   75

6. Henceforth My-Beauty should look for ways[3]
   To compensate for behaving so vilely.
   So far she hasn't bothered to work
   At bettering herself.
   I don't know her equal in the world   80
   When it comes to joy and talk
   And courting.[4]

7. Lady whose heart is stingy
   In promising and giving,
   Since you don't want to go to bed with me   85
   May you give me one kiss,
   For thus you can make me rich
   And make up for all my damages,
   So long as God and the Saints protect me.

8. Papiol, go tell   90
   My-Lord about my song.
   For love of Sir Aimar
   I give up on waging war.

---

[1] This would presumably be Richard, who would have also reasserted his authority over his vassal at nearby Monfort (Paden et al., 235).

² This is the stanza that the razo singles out as having brought Bertran and Richard to peace. The metaphor of friendship-as-money is interesting in terms of similar references in other songs to love-as-money.

³ Stanzas 6 and 8 are not included in the manuscripts which contain the razos.

⁴ Paden et al. suggest that this lady who is suddenly addressed in the midst of this song about treachery and war is a thinly disguised figure for Richard. The kiss of forgiveness conferred in the first stanza would thus be echoed here in the erotic kiss. This lady being unequaled in "domneiar" (i.e. courting ladies, acting gallantly) is thus a doubly sly joke, particularly as Richard was reputed to be gay, as several sources document (Paden et al., 232; Boswell, 231; Brundage, 257).

23. Bertran de Born 80, 13 (B/S 113)
MSS: F 78, I 181, K 167.
Base Text: I

During the period after the Young King had made peace with his brother Richard and, as per the wishes of his father, had ceased making demands on his lands as he had been doing, the father sent him regular shipments of money for his food and needs. He had no land of his own nor did he govern any land, and no one came to him for support or aid in war. Sir Bertran and all the other barons who had supported him against Sir Richard were deeply saddened. The Young King went off to Lombardy to participate in tournaments and amuse himself and abandoned all those barons to their war with Sir Richard. The latter seized towns and castles, and took over lands which he then devastated, burned, and set on fire. Meantime the Young King was jousting and sleeping and enjoying himself. This is why Sir Bertran composed this sirventes which begins:

I don't feel like putting off a sirventes any longer...

Song 80, 13   Bertran de Born: "D'un sirventes no·m cal far loignor ganda..."
Source: Paden et al., 184.
MSS: A 195, C 138, D 123, F 78, I 181, K 166, N 247, R 7, M 240 (Attributed to Raimon de Miraval)
Other English translations: Paden et al., 184; Smythe, 78.

1. I don't feel like putting off a sirventes any longer;
   Such desire I have to tell it and spread it!
   For I have a great new story about the Young King
   Who has given up his claim
   On his brother Richard because his father ordered him to.   5
      That's how much he is controlled by others![1]
   Since Sir Henry neither owns nor governs any land,
      Let him be the king of the bums!

2. He's acting like a bum, for that's how he lives,--
   Off an allowance that is counted out and rationed to him. 10
   A crowned king who lives off another
   Doesn't much resemble Arnaut, the marquis of Bellande,
   Or that valiant Guillaume who conquered the tower of Miranda;
      How greatly he was esteemed![2]
   Since he lies to them in Poitou and treats them like dirt 15
      He will never be much loved there.

3. Never by sleeping will he be king
   Of the English at Cumberland or conquer Ireland;
   Nor will he have Angers or Montsoreau or Candes,
   Or control the watchtower of Poitiers.   20
   He will never be the duke of the Norman lands
      Or the count palatine
   Of either Bordeaux or of the Gascons beyond the Landes,
      Or even lord of Bazas.

4. I want to send some advice over there to Sir Richard,   25
   To the tune of Lady Alamanda, even though he hasn't asked for it.[3]
   May he never pay court to his men out of fear of his brother;

Not that he even pretends to; rather, he attacks and assails
   them,
Takes their castles, destroys and burns what they have
   All around them   30
While the king is off tourneying with the men from Guarlanda
   And that other one, his brother-in-law.[4]

5. I wish that Count Geoffrey, who has Brocéliande,[5]
   Had been the first born,

6. For he is courtly; and that the kingdom and the duchy   35
   Were under his command.

[1] There is word play here between "forsatz," meaning coerced, and "forcatz," meaning split down the middle, forked, unable to make up his own mind.

[2] References to the Guillaume d'Orange cycle of *chansons de geste*.

[3] This is an allusion to the fact that this song was to be sung to the tune of Guiraut de Borneilh's well-known tenso, "S'ieu.us quier conseill...", song 242, 69 under razo 5 in this collection. (Paden et al., 189).

[4] King Philip of France (Paden et al., 189).

[5] The place names in this song are often synecdoches: the watchtower of Poitiers represents the residence of the dukes of Aquitaine at Poitiers; Guarlanda was a fief within Paris, so here refers to Parisians; and Brocéliande refers to Brittany, which was under Geoffrey's rule (Paden et al., 189).

24. Bertran de Born 80, 26 (B/S, 115)
    MSS: F 96, I 183, K 169.
    Base Text: I

The planh[1] that Sir Bertran de Born composed for the Young King was written for no other reason than that the Young King was the finest man in the world and Sir Bertran loved him more than any man in the world and the Young King loved him more than any man in the world and trusted him more than any man in the world. This is why King Henry, his father, and Count Richard, his brother, wished harm upon Sir Bertran. For the sake of the valor of the Young King and for the great sadness that his death inflicted upon all people, he composed this planh about him which says:

I end my song in sorrow and suffering...

[1] The Young King had died in June of 1183. Bertran composed this and another song (80, 41) lamenting his death. Songs of public lamentation of this sort were referred to as planhs.

Song 80, 26   Bertran de Born: "Mon chan fenis ab dol et ab maltraire..."
Source: Paden et al., 215.
MSS: A 189, B 113, C 144, D 122, E 99, F 97, I 183, K 169, Mh 2 (anonymous).
Other English translations: Paden et al., 215.

1. Forevermore I end my song in sorrow and suffering
And consider it over and done with,
For I have lost my wits, and my joy,
And the best king ever born of a mother:
    Generous and well-spoken,   5
    A fine horseman,
    Beautiful to look at
    And of humble appearance,
    So as to confer great honors.
    I believe this grief has such a grip on me   10
    That it has taken me over completely
    And this is why I go on talking about it.
    I commend him to God,
    That he put him in the place of Saint John.

2. King of the Courtly and Emperor of the Brave: 15
   These would have been your titles had you lived, Lord.
   But you carried the name of Young King
   And indeed you were the father and leader of all who are young.
   Hauberks and swords,
   Beautiful buckram,   20
   Helmets and banners,
   Doublets and garments,
   Joy and love
   Have no one to maintain them
   Or to bring them back.   25
   They will follow you there,
   They will flee with you
   And all fine and perfect deeds.

3. A fine welcome, giving without a fickle heart,
   Lovely conversation and "How glad I am to see you!";   30
   A great court, paid for and well maintained,
   Gifts, arms, and well-being without wrong-doing,
   Eating to the lively sounds
   Of song and viol,
   And tons of companions,   35
   Strong and brave,
   The very best there are.
   I want people to stop all this
   So that none of it is retained
   In this vile world   40
   During this ill-fated year
   Which once seemed so fair.

4. Lord, in you there was nothing to improve upon;
   All the world had chosen you as
   The best king ever to carry a shield   45
   And the bravest, the champion tourneyer.
   Since the time of Roland
   Or even before
   Never has there been seen so noble a man,
   So skilled at war,   50
   Whose praises
   Have left such a mark on the world
   Or brought it such vitality.
   Nor one who has gone off to in search of that praise

        From the Nile to the land of the setting sun,   55
        Expecting it wherever he went.

    5. Lord, in your honor I wish to give up on joy;
        All those who ever set eyes on you
        Must now stand grief-stricken and mute
        And may no joy ever transform that sorrow: 60
        Bretons and Irishmen,
        English and Normans,
        Aquitanians and Gascons,
        And Poitou suffers over it
        As do Maine and Tours.   65
        May all of France, up to Compiègne,
        Be unable to hold back her grief,
        And Flanders, from Ghent
        All the way to Wissant;
        Even the Germans weep!   70

    6. When the men from Lorraine and Brabant
        Hold their tournaments
        They will be so saddened not to see you there.

    7. The world isn't worth a penny
        Or the drop of an acorn to me   75
        Nor are those who are left within it.

    8. Because of the burdensome death
        Of the good and venerable king
        We must now, all of us, suffer.

25. Bertran de Born 80, 35 and Guillem de Berguedan 210, 10 (B/S, 117)
    MSS: F 70, I 179, K 165.
    Base Text: I

You have surely heard about the harm that the King of Aragon had brought Sir Bertran de Born and how Bertran remembered what the king had done to him and to others. After a long period during which Bertran heard about other evil deeds that the king had done, he decided to tell all in a sirventes. Bertran had been told about a knight in Aragon whose name was Sir Espaingnol, and who had a good strong castle named Castellot which belonged to him and was near the Sarrazin border. He was therefore involved in a great war with the Sarrazins. The king was very desirous of this castle so he came one day to this area. Sir Espagnol came to meet him, to offer his services and his castle and immediately led him there with all his retinue. And the king, when he was inside the castle, had Sir Espagnol taken and led outside and he took possession of the castle.

And it is true that when the king had left to serve King Henry, the count of Toulouse inflicted upon him a defeat and took hostage a good fifty knights. King Henry gave him all the money that the knights were to pay for their ransom but the King of Aragon did not give this money to the knights but took it back with him to Aragon. And the knights got out of prison and paid with their goods.

And it was true that a joglar whose name was Artuset lent him two hundred marabotis and the king took him along with him for over a year and never gave him a cent.[1] One day Artuset got into a quarrel with a Jew and the Jews attacked Artuset and wounded both him and his companion badly. So Artuset and his companion killed a Jew. For this the Jews went to the king and begged him to seek revenge, saying that they would give him two hundred marabotis if he would give them Artus and his companion to kill. The king gave over both of them and took the two hundred marabotis. The Jews had them burned on the day of the nativity of Christ, as Guillem de Berguedan tells it in one of his sirventes which speaks badly of the king:

> And he committed a crime
> Which no man should try to justify,
> For on the day of the Nativity
> He had two Christians burned,
> Artus and his companion;
> And one should not condemn
> To death or torture
> Two men for one treacherous Jew. (210, 10)[2]

Another, whose name was Peire the Joglar, lent the king money and horses. This Peire the Joglar had said many evil things about the old queen of England who was occupying Fontevrault, an abbey where rich old women retire. So she had him killed with the consent of the King of Aragon.

Sir Bertran de Born remembered all these shameful deeds committed by the King of Aragon in this sirventes which says:

When I see in the fields
the yellow, purple and blue banners unfurled... (80, 35)

[1] Note that the king is borrowing money from two different joglars, an indication not only that the king had lost most of his money in wars but that the joglar is someone who is wealthy enough to provide the king with cash. This information reinforces other songs which emphasize the economic arrangements between singer and patron. The truly despicable deeds of the king all hinge upon his refusal to reciprocate once a gift has been given. The fact that his victims lose their lives and/or land is bad enough, but the author is underlining that this is a man who does not repay service, the ultimate insult in the patronage system within which the singer operates.

[2] This anti-Semitic note should be seen in light of the fact that Spain was at this time a three-cultured land in which learning and power were shared among Christians, Jews and Moslems (Menocal, 1987). This fragment of song by Guillem de Berguedan is the only portion of the song extant.

Song 80, 35   Bertran de Born: "Qan vei pels vergiers despleiar..."
              Source; Paden et al. 274.
              MSS.: A 195, C 138, D 123, F 71, I 179, K 165,
                 R 96, T 170, V 81.
              Other English translations: Paden et al., 274.

1. When I see in the fields
   The yellow, purple and blue banners unfurled,
   The neighing of the horses soothes me,
   As do the songs that the jongleurs perform
   As they go fiddling from one tent to another;   5
   And the trumpets, the horns and the clarion call.
   Right then I want to compose a sirventes
   So that Count Richard will hear it.

2. I want to reconcile with the king
   Of Aragon and return to peace,   10
   But he was far too rude and insulting
   When he came up here to make war;
   It's only right that I criticize him.
   I am only saying this to teach him a lesson,
   And I want him to learn it from me,   15
   For it hurts me to see him acting like a fool.

3. They all want to join me in accusing him,
   For one of his vassals told me
   That he was roundly criticized for Chastellot
   When he had Sir Espaignol thrown out.   20
   And it doesn't seem to me that he can defend himself
   Against him if he dares to bring it to a head.
   And when he did go in and take over by invitation
   He certainly got little income out of it.

4. From now on I can hide nothing from him;   25
   No, I will be his loyal friend.
   Gaston, lord of Béarn and Pau
   Sent me a little story to tell
   About how he accepted ransom money from the king,
   To buy the freedom of his men, held as prisoners,   30
   But he preferred to carry off the money himself
   Rather than have his men returned to him.

5. This is what joglars have told me about him:
   That they gave him their praises and got no recompense.
   If ever he gave them green or blue clothing   35
   Or allowed them to be paid a single penny
   It displeased him greatly if anyone caught him doing it.
   Only one found a way to pay him back,

Artuset, and for what he did he deserves to be criticized,
   For he put him up for sale to the Jews.   40

6. He knew how to cheat Peire the Joglar,
   Who had lent him money and horses;
   For the old lady who watches over Fontevrault
   Had him cut to pieces.[1]
   Not even the insignia given to him by the king at arms   45
   With its band of metal from the king's own skirt
   Could save him from being cut up
   When they attacked him with knives.

7. Pedro Ruiz was able to guess
   As soon as he saw him as a royal youth   50
   That he would not be courageous or bold;
   He knew it by the way he yawned.
   A king who yawns and stretches
   When he hears people talking about battles to come
   Looks like he does it out of weakness   55
   Or because he isn't interested in arms.[2]

8. I forgive him if he made the Catalans
   Or the Larans go against me;
   Since it was the lord of Poitou
   Who ordered him to do it, he didn't dare do anything but.   60
   A king who expects that a lord is going to pay him
   For a service rendered had better do something in return.
   And he did come here for profit
   More than for any other agenda.

9. I want the king to know my sirventes, to learn it   65
   Of his own free will, to have it sung
   Before the king of Navarre,
   And to spread it throughout Castille.

---

[1] Though the razo identifies the "old lady" as Eleanor of Aquitaine, who did indeed end her days at Fontevrault, Paden et al. note that at the time when this song was composed the lady presiding over the abbey would have been Mathilde, the sister of Philip of Flanders (Paden et al., 279).

[2] There is a pun here that extends over three lines based on the words "badaillar" (to yawn), "badaill" and "batailla" (battle).

26. Bertran de Born 80, 39
MS: m
Base Text: Crespo, 790.

When Sir Richard was a count, he fell in love with a lady from Gascony who was the wife of the lord of Blancfort whose name was Guillem and her name was my lady Biatrix, the sister of Sir Arnaut of Marsan. The lady was beautiful and courtly and learned; she was glad to listen to the beseechments of the count, for she considered his attentions an honor. For a long...[1]

[1] This is one of the three new razos found written on eight fragments of vellum in the Koninklijke Bibliotheek in the Hague and published for the first time by Roberto Crespo in 1983. All of the texts concern Bertran de Born. All of the six songs in the fragments can be found in other manuscripts as well as three of the six razos. The remaining three, including this one, are therefore not included in the B/S edition. Though there is no song mentioned in what text remains of this razo, Crespo determined that it was intended as commentary on song 80, 39 (Crespo, 789). The text has been grouped here with other songs which discuss the revolt of 1183, as determined by the Paden et al. edition.

Song 80, 39   Bertran de Born: "Seigner en coms, a blasmar..."
Source: Paden et al., 224.
MSS: A 194, D 121, I 175, K 160.
Other English translations: Paden et al., 226.

1. My lord, the count, it makes one
   Criticize you, there's no doubt about it,
   That you didn't dare go
   Talk to the lady
   When she wanted you to.   5
   And in the manner of Catalogne,
   I am ashamed of you on your behalf
   That you made her wait in vain.

2. A fine lover shouldn't delay
   If a message comes to him;   10
   He should get ready to leave
   And hit the road
   Since he doesn't know his lady's
   Concern or need.
   Maybe she wants him to go away;   15
   That's why he'd better not delay.

3. And when you saw your joglar
   Coming back from having seen her
   You shouldn't have waited,
   Even if you were given Normandy!   20
   If you had truly wanted to go
   Into the area between Beira and Dordogne
   You wouldn't have been overcome with fear,
   And you shouldn't have thought about it.

4. But now you can prove   25
   Whether what I've been saying is true:
   That it's not good to love
   A rich man and expect to share love's pleasures.
   They have so much to worry about;
   That's why the joy of love keeps its distance.   30
   I don't want to have Burgundy
   If it means not fearing and hiding it.[1]

5. I don't ever want to be a baron
   Or a man of great wealth
   So that some man   35
   Could accuse me of villainy.
   I'd rather laugh and joke
   With My-Lord, who invites me to be with her,

>   Than rule over Gascony
>   Or Brittany.   40

6. My song turns to Sir Azemar[2]
     Who should recognize in it his honor/land.
     May our lord cut it into quarters![3]
     He knows how to court
       That little Lombardy so nobly[4]   45
     That he doesn't change his course or take up arms
     Over threats; rather, he doubles his attentions
     And tightens his grip on Limousin.

7. If Count Geoffrey doesn't go away,
     He'll have Poitou and Gascony[5]   50
     Even if he doesn't know how to court ladies.[6]

[1] Bertran is parodying here some of the topoi of fin'amor. According to the topos of secrecy, the love for the lady must be concealed. Bertran's lady in this case is first revealed in line 28 to be a rich man, and then, in line 31, it is Burgundy itself that he wishes to love in secret.

[2] Bertran had previously reconciled with Aimar V of Limoges but in this song has reverted to his previous disdain. (Paden et al., 229)

[3] Henry II.

[4] The comparison is with the rebellious Lombard League (Paden et al., 229).

[5] The lands of Richard.

[6] This song is one of the most remarkable of the corpus for its candor concerning its use of the verb "domnejar" (the courting of ladies) as a metaphor for political, social and economic domination and advancement.

27. Bertran de Born 80, 36
   MS: m
   Base Text: Crespo, 785.

There had been a great war that involved the barons of Limousin and Sir Bertran de Born, as you have heard elsewhere. And it happened that all those barons made peace with the count without conferring with Sir Bertran. He was as sad and mournful over this as he could ever possibly be, and he complained about it to the courtly Count Geoffrey, with whom he shared the name "Rassa," and who had supported them in that war, and then they went and made peace without conferring with the count. And so he wrote a sirventes about his recriminations that begins:

   Rassa, they've put themselves first...

He showed just how they had been the first to get involved in the war, and how, once they had gotten him into the war, each one of them left him so that he was the last fighting. Then, when his land had been set aflame and burned, they told him that he really should seek vengeance, if he felt like it. So he exposed them, saying that they were all getting rich, with their hunting dogs and crane falcons and bloodhounds all for themselves; they were getting themselves up all rich-looking with their Salisbury hose, and that they didn't care about anything else anymore. And here is the sirventes:[1]

   [1] See note 1 to the previous razo.

Song 80, 36   Bertran de Born: "Rassa, mes si son primier..."
               Source: Paden et al., 242.
               MSS: A 193, C 143, D 120, I 175, K 160, M 230, m.
               Other English translations: Paden et al., 244.

1. Rassa, they've put themselves first
   In this truce they've declared,
   Those lords and lieutenants
   And the barons from that region.
   And if they're all headed in your direction   5
   What harm do I deserve from you,
   I, who haven't even recovered my land?

2. Each of them leaves me behind
   Once they've gotten me into the melee,
   The noble ones and commoners both.   10
   Then after they've laid waste my land,
   Set it aflame and burned it,
   The folks from Colombier
   Tell me I can seek revenge, if I feel like it.

3. There are about thirty of us warriors,   15
   Each one has a cape full of holes;
   All of us, lords and their partners,
   With our hearts set on a messy war,
   For we never got a dime out of it.
   Rather, when it's time for blows   20
   They have already offered their demand.[1]

4. From now on they'll be rich gatekeepers
   Who'll keep the gate locked!
   And crossbowmen will know
   There is peace in the region   25
   For no one will be giving them wages!
   It's dogs and greyhounds who'll be sharing in
   The count's intimate love.

5. Goshawks and crane falcons,
   Horns and leather drums,   30
   Hunting dogs and bloodhounds,
   Bows with barbed arrows,
   Huge, lined overcoats
   And hose from Salisbury
   Will now be part of their household.   35

6. I have searched from Montpellier
   All the way to the salty sea

Without being able to find an unsullied baron
Of perfect prowess
Who's not cracked down the middle   40
Or chipped on one corner.
There isn't one of them who pleases me anymore.

7. Beautiful lady, I beg God to let me have you
For I have so desired you
That desiring has killed me,   45
Lovely and esteemed lady.
Sir/Lady Temperance, the noblest one pleases me,
For through his/her messenger he/she has hidden from me
The meaning of the world.

8. Papiol, take the straight road   50
And fear neither wind nor frost.

9. Tell my Rainier for me
That his prowess pleases me.[2]

[1] Paden et al. translate this line as: "the others were the ones to complain." It seems equally possible that these supposed allies have already offered/extended ("prestada") their demands for a peace treaty ("lor coreilla").

[2] Sir or Lady Temperance is unidentified, as is the lady who appears quite suddenly, though in keeping with Bertran's tendencies in other of his songs, at the end of the sirventes. Peire Vidal also used the senhal "Rainier" and in his case it referred to Sir Barral, viscount of Marseille. Stronski theorized that Bertran was using the same name to refer to the same person, especially since his reference to what lies beyond Montpellier and the salty sea could be a reference to Marseille (*Folquet*, 32).

28. Bertran de Born 80, 31 (B/S, 121)
   MSS: F 65, I 178, K 164.
   Base Text: I

In the past, during the time that King Richard of England was at war with King Felip of France, they were both encamped with all of their men. The King of France had with him the French and the Bourguignons, the Champenois, the Flamands and those from Berry. King Richard had with him the English and the Normans and the Bretons and the Poitevins and those from the Anjou, Turenne, Maine, Saintonge and Limousin. They were at the bank of the river Sèvre, which flows by the foot of Niort. One army was on one bank of the river and the other was on the other side and they stayed like this for fifteen days. Every day they would arm and equip themselves to come into battle. But the Archbishops and the Bishops and the Abbots and the men in religious orders who were all seeking peace came between them and forbade that the battle should take place.

One day all of King Richard's men were armed and in battle formation and ready to cross the Sèvres and the French too armed themselves and took their places. The good men of religion with their crosses in their arms were there, imploring Richard and King Felip that the battle not take place. But the king of France said that the battle would not be put off unless King Richard acknowledged him as lord of all that he possessed on that side of the sea, including the duchy of Normandy, the duchy of Aquitaine and the county of Poitiers; and that he return Gisors, which he had previously taken. Sir Richard, when he heard the text of what Felip was demanding, was full of confidence, for the Champenois had promised him that they would not oppose him in battle due to the large amount of silver that he had distributed amongst them. He mounted his horse, put on his helmet. had the trumpets sound and had his banners unfurled at the edge of the water to lead them as they crossed the river. He then ordered the formations of barons and of his own men to cross over onto the battlefield. And when King Felip saw him coming, he mounted his horse and put his helmet on his head. All his men climbed upon their horses and took up their arms to come into battle except for the Champenois, who did not put on their helmets.

King Felip felt dishonored and horrified when he saw Sir Richard and his men coming toward him with such vigor and saw that the Champenois were not going to do battle. He began to have the Archbishops and Bishops and men of religion called for, all those who had implored him to make peace. He begged them to go to Sir Richard and beg him to make peace and reinstitute concord; and he himself promised to make and uphold that peace (without) demanding the return of Gisors or the vassalage that Sir Richard was to accord him. The holy men went with their crosses in their arms to King Richard, and crying, they asked him to have pity on the many good people on the battlefield, for all would die; and they asked that he choose peace. They said that they would have Felip leave Gisors and abandon King Richard's lands. The barons, when they had heard the great honor (goods) that King Felip was ceding, all went to King Richard and advised him to accept the plan for peace and reconciliation. And Richard, on the prayers of the good men of religion and the counsel of his barons, made a peace and reconciliation agreement such that King Felip ceded Gisors to Richard with no payment and the question of vassalage remained as it had been left. Felip departed and King Richard stayed on.

They both swore to a ten-year peace; disbanded their armies; gave their soldiers leave; and became cheap and miserly, both of them. In their cupidity they did not want to raise armies or spend their money except on falcons and hawks, dogs and hounds, buying property and possessions and hurting their barons. For this reason, the barons of the King of France as well as those of King Richard were sad and mournful, for it appeared that peace had been declared so that the two kings could become miserly and discourteous. Sir Bertran de Born was the angriest of all the barons, for he was no longer able to delight in his own or in others' wars or in the wars between the two kings. When the two kings were at war with one another, Bertran was able to get from Richard all that he wanted in goods and honor and he was feared by both kings for the power of his tongue. And so Bertran, out of desire to see the kings return to warring, and seeing that the other barons had much the same wish, composed this sirventes which begins:

Since it troubles and annoys the barons...[1]

---

[1] The razo author is clear-sighted about Bertrand's stake in this affair. His righteous anger is based on the principle that rulers are in power to keep the economy moving through active participation in warfare. Any ruler (see e.g. razos 21, and especially 23, in which the Young King is blamed for the same fault of spending on his own pleasure while neglecting the call to war) who shirks the responsibility he has to keep his men in his service and reward them with plunder is seen as "vilain," the opposite of all that courtliness demands. Ladies who favor other pretendants and no longer reward poets with their patronage come in for similar attacks. This poet sees his role as one of editorialist. He does what he can to prod

leaders into action and keeps them in his control through their fear of what he might otherwise broadcast about them.

Song 80, 31   Bertran de Born: "Pois als baros enoia en lur pesa..."
Source: Paden et al., 362.
MSS: A 196, B 116, C 141, D 121, E 97, F 67, I 178, K 163, R 20, U 143, V 49.
Other English translations: Paden et al., 362.

1. Since it troubles and annoys the barons,
This peace that the two kings have made,
I will compose such a song that once it is learned
Every one of them will be dying to go to war.
I don't like the look of a king who accepts peace   5
After he's been disinherited, or loses what is his by right;
Not until he gets what he has demanded.

2. They are both thought to have behaved disgracefully
For they made an agreement which leaves them both sullied.
The French crown has five duchies   10
But if you count them, three are spoken for.[1]
He is losing the taxes and revenues from Gisors,
And Quercy over there is still in trouble
As are Brittany and the land of Angoulême.

3. A peace like this doesn't improve one's prowess;   15
Nor does any other, no matter how much it hurts him to hear it.
And he shouldn't let people debase his noble standing.
Since Issoudun has turned to King Henry
And is placed under his jurisdiction,
He shouldn't think that he is going to declare himself his man   20
If his Angevin fief is diminished by a log.

4. If the English king gave a gift or showed any generosity
To King Philip, it is only right that he thank him;

    For he had English money brought to France
    And now sacks and belts have added value there![2]   25
    It wasn't the Angevins or those from Maine
    Who defeated the troops from Champagne.
    It was sterling, the crucial equipment.

5. Guerri the Red responded with courtly discourse
    When he saw his nephew come running back in fear.   30
    For when disarmed, he would have liked to see a peace
        settlement
    But armed he wasn't willing to accept any treaty at all.[3]
    He wasn't at all like the lord of Orleans[4]
    Who, when disarmed, showed less willingness to yield
    Than when he had his helmet on his head!   35

6. It is considered a sign of weakness for an armed king
    To go seeking a peace accord when he is on the battlefield.
    They really have traded honor for greed,
    These Burgundians and French, from what I hear.
    In the name of the faith I owe you, I say it would be better
    For King Philip to begin his assault   41
    Than to negotiate a peace treaty in full armor, in the mud.

7. Be off, Papiol, and carry my sirventes
    Straight away to the land beyond Crépy-en-Valois
    To my Isembart in the land of Artois.[5]   45

8. And tell him I bow to a lady such that
    I can truly swear on my faith
    That she is the best in the world and the most courtly.

---

[1] The five duchies of the French crown were: France, Burgundy, Brittany, Normandy and the Aquitaine. Philip had lost control over the last three. (B/S, 130)

[2] Because he has convinced the Champenois not to support Philip by filling their sacks with sterling.

[3] Reference to the chanson de geste, *Raoul de Cambrai*.

[4] "The lord of Orleans" is another way of referring to Philip (Paden et al., 367).

⁵ The senhal "Isembart" refers to the northern French poet Conon de Béthune, and may have been inspired by the protagonist of the *chanson de geste, Gormont et Isembart* (Paden et al., 369). The song is thus an object of exchange between two male poets. The throw-away reference to the lady in the last line of a song which has to this point been patently political is merely a framing device, a bow to convention, and an admission that in the song the lady is often just a pretext for discussions of political and economic issues.

29. Bertran de Born 80, 2 (B/S, 127)
MSS: F 68, I 179, K 164.
Base Text: I

After Sir Bertran had composed the sirventes which says:

Since it troubles and annoys the barons...(80, 31)

and finished telling King Felip that he was losing three duchies out of five and the revenues and profits from Gisors; that the Quercy was still at war and unsettled, as was the Angoulême; that the French and Burgundians had exchanged honor for greed; and how King Felip had gone to the river bank to plead for peace; and how he had not wanted peace before putting on his armor but, to his disgrace, lost his strength and drive as soon as he dressed; and how little he resembled Gueric-the-Red, the uncle of Raol de Cambrai, who, when he was out of armor, wanted peace to be established between his nephew, Raol, and the four sons of Sir Albert, but who wanted neither peace nor reconciliation as soon as he was dressed for battle; and how any king who undertook a war with another king over land that the other had taken from him was shamed and dishonored if he accepted a truce or peace agreement before he had conquered and recovered the land that he had demanded, which was his by right and by reason, and that this is why the other kings thought he had been dispossessed; he shamed the Champenois for the silver that had been distributed among them and on account of which they did not wish to return to war. And all the barons of the Poitou and Limousin were very happy about Bertran's messages. This peace had left them downhearted for they were now less well remunerated and of lesser importance to both kings.

King Richard was full of pride because of this peace treaty, and he began to commit illegal and unjust actions in the territories of the French king which bordered his own. King Felip protested to those who had set up the peace treaty between them but Sir Richard didn't want to listen to the accusations of wrong-doing and did not change his behavior. So they ordered that an assembly be held between the Turenne and the Berry and there both sides met. King Felip made many accusations against Sir Richard and they had a huge and bitter argument. Sir Richard refuted what had been said of him and called Felip a base coward. They defied one another, and parted acrimoniously.

When Bertran de Born heard about their acrimonious parting, he was very happy. This occurred at the beginning of summer and because of it Bertran wrote the sirventes that you will now hear:

> In the new, sweet, white season
> Of Easter I see signs...

In that sirventes he strongly urged King Felip to begin a war of fire and blood with King Richard. He said that King Felip wanted peace more than a monk and that Sir Richard, with whom he shared the nickname Yes-and-No, wanted war more than any of the Algais brothers. They were four brothers, great thieves, who went around robbing at the head of a thousand thieves on horseback and two thousand on foot, and who had no other income or profit.

Song 80, 2   Bertran de Born: "Al nou doutz termini blanc..."
              Source: Paden et al., 354.
              MSS: A 195, C 137, D 124, D^c 256, E 101, F 69, I 179, K 164, N 247, a^1 452.
              Other English translations: Paden et al., 354.

> 1. In the new, sweet, white season,
>   Of Easter I see signs
>   Which the new age uses to please the senses,

A time when the season is kinder,
   More gracious, more precious; 5
   When one should be at his gayest
   And joy seems more delectable.

2. This is what is bothering me: I'm stuck
   And I can't enjoy the feast day right now;
   For one single day seems like thirty to me 10
   On account of a gracious promise
   Which has brought me pain and sorrow.
   I wouldn't want to make Doais mine[1]
   Without any hope of ever getting Cambrai!

3. A pustule and canker in the eye 15
   To whoever has been encouraging him in all of this.
   For never will miserable cowardliness
   Come to be worth a gracious payment of what is due,
   Or lounging around in a state of ennui
   Be the equal of war, trouble-making and hard work. 20
   May the lord of Roais be aware of this![2]

4. Never have we seen him take a slice
   Of an arm or ribcage, or strike a leg or head
   And leave it with a painful wound.
   And we didn't see him at Roam or Sais either 25
   With any great and noble army.[3]
   Let him remember what was said about him:
   That he has never broken a lance on a shield.

5. War without fire and blood
   Waged by a king or powerful figure 30
   Whom one can scorn or insult
   Is not a word that lives up to its reputation;
   Especially when he then turns to lounging and getting fat.
   Any young man who doesn't take to war
   Soon grows fat and wicked. 35

6. King of France, I consider you an upstanding man,
   For no one in Tours is paying his dues
   And in Gisors they are not offering
   Peace or a treaty that could be considered honorable.
   There you have it--war and peace, 40

And until a man throws himself into it
His reputation will never be dependable and true.

7. I will never complain about 'Sir Yes-and-No'
For I am sure that in him desire for war
Will never cease or slow down;   45
For peace and treaties have never been noble.
No man throws himself into it more willingly
Or leads raids and assaults
With so few men and under such great strain.

8. King Philip loves peace   50
More than the good man of Tarantais.[4]

9. Sir 'Yes-and-No' desires war even
More than one of the Algais clan.[5]

[1] "Douai, among the most important cities held by Count Philip of Flanders, a dependency of the French crown; Cambrai, capital of the county of Cambrésis, the point of furthest penetration of the Roman empire into French terrain" (Paden et al., 357: notes 13-14).

[2] Appears to be a reference to King Philip. Roais would then be the Arrouaise, a place which in *Raoul de Cambrai* is reputed for the baseness of its men: "Hom d'Aroaise ne vaut une cinele" (Paden et al., 357).

[3] Rouen and Sées, two sites in English-controlled Normandy that Philip had been threatening to invade (Paden et al., 359).

[4] Archbishop Peter of Tarentaise, while serving as papal legate, worked to keep the peace between Henry II and Louis VII and later between Henry and the Young King. He was canonized in 1191 (Paden et al., 361).

[5] Infamous thieves, known to have terrorized travelers and served as mercenaries. One of the brothers, Martin, is mentioned in chronicles from 1196 to his death in 1212 (Paden et al., 361).

30. Bertran de Born 80, 29 (B/S, 132)
MSS: F 64, I 178, K 163.
Base Text: I

Nothing that Sir Bertran de Born ever said about King Felip in verses or sirventes, not even his reminders of the wrongs and insults that had been done to him, could make him go to war with King Richard. But Sir Richard set out for war when he saw the weakness of King Felip. He robbed, took over castles and burned them along with towns and cities, and he took men as prisoners and killed them. All the barons who were unhappy with the peace were greatly pleased by this and Sir Bertran de Born more than any other for he loved war more than any other man and believed that it was on account of what he had been saying that King Richard, with whom he shared the nickname Yes-and-No, undertook this war. All this you will hear about in the sirventes that he composed as soon as he heard that Sir Richard had set off to start a war. He composed this sirventes which begins:

I can't prevent my song from spreading about..

Song 80, 29   Bertran de Born: "Non puosc mudar mon chantar non esparga..."
Source: Paden et al., 370.
MSS: A 193, C 138, D 120, F 64, I 178, K 163, M 232, R 7, T 172, U 140, V 27, a^1 447.
Other English translations: Blackburn, 164; Bonner, 151; Lindsay, 149; Paden et al., 370; Smythe 83.

1. I can't prevent my song from spreading about
   Since Sir Yes-and-No has set fires and drawn blood.
   A great war makes a stingy lord generous;
   That's why I love to hear the clash of kings.
   Let's hope they need stakes and cords and tent-knobs   5
   And that their tents will be set up outside for sleeping
   And that we'll meet them by the hundreds and thousands
   So that after us they will sing epics about our deeds.

2. By now I would have taken blows on my shield
   And turned my white banner bright red   10
   But for this: I hold off and bide my time
   For I see that Sir Yes-and-No is loading my dice.
   I don't even have Lusignan or Rancon

And I couldn't very well wage war at a distance without funds.
But I can help out with my know-how, 15
My shield at my neck and my helmet on my head.

3. If King Felip had burned his boat
Before Gisors, or let loose a dam,
Or entered the park in Rouen by force
And attacked him by hill and vale 20
So that no letter could get out except by pigeon,
Then I am sure that he would want to be like
Charlemagne, the best of his lineage,
Who conquered Apulia and Saxony.

4. War brings shame and takes away the good reputation 25
Of any man who is found not to give it his all;
That's why I don't think my Yes-and-No will give up
Cahors or Cajarc, since he knows so much about sudden
    reversals.
If the king gives him the treasure of Chinon,
He'll then have might; the heart for war he already has. 30
He gets so much pleasure out of trouble and spending
That he assails both his friends and his enemies!

5. Never did a seagoing ship, having lost its lifeboat
In bad weather and wanting to veer away from the reef,
Plunging forward with more force than an arrow from a bow,
Being lifted on high, then plummeting down below, 36
Have it any worse than what I go through for her;
And I'll tell you why: because she doesn't want to take me on.
She won't keep me for a day or night, or keep her promises;
And that is why my joy, which once blossomed, now withers.[1]

6. Go forward, sirventes, now, fast and running 41
To Treignac, and may you be there before the feast day.

7. Tell Sir Roger and all my family for me
That I can't find any more "ombas," "oms" or "estas."[2]

[1] The appearance of the lady at this point in the song is unexplained. Bertran is very likely referring to Richard (Yes-and-No) in the person of an indecisive and inconstant lady.

[2] Reference to the rhymes of the original Provençal text.

31. Bertran de Born 80, 8 (B/S, 134)
MS: F 78.

After Richard had made peace with Bertran de Born and returned to him his castle of Hautefort, he went overseas on a crusade. Bertran stayed behind, at war with Sir Aimar, the viscount of Limoges, and with the count of Périgord and all the other barons of the surrounding areas. And, as you have heard, while Richard was on his way back he was taken prisoner in Germany and he spent two years in prison and won his freedom with ransom money.[1]

And when Bertran de Born found out that king would be getting out of prison, he was very happy on account of the good favor he would receive from the king and the blow it would be to his enemies. You should know that Sir Bertran had inscribed in his heart all the wickedness and damages that those warriors had perpetrated in Limousin and in King Richard's lands. And so he composed this sirventes:

I wish the king were a mind-reader...

[1] B/S remind us that we have not, in fact, heard this previously (135, n. 1). This would imply that there were at one time other razos on Bertran de Born which were lost by the time the compiler of ms. F put together his collection and that this collector was not the original author. Richard did leave for the crusade in 1190, was taken prisoner in 1192 by Duke Leopold of Austria and delivered to the emperor, Henry VI, and was not released until 1194.

Song 80, 8   Bertran de Born: "Be.m platz car trega ni fis..."
            Source: Paden et al., 434.
            MSS: A 193, D 120, F 79, I 175, K 160.
            Other English translations: Paden et al., 434.

1. I wish the king were a mind-reader[1]
   And would travel over here to be among us
   So he could see which of the barons
   Are true to him and which are false,
   And learn about the spirit of evil   5
   Resounding throughout Limousin.
   It used to be his, and could be of some use to him,
   But for one sore spot that's infecting the whole place.

2. I would love him for it if he would listen
   As soon as he's free   10
   And acquit himself twice of his gifts
   Before it hardens up on him.[2]
   As soon as he has returned from Germany
   I want young Sir Aimar
   And Sir Guy to split things   15
   Equitably so that no one is left complaining.

3. There will be laughter once again
   And soon enough they'll love us
   And welcome the finest people
   And give us coins   20
   If they want us to stay with them![3]
   For you'll never win over outsiders
   Just by yelling "Paris"
   Without any other flow of money.[4]

4. It pleases me well that there is no truce or treaty   25
   Left in force among these barons
   Who were forever planting bushes.
   They so love gardens of every kind
   And residences where few companions are welcome
   That you'd think they were hiding out from the Anssessis![5]
   For you won't get into wherever one of them might be   31
   Without a struggle.

110

5. Don't ever think that some weakling
   Can climb two steps on the ladder of merit;
   He's fine down there on the bottom,   35
   All bent over and forgotten.
   And let him stay there!
   Because even for a thousand marks in sterling
   He couldn't manage to climb two steps
   He's so afraid his money will run out!   40

6. Papiol, Sir Frederick would never
   Have struck a bargain
   Like his son, Sir Henry, did
   When he took pilgrims with their walking sticks
   In order to take Apulia and Romagna.[6]   45

[1] Ms. F's version of this song differs markedly from others. Since the only razo extant is from that manuscript, I have included the song as it is written there, since it is clear that it is to that text that the razo author is referring. The line from the song cited in the razo is the first line of the first stanza in manuscript F, but this stanza is the fourth stanza of the other manuscripts' versions.

[2] These lines in manuscript F read: "Ben volgra l'en si aucis, E q'en passes dos so dos..." Since "dos" can be read as "back," "gifts," "sweet"; and "so" as "that," "his," "music," there are multiple interpretations suggested by this configuration of words.

[3] Here Bertran equates the singing of songs and serving of lords with political alliances and an active economy.

[4] The battle cry of "Paris" is probably a reference to the fact that some of the Limousin barons had taken to supporting Philip of France in Richard's absence (Paden et al., 437).

[5] The Anssessis (assassins) refer to the members of a radical Islamic sect often sent out to kill on the orders of their chief, the Man of the Mountain (Paden et al., 437).

[6] Frederick Barbarossa, father of the emperor Henry VI.

32. Bertran de Born 80, 34 (B/S, 136)
MSS: F 80, I 184, K 170.
Base Text: I

When King Richard had departed on his voyage overseas, all the barons of Limousin and Périgord swore a pact together, built a great army and went to the castles and towns that Sir Richard had taken from them. They fought and overcame all those who put up resistance and in this way recaptured a good deal of what Sir Richard had taken from them. After Richard returned from overseas and was let out of prison, he was distressed and angry to find that the barons had taken possession of their castles and towns and he began to threaten that he would soon strip them of their possessions and destroy them. The Viscount of Limoges and the Count of Périgord discounted these threats because of the support the king of France had given them and continued to give them. They answered him, saying that he had become too proud and obnoxious and that in spite of himself they would make him affable, courtly and humble and that they'd teach him a lesson by declaring war on him.[1]

Now Bertran de Born, like a man who has no greater joy than to get barons involved in wars, was very happy to hear that the King was threatening those barons who showed him no respect, disregarded his pronouncements and had messages sent to him saying that they would make him affable and courtly again, even if it be against his will. Sir Bertran knew that the King was distressed and angry about what they had said and about the castles of Nontron and Agen which they had taken from him, so he composed a sirventes to encourage King Richard to set off for war.

When he had composed his sirventes, he sent it to Sir Raimon Jauzeran, the lord of Pinos, from the county of Urgel, a valiant, generous, courtly and noble man. There was no man in Catalogne who could equal him in dignity. He was courting Lady Marquesa, the daughter of the Count of Urgel and the wife of Sir Giraut de Cabrera, the most powerful and noble man of all Catalogne with the exception of the Count of Urgel, his lord. And the sirventes begins like this:[2]

When the first flower appears on the branch. (80,34)

[1] B/S note that this song could not have been composed after Richard's return, as the razo says, since in it he addresses Geoffrey of Brittany, who died four years before Richard's departure (B/S, 138).
[2] The localities and people mentioned have all been identified as being in and of Catalonia. Marquesa was sung of by Peire Vidal, Pons de la Gardia, Guiraut del Luc and Guillem de Berguedan (B/S, 139).

Song 80, 34   Bertran de Born: "Qan la novella flors par el vergan..."
Source: Paden et al., 282.
MSS: A 192, C 143, D 119, F 81, K 169, M 229, T 173, Frammento Romegialli A.
Other English translations: Paden et al., 282.

1. When the new flower appears on the branch[1]
   And the twigs are all scarlet, green and white,
   With all the sweetness that I feel at the changing of the year
   I sing like the other birds do;
   For in many respects I think of myself as a bird   5
   Because I dare to desire all the best the world has to offer.
   I dare to desire her and to have a yearning heart
   But I do not dare speak my heart to her; instead I hide it from her.

2. I am no lover and, as for love, I don't even fake it enough
   To explain myself to a lady, or to ask her for it,   10
   And I don't go courting. Yet I might just as well,
   For the scandal-mongers --an ignominious, lying, meddling,
   Unlearned, base and villainous bunch,
   Have said such things about me, and gotten so involved,
   That they make it seem that the noblest lady in the world
   Is keeping me gay, satisfied, and desirous.   16

3. A man without a lady cannot compose a love song
   But I will make a sirventes, a fresh, new one.
   Since our barons are thinking of teaching the lord of Bordeaux
   A lesson by attacking him,   20

Making him open and courtly, by means of force;
   It won't look right if he's not so rude to them
   That each of them would be overjoyed if he even answers them.
   And let them not be upset if he shaves them down and skins
      them alive!

4. It will be a disgrace if all his hard work is for naught
   In Limousin, where he captured so many weapons,   25
   So many towers and walls and parapets,
   Ripped into them and tore them apart, knocked down so many
      castles,
   Took, gave, and spent so much money,
   Dealt, received and withstood so many blows,   30
   And underwent such hunger, thirst and fatigue
   Like he has, all the way from Agen to Nontron.[2]

5. Rassa, they are still complaining about you
   In Limousin, from here to Montsorreau.
   It was for your own profit that you inflicted those
      damages;   35
   That's what Sir Aimar and the lord of Martel tell me,
   As well as Sir Taillafer, Sir Rostand and Sir Golfier
   And all the rest of those who allied themselves with you.
   The peace they have found has nothing to do with you;
   It's to Count Raimon, way over there, that they give
      thanks.   40

6. There's one thing the Bretons and Normans should know,
   And the Angevins, Poitevins, and people from Maine as well:
   That from Ostabat to Montferrand
   And Rosiers to Mirebeau
   There won't be a man who won't see his armor;   45
   And since a count wants a rest, and that's his right,
   Let him ask at once for the land of Saint Haimon,[3]
   Before they put the sacred oil on his forehead.

7. Sirventes, be off to Sir Raimon Gausseran,
   Over there in Pinos, for I show in my explanation[4]   50
   That his words and demands
   On the lady who comes from Urgel and rules Cabrera are
      excessive.

> To my brother from Berguedan I give thanks and
> recognition
> For the fine joy he brought me; as a result of what he did
> My whole heart turned to rejoicing   55
> When we parted from each other at the end of the bridge.[5]

8. As birds are beneath the alerion,
   So are other ladies beneath the noblest in the world.

[1] This opening stanza is a response to the tornada of a song by Guillem de Saint Leidier in which he (Guillem) refers in the tornada to "Friend Bertran." This song by Bertran uses the same form and rhymes as the one by Guillem and plays on some of the words in Guillem's tornada ("cor volon"); (Paden et al., 283).

[2] That is, from one end of the Aquitaine to the other.

[3] Saint Edmund, the protector of the kings of England (Paden et al., 289).

[4] The original reads: "...q'en ma razon l'espel...," i.e., that in my razo....Here is a case in which Bertran is referring to the exposition of facts presented in a song as a 'razo.' However, the facts in this song do not pertain to a love affair with a lady. It may be once again that he is referring to an allegorical love affair that in fact refers to a political alliance, or it may be that Bertran means that he has elsewhere set out the facts of this affair in a text quite separate from the song in question.

[5] The reference is to the troubadour Guillem de Berguedan. See razo 25.

33. Bertran de Born 80, 28 (Crespo, 784)
MS: m

There was a time when Count Richard of Poitiers had agreed to a truce with Sir Aimar, the viscount of Limoges, with the viscount of Turenne, with Sir Archimbaut, count of Périgord, and other barons from the Limousin and surrounding areas. Sir Bertran de Born was never sadder than when the barons were at peace with each other during times of truce; he was never happier than when there were wars and skirmishes. And so he composed this sirventes, which says:

> It brings me down that...(80, 28: 1)

[Lose war?] ; and so he recalled the act of treachery that King Amfos of Aragon had committed against him in a verse that says:

> The Aragonese...are lamenting... (80, 28: 33)

Then he talked about his lady and accused her of jealousy and put up with......suitor if she......and he accused her of treachery, and these were her suitors: the Young King of England, his brother, Count Geoffrey, and the good Count Raimon of Toulouse; and it appeared very likely to him that she loved him more than any of these others. And so, out of jealousy over her he said that he knew a young goshawk with whom he shared the name "Tristan"; and, to get her jealous, he said that she (the goshawk) had taken him on as a suitor and that for this he felt richer than if he had been made lord of the city of Lucerne. This lady was the sister of King Richard and the Young King, as you have heard elsewhere, and the wife of the duke of Saxony; she was also the mother of the emperor Otto, and her name was Lady Elena. He said that out of love of her, the champions of the tournaments would see him in Poitou and the surrounding lands, so as to bring pleasure to the one lady and make the other one, my Lady Maeuz of Montaingnac, wife of Sir Talleyrand and daughter of the viscount of Turenne, jealous. And here is the sirventes that treats this subject:[1]

[1] This is one of six razos and songs found written on eight fragments of vellum in the Koninklijke Bibliotheek and first published by Roberto Crespo in a 1983 article. All of the texts concern Bertran de Born. All six songs can be found in other manuscripts but three of the razos were unknown before Crespo's paper. They are therefore not part of the B/S critical edition and have been placed here in light of Paden et al.'s determination of the songs' chronology. There are obvious gaps in the text.

Song 80, 28   Bertran de Born: "Molt m'es dissendre car col..."
               Source: Paden et al., 326.
               MSS: A 193, C 140, D 120, I 174, K 160, R 7, T
                   173, U 141, V 48, a 120 (attributed to Peire Vidal),
                   m.

1. It brings me down that
   We haven't seen me wage war from a castle
   Or attack or ambush
   For more than a year now.
   And that keeps me in a state of great torment   5
   For there are some who are like that out of fear,
   And others of us who are like that out of love
   Of the lord of Mouliherne.[1]

2. He really sharpens them and grinds them
   And tests them, like knives,   10
   That lord who holds Bordeaux.[2]
   But they're too thick in the front
   And weak at the cutting edge.
   They're more loyal than a prior,
   Thanks to the grinder,   15
   And all will come to enjoy *vita eterna*.

3. Sir Berlay de Mostairol
   And Sir Guillem de Monmaurel[3]
   Wouldn't have hearts as fickle
   As our lords do each year   20
   When they've started into winter
   And are in the summer heat.
   Their courage goes soft
   When the bright season darkens.[4]

4. I don't believe the lord of Mirandol,   25
   Who holds Creysse and Martel,
   Will revolt this year
   Until he's seen what the French,
   Who are threatening, will do;
   And they aren't quite as talkative.   30

They'd better not wait until spring
   For from now on it's going to rain and be like winter.

5. The Aragonese, the Catalans
   And the people from Urgel are lamenting,
   For they have no one to defend them   35
   But a big, soft lord
   Who praises himself in song
   And would rather have money than honor.
   He hung his ancestor;
   That's why he's destroying himself and condemning himself to
     hell.⁵   40

6. I turn to where my tooth is aching,
   To the one I enjoy
   Reproaching and accusing
   Of treason and trickery,
   For through her fickle desire   45
   She allows false pretenders
   To go around feigning that they have the love
   Of her who reigns over good reputation.

7. I know a young moulted hawk,
   Quick, honest and courtly,   50
   Who has never caught a bird,
   And with whom I call myself Tristan.⁶
   And because of this resemblance
   He/she has taken me on as a suitor
   And given me more riches   55
   Than if I were the king of Palermo.⁷

8. Tristan, for love of you
   The tourneyers will see me
   In Poitou, regardless of who mocks me for it.

9. But the queen of love   60
   Has taken me on as a suitor.
   I can throw a five and she can get double threes!⁸

[1] Henry II of England (Paden et al., 329).

[2] Richard, the count of Poitiers, and future king of England.

[3] Both of these men's names are used to refer to "the good old days." In the mid-twelfth century Berlay had revolted against Henry II's father, and Guillem was a lieutenant of the poet/duke Guillem IX in the early part of the century (Paden et al., 329).

[4] This stanza is not included in manuscript 'm' but is included in manuscripts I and K. Stanza 6 in the Paden et al. text is not in any of the three. It is found only in manuscript 'a' and has therefore not been included here.

[5] Alphonse II of Aragon and Barcelona was said to have hung his great uncle (Paden et al., 331).

[6] There is no indication that this hawk is a lady rather than a patron. Since the senhal, Tristan, is said to have been reciprocal, it seems likely that the reference is to a poet/patron, someone of Bertran's own standing. Tristan is used as a senhal by other poets as well. Bernart de Ventadorn used it in song 70, 43, under razo 1, and it has been claimed that this was a code-name he shared with Raimbaut d'Aurenga (Meneghetti, 108). The final tornada's reference to the queen of love may be to the same person as the hawk or may refer to the first lady mentioned in the song. It may also be an arbitrary closing addressed to a lady, the same sort of framing device seen in many of Bertran's sirventes.

[7] The King of Palermo was William II of Sicily. He is said to have lived in cloistered luxury, like an Oriental potentate, with his wife, Joanna, the daughter of Henry II (Paden et al., 333).

[8] Paden et al. explain this line as a reference to dice throwing, i.e. the poet would be glad to let the lady win. It seems also to be a joke, as in: "I can do five and she threesomes." This is especially likely if he is referring to the same lady he castigated in the sixth stanza as being known to allow many men to claim her as their lover.

34. Bertran de Born lo fills 81,1 (B/S, 140)
MSS: F 91, I 185, K 170.
Base Text: I

When King Richard died, he was survived by one brother, called John Lackland because he had had no portion of the land. He was made King of England and he possessed that kingdom along with the duchy of Aquitaine and the county of Périgord. As soon as he was made King and lord of the county and of the duchy of the Poitiers, he went off to the Count of Angoulême. The Count had a very beautiful young daughter of fifteen who had been promised by Sir Richard to Sir Ugo lo Brun, the Count of the Marche and nephew and vassal of Sir Jaufre de Lusignan. The Count of Angoulême had promised him his daughter as his wife and had taken him as his son, for he had no other sons or daughters. John told the Count of Angoulême that he wanted his daughter as his wife. He made him give her over; married her on the spot; mounted his horse and went off with his wife to Normandy.

When the Count of the Marche found out that the King had taken his wife from him he was greatly distressed and went to announce to all his relatives and friends what had happened. They were all very angry and advised him to go to Brittany and take prisoner the son of Count Jaufre, whose name was Arthur, and name him as their Lord. This they could justify doing for he was the son of Count Jaufre, who was born before King John. And so they did this and they made Arthur their lord. They swore to him their loyalty and brought him to Poitiers and they took Poitou from the King, leaving him only a few castles and fortified towns that he had in that land. John remained in Normandy with his wife, never leaving her side, night or day, whether in eating, drinking, sleeping or waking. He brought her hunting with him, through the forest and the plains, with his hawks and falcons. Meanwhile those barons took from him all his lands.[1]

One day, however, there occurred a very unfortunate incident. Jean's mother was being held in a castle named Mirabel and he, with the help of others, came to her aid without anyone knowing it. He did it so secretly that he was able to enter into the fortified town where they were without being discovered. He found them sleeping and took them all prisoner: Arthur, the barons and all those who were with them. Due to jealousy over his wife, however, for he could not live without her, he gave up Poitiers, returned to Normandy and left the prisoners behind in return for oaths and hostages. He then departed for England and took with him Arthur, Sir Savaric de Maleon, and the Viscount of Châtellerault. He had his nephew, Arthur, drowned, and had Sir Savaric de Maleon put in the Tower of Corf, a place where one could neither drink nor eat, and he did the same with the Viscount of Châtellerault. As soon as the King of

France heard that King John and his wife had left for England, he entered into Normandy with a great army and took over the land. The barons of Poitiers rose up and took all of Poitou from him except for La Rochelle. Sir Savaric de Maleon, a valiant, wise and generous man, used his wits to escape from the prison and took over the castle where he had been held.[2] King John then made peace with him, let him go free and put him in charge of all the land that he had not lost in Poitou and Gascogne.

Sir Savaric went off and began wars with all of King Jean's enemies and got back from them all of Poitou and all of Gascogne. The King remained in England, in his bedroom with his wife, and gave no aid or reinforcement to Sir Savaric de Maleon, neither in funds nor in men. And so the younger Bertran de Born, the son of the Sir Bertran de Born of those other sirventes, composed this sirventes on behalf on the needs of Sir Savaric and of the complaints of all the people of Aquitaine and the County of Poitou:

When I see the season change...(81,1)[3]

[1] The king's behavior reminds us of Chrétien de Troye's *Erec et Enide*, in which excessive devotion to one's wife at the expense of knightly duty is criticized.

[2] Savaric de Malleo is himself the subject of razos 46 and 47.

[3] According to Stimming and Boutière/Schutz, much of this razo is factual. John did take as his second wife Isabelle, daughter of the Count of Angoulême, though she was to have married Hugo IX of Lusignan. After John's death, she married Hugo's son. Arthur, the king's nephew, was indeed killed on the king's orders (see B/S, 144; Egan 22).

Song 81, 1   Bertran de Born lo Fills: "Quan vei lo temps renovelar..."
            Source: Stimming, 148.
            MSS: A 194, B 115, D 122-423, D^a 185-662, F 93, G 107,
                I 184, K 170, N 246-393, Sg (attr. to Bertran de Born)

1. When I see the season change
   And the leaves and flowers reappear,
   Love gives me the ardor,
   The heart, and the knowledge to sing.
   And since I see I have all I need,   5
   I will compose a stinging sirventes
   Which I will pass along as a present
   To King John, who brings shame upon himself.

2. He truly should be ashamed
   If he thinks of his ancestors,   10
   For he leaves Poitiers and Tours
   To King Philip without even laying his claim.
   This is why all of Guyenne mourns
   King Richard, who put so much
   Gold and silver into defending them,   15
   While John doesn't seem to have given that a thought.

3. He prefers feasting and hunting,
   Hounds, wild hares, hawks
   And amusement; and this is why honor eludes him
   And he allows himself to lose his inheritance in his own
       lifetime.   20
   He little ressembles Gawain in ardor,
   For it is right here that we most often see him.
   And since he will take no one else's advice,
   He gives up his land to the lord of Gronh.[1]

4. Ludovic knew better how to set free   25
   Guilhem and lend him his powerful aid
   At Orange when the almanzor
   Had Thibaut lead a siege against him.[2]
   For that he got reputation and honor with interest.[3]
   I say this so as to chastise   30
   King John, who is losing the support of his people,
   For he sends them no aid, be they close or far away.

5. Barons, I now turn my blame on you
   For the foolishness
   You have shown; and it hurts me   35
   To have to talk about you.
   You have dashed merit to the mud

>   And learned a mad kind of reasoning,
>   For you fear no chastisement;
>   Rather, you flatter those who speak ill of you. 40
>
> 6. Lady whom I desire and hold dear,
>   Fear and esteem as above all others,
>   So true is the praise about you
>   That I know neither how to speak it or spread it.
>   For just as gold is worth more than pewter 45
>   So are you worth more than the hundred finest;
>   And you are more faithful to youth
>   Than those from Cadouin are to God.
>
> 7. Savaric, a king who lacks heart
>   Will have trouble mounting a successful attack, 50
>   And since his heart is weak and cowardly
>   May no man ever make the effort on his behalf.

[1] Logroño in Castile.

[2] This is a reference to a lost version of the *Siege of Orange*, part of the epic cycle of William of Orange (de Riquer, 953; Pirot, 389).

[3] A particularly clear example of the way in which reputation is equated to currency.

35. Richart de Berbezill 421, 2 (B/S, 153)
MS: P 46.

You have certainly heard who Ricchaut de Berbesiu was and how he fell in love with the wife of Jaufre de Tonnay, who was a beautiful, noble, young lady. He loved her beyond all measure and called her "Better-than-a-lady" and she loved him in the courtly manner. Ricchaut beseeched her to give him "pleasure in love" and called for her mercy.[1] The lady responded that she was very willing to give him pleasure so long as it would bring her honor. She told Ricchaut that if he loved her as he said he did then he should not want her to say any more about it, or do anything more for him than what she was already doing and saying.

So it stood, and their love went on in this fashion until a lady from that land, the chatelaine of a powerful castle, called for Ricchaut and he went to see her. The lady began by telling him that she was amazed at what he was doing, for he had loved his lady for such a long time and never had she given him "pleasure of love" according to "the rights of love".[2] She said that Sir Ricchaut was such a handsome man, and so worthy, that all good ladies should be willing to give him pleasure. If Ricchaut agreed to leave his lady, she said that she would give him as much pleasure as he wanted to ask for, and she added that she was a more beautiful and powerful lady than the one he was then courting.[3]

And so it came about that Ricchaut, on account of all the great promises that she had made, said that he would leave the other lady. The lady ordered him to go and take his leave of that other lady and warned him that he would get no pleasure until she knew that he had really left her. Ricchaut departed and appeared before the lady he was courting. He began by telling her that he had loved her more than all the other ladies in the world, and more even than himself, but that since she had never consented to give him any "pleasure in love" that he was going to leave her. She was very sad and mournful and beseeched Ricchaut not to leave her. She said that even if in the past she had not given him pleasure, she was now willing to do so. Ricchaut answered that he wanted to leave as soon as possible and thus he left her.

Then, after he had left, he came to the lady who had made him leave and told her that he had done all she had ordered, and was beseeching her to come through with all that she had promised him. The lady answered that he was no man to whom any lady should give or speak of pleasure; that he was the wickedest man in the world for having left his lady, who was so beautiful and gay and who so loved him, just on the say-so of another lady; and that just as he had left that lady, so would he leave another. Ricchaut, upon hearing what she said, was the saddest man in the world, and the most miserable who had ever been. He went off, hoping to reenter the favor of the first lady, but she did not wish to retain his services. In his great sorrow, he went off to a wooded area where he built a home and took refuge in it, refusing to come out until he had found the forgiveness of his lady. This is why he says in one song:

Better-than-a-lady, from whom I fled two years ago...(421, 2: 50)

The good ladies and the knights of the surrounding lands, seeing the wretched state of Ricchaut, lost as he was, came to him in his house of reclusion and begged him to come out and leave that place. Ricchaut said that he would never leave until his lady had pardoned him. The ladies and knights then went before the lady and begged her to give her pardon, but the lady said she would never do such a thing until one hundred ladies and one hundred knights who all loved each other in true love came before her on their knees, with their hands joined, to beg for her mercy to pardon Ricchaut.[4] Only then would she pardon him, if they could arrange this. The news reached Ricchaut and this is why he composed this song, which says:

> Like the elephant
> Who, when he falls, cannot get up
> Until the others, with the cry
> Of their voices raise him up,
> I, too, wish to follow that custom;
> For my crime is so grave and weighty
> That if the court of Puy with all its ostentation
> And the fine prayers of loyal lovers
> Cannot raise me, then I will never be raised.
> May they deign to beg for mercy for me
> There where prayers without mercy do me no good. (421, 2)

When the ladies and knights heard that he could find forgiveness from his lady if one hundred ladies and knights who loved one another in true love went to beg Richaut's lady to forgive him, and that she would then do so, they assembled and all went and begged for her forgiveness of Ricchaut. And the lady forgave him.[5]

---

[1] "Far plaser d'amor" is one of the ambiguous references to compensation in love that one finds in the songs as well as the razos. It clearly refers to a payment on the part of the lady that is due to the singer who has already performed a service for her. In some cases it clearly refers to sexual favors. It could also be an admission, probably public, that this singer is the favorite of the lady, thus acknowledging him as the finest singer/composer. If the term refers exclusively to a private love affair and the exchange of sexual favors, it is difficult to determine how such knowledge would be so well known that a lady from a neighboring land could know exactly how much "plaser d'amor" the poet had received.

² "En dreit d'amor" is another technical term that one finds used repeatedly to indicate the contractual side of the poet/lady relationship. It appears that if an agreement is reached "according to the rights of love," the poet can reasonably expect some public recognition that he is the favorite of the lady in return for his service, or he can expect some sort of sexual recognition.

³ This triangular formation is typical of a certain type of razo. Note that the poet has value to the second lady only so long as he is unavailable. It could be interpreted that the second lady is somehow defending the rights of the first in luring Richart away and punishing him. It is much more likely that she wishes to enhance her own renown by luring him from another court but realizes that he is of no further value unless he is desired by a rival.

⁴ "Amar per amor" is yet another term that refers ambiguously to the relations between a couple. This seems to mean love in the sense of shared, sexual relationship. It is opposed to the other type of love about which many of the troubadours are singing which refers to a public expression of praise.

⁵ This razo served as source for a story in the *Novellino*, "D'una novella che avenne in Provenza alla Corte del Po" (B/S, 595).

Song 421, 2   Richart de Berbezill: "Atressi con l'orifanz..."
               Source: Braccini, 24; Varvaro, 106.
               MSS: A 165, B 103, C 219, D^a 180, D^c 254, G 63, H 30, I 88, J 9, K 72, L 13, N 73, O 18, Q 44, R 60, U 104, Ve. Ag. I 167 and 291, W 195, X 84, a^1 421, b 1, f 47.
               Other English translations: Wilhelm 200.

1. Like the elephant,
   Who, when he falls, cannot get up
   Until the others, with the cry
   Of their voices, raise him up,
   I, too, wish to follow that custom.   5
   For my crime is so grave and weighty
   That if the court of Puy and its ostentation
   And the fine prayers of loyal lovers

Cannot raise me, then I will never be raised.
May they deign to beg for mercy for me   10
There where judgement and reason do me no good.

2. And if I cannot rejoin in joy
The other fine lovers,
I give up singing forever;
For there is nothing left of me.   15
Instead I will live as a recluse
Alone, without companionship, for such is my desire.
My life is but pain and irritation;
Ecstasy hurts me; pleasure is sorrow.
I am not like the bear   20
Who, when he is beaten and mistreated without mercy,
Grows fat, revives and prospers.

3. I know well that love is so great
That it could easily forgive my
Having failed through over-loving.   25
I acted like Dedalus,[1]
Who said he was Jesus
And wanted, in his arrogance, to fly to heaven.
But God laid low his pride and arrogance.
My pride is nothing more than love   30
And for that reason mercy must come to my aid:
For there are many places where reason beats mercy
And others where justice and reason hold no sway.

4. I blame myself before the whole world
For my behavior and for having talked too much;   35
And if only I could be like the phoenix,
Of whom there was only ever one,
And who burned and then rose up again,
I would set myself aflame. For I am so miserable
And my false words are so full of lies and deceit   40
That I would rise from them with sighs and tears
To a place where there is beauty, youth and merit.
It takes only a little bit of mercy
For all that is good to be united.

5. My song will be my spokesman 45
   At the place I dare not approach
   Or even look full in the face;
   So evil and finished am I,[2]
   That I should never be excused for it.
   Better-than-a-Lady, from whom I fled two years ago, 50
   I now return to you, mournful and in tears.
   For like the stag who, when he has finished his run,
   Returns to die at the cry of the hunters,
   So do I return to you, Lady, in your mercy,
   But it matters little to you since you do not recall our
       love. 55

6. I have such a lord, in whom there is so much good,
   That on a day when I see him I can do no wrong.

7. Beautiful-Emerald, joy and renown support you;
   When I think of you I have everything I could want.

[1] Braccini uses the more logical "Le Magus" in his edition but it is found in only two manuscripts. Varvaro retains "Dedalus," which appears in seventeen, and is plausible as an allegorized version of Ovid's tale.

[2] OR: as in 10 manuscripts: "So evil and conquered am I."

36. Raimon Jordan 404, 9 and 404, 12 (B/S, 161)
    MSS: A 128, B 78, I 81, K 65.
    Base Text: I

The Viscount of Saint-Antonin was from the bishopric of Cahors, a lord and viscount of Saint-Antonin.

He loved a noble lady who was the wife of the lord of Penne d'Albigeois, a strong and powerful castle. The lady was noble and beautiful and worthy, much esteemed and much honored; and he was valiant, learned, skilled at arms, attractive, and a good composer of song and his name was Raimon Jordan. The lady was called the Viscountess of Pena. The love between the two of them was beyond all measure, so much did they love one another.

One day the Viscount went into the territory of one of his enemies dressed in his armor. There was a great battle and the Viscount was wounded to death. His enemies announced that he was dead. The news reached the lady that he had died and she, in the great sorrow and pain that she felt on hearing the news, went straight away to a convent of heretics and gave herself over to them.[1]

As was God's will, the Viscount got better and recovered from his wounds. No one wanted to tell him that she had committed herself. When he was completely cured, he went to Saint-Antonin where he was told that she had committed herself over the sadness she felt when she heard that he had died. When he heard this, he lost his delight in company, his laughter, his singing and his happiness; they were replaced by moans, tears, sighs, worry and sorrow. He no longer participated in knightly activities nor socialized with good company.

For more than a year he remained in a state of great mourning. This is why my lady Elis de Montfort, the wife of Sir Guillem de Gourdon and daughter of the viscount of Turenne, in whom there was youth and beauty, courtliness and merit, called for him, beseeching him in a pleasing manner to leave behind his sorrow and sadness and become happy through her love for him. She said that she would make a gift of her heart and body and love to make amends for the sorrow he had had to suffer and begged him, asking for his mercy, to deign to come and see her or to allow her to come and see him. When the Viscount heard the magnificent message that the noble, worthy lady sent him, there began to grow in his heart a sense of the great sweetness of love. So much so that he began to be happy and to feel joy again, to go out in public, to participate in gatherings of good company, to dress himself and his companions, to take up once again his equipment and his arms and his delight in living. He dressed himself up in fine and honorable style and went off to see my lady Elis de Montfort and she received him with great pleasure and showed him great honor. He was gay and cheerful upon receiving the honor and pleasure that she was bestowing upon him and she was very happy with the goodness, valor, intelligence, learning and courtesy that she saw in him. She did not renege on the promises of pleasure and love that she had sent him. He, for his part, found ways to thank her and beg for her continued grace, asking that she show him so much love that he might believe that she sent him her pleasing invitations to pleasure out of her own free will and good heart; and he told her that he carried them written within the chamber of his heart. She did this so well that she took him on as her knight and accepted his homage and she gave herself to him as his lady, kissing and hugging him, and gave him the ring from her finger as a guarantee and token of their sure union.

And so the viscount departed from her very happy and gay and began again to compose and sing and socialize.[2] So he composed for her the song which says:

To you I bow, in whom I have placed my affection.. (404, 12)

And even before he had composed that song, one night while he was sleeping it seemed that Love assailed him with a verse which says:

Raimon Jordan, I want to hear it from yourself
Why you have given up socializing and singing.
You used to be so interested in courting ladies
According to all the rules, or made it seem as if you were
By pretending and making yourself look gay.
But now I see that you have given up on lais (songs);
For this you are to be blamed if there is no one to stand up for
    you... (404, 9)

He composed many good songs, some of which are written here, as you will hear.[3]

---

[1] One of the rare mentions in the prose texts of the heretical movements in the South whose influence served as the pretext for the Albigensian Crusade and Inquisition.

[2] It is interesting to note that once their pact has been satisfactorily concluded, both sides delivering what had been promised, the poet is said to depart to resume his life. This first visit to the lady resulted in his being accepted as her lover and liege man, but he will now go off on his own to continue singing her praises.

[3] Again we note that writing and hearing are not mutually exclusive, that in fact they are at this point mutually supportive

activities, neither of which seems to have displaced the other (Stock, 1983).

Song 404, 9   Raimon Jordan: "Raimon Jordan, de vos eis volh aprendre..."
Source: Kjellman, 91.
MS: C 153.

1. Raimon Jordan, I want to hear it from you yourself
   Why you have given up socializing and singing;
   You used to be so interested in courting ladies
   According to all the rules, or made it seem as if you were
   By pretending and making yourself look gay.   5
   But now I see that you have given up on lais (songs);
   For this you are to be blamed if there is no one to stand up for you.

2. Love, from now on I must contend with you
   But you yourself provoke me so much
   And I think I can make you see, through my argument, 10
   That this will never suit you or bring you honor.
   I have put all of my efforts into serving you
   And you treat me like someone who betrays his own,
   And so I perish like a ship on the waves.

3. You seem upset, Raimon, by my criticism   15
   But it isn't true, no matter what you go around saying,
   That any one of mine has ever been betrayed by waiting.
   I consider those who follow my orders as my own
   And those in whom trickery is born are not.
     20
   This is all so painful for me that I don't know where to hide.

4. *(This stanza has been almost entirely obliterated in manuscript C)*

5. It looks as if you want to break away,
   Raimon Jordan, from everything that is agreeable.
   This is why I will make your heart ignite once more
   From the sweet desire that a lover will inspire; 25
   And I will make of one kiss such a compensation
   For that which your mouth so often enjoyed
   That all of these wrongs and trouble will end.

6. Let it be seen, Love, whether you conjure the mercy
   Within you before you go promising me so much. 30
   For my affair would be much too insignificant
   If you were to restrict me to a desire from yesteryear.
   Again it happens that I let you control me,
   But be careful that no plaint should follow
   Over what that mouth so desired. 35

7. Raimon Jordan, a great deed like this can never be accomplished
   With just one bold stroke,
   As easily as a swallow whirls in the sky.

Song 404, 12 Raimon Jordan: "Vas vos soplei en cui ai mes m'entensa..."
Source: Kjellman, 94.
MSS: A 370, B 137, C 152, D 401, E 135, I 83, K 66, M 191, R 272, T 215, (Attributed to Gui d'Uisel in M and to Guiraut de Calanson in E).

1. To you I bow, in whom I have placed my affection,
   For never could anything else so please me.
   There I join my hands to become your man
   As my reason and knowledge direct me.
   She and Love and my heart, when they join together 5
   To assault me, are all three against me.
   Each grows in strength and conquers me, so great
   Is the power that they have; and I willingly
   Accept the suffering which keeps me from all joy.

2. Lady, by whom the world is refined and improved,   10
   You have my heart; you know so well how to betray me.
   I feel sorrow and joy, and when I think of you
   I lose all sense and I know it.
   So why should one who loses all hope right there,
   Just seeing you, ask you for anything?   15
   Even thinking of you makes me fear scandal-mongers.
   What can someone who doesn't even speak lie about?
   This much I know, Lady: I have great fear of you.

3. Good lady, in deed and attitude
   I love you so much, if only I dared to tell you.   20
   If it's through love that a man should come to mercy,
   Then you should have mercy on me without consent;[1]
   For a lady conquers with love and mercy.
   May you have mercy, for mercy is what's needed,
   Good lady; I desire and seek nothing   25
   More than that; I am desperate
   That mercy should gain the consent of love.

4. I will not believe that there might be a cure
   In death such that I no longer sigh for her;
   Nor do I believe that any man can withstand   30
   The firm will I so fear.[2]
   And if I die thus, what good does it do; where does it get me;
   If she for whom I endure it doesn't know about it?
   Shall I tell her or not? Now I am being too hasty.
   Neither I nor any other will bear that message: 35
   Just think of how she would remember it.

5. Love, you are truly cowardly and false
   To come and strike me when I am beaten,
   And leave her whom neither I,
   Nor mercy, nor you, nor good judgement can convert.   40
   But if you could make her love me
   You would never again fail in any way.
   Working on cold steel is not as hard
   As making her hard heart pleasant;
   She is against me and from this comes my harsh penance.

6. If the one whose aid I so need   46
   Knew how deeply she was disturbing my peace of mind

It would be easy for her to deign to acknowledge me.
If only she would give me credit for my good behavior.
I opened my heart to her; she doesn't even remember it;   50
So, by my faith, I have neither myself nor her.
Nor do I dare seek more than the penitent,
But my song will act as my latin-speaker before her[3]
For whom I endure such painful abstinence.

7. I will not go on too much about praising her   55
For they would understand whose knight I am
If I mentioned even one quarter of her merits.[4]

  [1] "Without all falseness" is found in mss. E and R. There may also may be a play on the words "cossensa" (consent) and "cozenza" (burning pain).

  [2] "Lo ferm voler" is an expression found in other troubadours, notably in Arnaut Daniel's famous sestina (29, 14), and later used by Dante.

  [3] "Latinier" means a speaker of many languages, a messenger, an interpreter, an educated commentator.

  [4] This song is built upon the conflation of eroticized religious and feudal metaphors and commonplaces of allegorical courtly poetry: being her man, the folded hands, the wounded lover, the penitent, the address to Love, fear of speech, fear of the woman, the intractable woman, the conspiracy against the poet etc.

37. Gaucelm Faidit 167, 43 and 167, 59 (B/S, 170)
MSS: E 191, N^2 24, R 1; p 1
Base Text: E

You have heard who Gaucelm Faidit was and where he came from and what he was like.[1] But he had so much heart that he fell in love with lady Maria de Ventadorn, the best and noblest lady known to exist anywhere in those days. And he sang about her and composed his songs about her, and beseeched her in his singing and exhorted her and praised her great nobility. And she permitted this on account of the great praise which he gave her but never did she make love with him. And so this love that he had for her lasted seven years, during which time he never received pleasure in the rights of love. Then one day Gaucelm came before her and told her that she would either have to give him pleasure in the right of love, after which point he would consider himself paid, or that she would lose him and he would serve another lady from whom would come great gifts of love. He then took his leave from her and went off greatly distressed.

Lady Maria then sent for another lady whose name was Lady Audiartz of Malamort, who was gracious and beautiful, and she told her all about Sir Gaucelm and herself and asked her for advice as to how to respond to what Gaucelm had requested and how she could hold on to him without making love with him. This lady responded that she would not advise her to hold on to him *or* to let go, but that she would make him give up on his love for her in such a way that he would hold no grudge against her and would not consider himself her enemy.[2] Lady Maria was very happy when she heard this and she beseeched her to do what she had proposed. Lady Audiartz went off and left lady Maria. She took one of her courtly messengers and sent him to Sir Gaucelm Faidit saying that he would do better to love a little bird in his fist than a crane flying in the sky.

Gaucelm, upon hearing this message, got on his horse and came straight to Lady Audiartz. She received him most warmly and she explained to him why she had sent him the message about the little bird and the crane. She told him, most warmly, that she had great pity for him, for she knew that he loved Lady Maria but that she did not love him except out of courtly respect and in return for the great praise that he dedicated to her and the exalted reputation that he had made for her throughout the world.[3] "And you should know that she is the crane flying in the sky and I am the little bird that you hold in your fist, to be talked to and done with as you please. Keep in mind that I am gracious, greatly endowed with riches, young in years and, according to some, very beautiful. Never have I given, promised, cheated or been cheated on. I have a great desire for esteem and to be loved by such a man who could bring me merit, nobility, wealth and honored friendship. I know that you are the one through whom I believe I could acquire all of these good things and I am the one who can reward all honored services rendered. I want you as lover, servant and master and I make of myself and my love a gift to you in return for the promise that you will take leave of Lady Maria de Ventadorn; that you will compose a song in which you fault her in courtly terms; that you say that since she does not want you, you will take another road; and that you have found another woman who is sincere, noble, loyal and gracious who will retain you with no conditions."

And Sir Gaucelm Faidit, when he heard about the pleasing pleasures that she was offering, saw the loving expression that she showed him, the sweet requests that she composed and recited, the magnificent goods she was offering, and her great beauty and fresh colors, was so overtaken with love that he lost his sight and hearing.[4] When his sight and hearing returned to him he began to thank Lady Audiartz, to the utmost of his capacities, and to do and say all that she had ordered, taking from Lady Maria his heart and love and prayers and songs and placing them all in the service of his love for Lady Audiartz, under the conditions of the promise that one had made to the other. Gaucelm then went off, full of joy and great happiness, thinking about how he could compose a song in such a way that Lady Maria would know that he had taken leave of her and found another who would retain him with promises of bestowing upon him great pleasures and honors. And for this reason he composed this song which says:

I have suffered great pain for so long now...(167, 59)

and which you will hear.

This song was sung so much that Lady Maria learned about it.[5] And she was very happy, Lady Maria, just as Lady Audiartz was very happy about this song, for she knew that he had taken his heart and song away from Lady Maria and that he had believed the false promises that she had made in exchange for this song.

A short time after this song was composed and sung, Gaucelm Faidit came to see Lady Audiartz in a state of great happiness, like one who thinks he can now enter into the bedroom, and she gave him a big welcome. Sir Gaucelm was at her feet and he told her how he had followed her orders, had left Lady Maria for her, and how he had now brought to her his heart, his mind, his knowledge and his singing so that she might see fit to say and do the pleasing pleasures that she had promised him and of which he was deserving, after all that he had done for her. And Lady Audiartz said this to him: "Gaucelm, it is true that you are very worthy and esteemed and there is no woman in the world whom you might want to love who would not consider herself well paid to have you as lover and servant, who should not feel happy when you feel happiness, and who should not be saddened when you feel sadness; for you are the father and master of nobility and courtliness. And what I said to you and promised you was done not through a desire to love you for love[6] but to get you away from that prison in which you were being held, and from that hope that you had held on to for over seven years. For I knew about Lady Maria's desires--that she was leading you on with words and promises without any desire to act on them. In every other way I will be a benevolent friend to you and to the degree that you should choose or order me."

When Gaucelm heard those words, he was sad, mournful and miserable and he began to beg the lady's mercy not to kill him, betray him or cheat him. She said that she would not kill or cheat him; that on the contrary she had saved him from cheating and death. When Gaucelm saw that begging for mercy and pity would do him no good, he got up and left her, like a man who has lost hope, for he saw that he had been cheated and betrayed; that she had made him leave Lady Maria, and that it was in trickery that she had wanted to love him. And he considered returning to Lady Maria and begging her mercy; and so he composed this song which you will hear, which says:

Neither songs nor the sounds of birds
Can cheer my angry heart... (167, 43)

But never, through prayers or songs or anything that he might say or do, was he able to induce the lady to pardon him or listen to his requests.

[1] Gaucelm's name may be a 'stage-name,' or professional name under which he sang. "Faidit" means 'banished,' 'unhappy.'
[2] This razo is one of the clearest in discussing the business aspects of the troubadour/lady relation. Maria wants him because of what he can do for her renown but wishes to avoid alienating him for fear that he should then destroy her reputation. Maria de Ventadorn also figures in razo 57 to Pons de Capdoill, throughout the other razos (38-41) and songs of Gaucelm Faidit, and in Savaric de Malleo's song 432, 3 under razo 46. Her own poetry is glossed under razo 45.

³ The author has made his story particulary vivid through the use of extensive direct citation of Lady Audiartz.

⁴ These physical reactions to pain or pleasure are found elsewhere in the prose texts, notably in the vida to Jaufre Rudel (B/S, 16; Egan, 61).

⁵ It is again interesting to watch the transmission of information in this razo. Gaucelm makes his song public; that is how both Maria and Audiartz will learn of his 'conversion'. Since this author is more explicit about these matters than others, he offers a glimpse into the process whereby public outcry, rumor, and scandal-mongers would enter into the dynamic of patron to poet and how the spread of a reputation from one court to another would hinge on troubadours' songs.

⁶ "Amar per amor" is another of the ambiguous terms for love that implies here a sexual relationship rather than (or in addition to) one based exclusively on economics.

Song 167, 59   Gaucelm Faidit: "Tant ai sofert longamen grand afan..."
                Source: Mouzat, 249.
                MSS: A 76, B 49, C 72, D^a 164, D^c 247, E 11, F 16, G 30, I 33, K 22, L 122, M 73, N 112, O 48, P 15, Q 59, R 46, S 113, U 51, V 33, a 137, b 5, f 58.

1. I have suffered great pain for so long now
   That if it were to go on much longer, without even noticing it
   I could die suddenly, and at any time, if she wished it.
   Sorrow will never count for much before that beautiful lady
   In whom there was a cursèd beauty and worth.   5
   When I look at her, my heart is forced to turn away.
   And since she doesn't want me, it will travel another road.
   She doesn't care or think it will hurt her
   To lose me or the beautiful lyrics of my song.

2. Yet sometimes a man can consider something worthless which is
      really valuable   10
   And he thereby loses something from which he says he actually
      got some benefit,
   And he later misses it and has fewer goods.
   The wealth of My-Lord is so great though
   That it means nothing to her if she loses me or I go elsewhere.
   I really committed an act of outrageous folly   15
   When I went out seeking my death and destruction
   With my own crazy heart. It made me reveal in my singing
   Things for which I should hide my desire more discreetly.

3. Since my body and eyes   19
   And my evil lady and my own good faith have betrayed me,
   Such that each one of them would have killed me if it had been
      able to,
   I must reproach them, the way I would a bad overlord.
   I will never believe my eyes again,
   Those lying traitors, nor any promise without a guarantee.
   Any man who gets himself into a crazy vassal relationship is
      mad;   25
   And any man who thinks he has at his command
   Everything he sees that seems pleasing or promising is crazy.[1]

4. I am really amazed; for in My-Lord there is such
   Merit and worth, pleasure and courtly discourse,
   How can there be no mercy there?   30
   And I am furthermore amazed that with the honor,
   Beauty and intelligence that she has in her, there is no love!
   And I am amazed that a lady of such noble birth,
   So beautiful and refined, is so evil in performing her lordly
      duties
   Or that she can act so contrary to her rank   35
   That she belies her frank and humble appearance.

5. All of this greatly amazes me
   And since it pleases her not to change a bit of it,
   Her evil reins will no longer keep me in check.
   I am leaving her now, even though it dishonors me;   40
   I have to leave this suffering behind.
   And since I am going to change my place of residence
   May God provide me with a good encounter and a good welcome,

And let me find a lady without a miserable heart,
For I have spent this year with an evil lord.   45

6. I would gladly remain with such an evil,
Cruel and hard lady, if only she wanted me to;
I'd prefer her to another who would do me more good.
But since she doesn't want that, I'll go to another for help,
Who brings sweet pleasures to my heart.   50
She's beautiful and noble, honest and of good habits,
And she sent me a message through a courtly messenger
That I should prefer a little bird who stays put in my fist
To a crane flying by in the sky.[2]

7. I send this to my Santongier and my Superguarantee,[3]   55
For through my madness I have bought a dose of good sense.
I know so much about the good and bad sides of love
That I will never again kill myself begging someone.

8. I send to my Superguarantee word that because of a Beautiful-Recompense
I have now acquired good sense from my madness,   60
And know how to pick from love the benefits and damages
And that I will never again kill myself begging someone.

9. I have now conquered some good sense from great madness
And know how to choose from love the benefits and the damages
And will never again kill myself begging someone.   65

---

[1] See Peire Vidal's vida for an illustration of this phenomenon (B/S, 351 and Egan, 80).

[2] This image can also be read as an erotic joke. In Italian folklore, for example, the little bird has for centuries referred to male genitalia (See Boccaccio's *Decamerone* for an example: story 4, day 5).

[3] Mouzat identifies Superguarantee (Sobregatge) tentatively as Raimon de Toulouse. He then goes on to say that an Audiartz de Malamort did live in this region, roughly between 1160-1180 and that if one were to believe the razo, Beautiful Recompense (Bel Gazaing) could be a reference to her. Since these senhals occur only at the end of the song, there could also be conflation between the

lady and patron, i.e. the song is written about patrons, male or female, in the name of ladies.

Song 167, 43   Gaucelm Faidit: "No m'alegra chans ni critz..."
Source: Mouzat, 393.
MSS: A 72, C 72, D 31, E 12, G 30, I 35, K 23, N 116, P 38, Q 51, R 43, U 52, V 36, a 142.

1. Neither songs nor the sounds
   Of birds can cheer my angry heart.
   I don't know why I should sing
   Or waste
   My words, for I would be wasting them   5
   If I said
   That prayers and pleas for mercy
   Did me any good before my lady.
   For it is unseemly
   That she should be begged for pardon by someone like me,
   So greatly have I failed her.   11

2. So then why should my song be listened to
   Since it wouldn't be right for her to pardon me?
   Oh God, so that I could beg her
   To take vengeance   15
   On me--For it once happened that
   Falsity
   And unfaithfulness
   And another's invitation so pleased me
   That I left her.   20
   It is right that I should be shamed:
   I thanked her so badly for her gifts.

3. Since the woman who made me fail
   Was a lying seductress,
   It is only right that   25
   That other lady now hang me,
   The one who took me from nothing

141

    And set me on the road
    To all good things.
    However, if all those who have made a mistake   30
    Were put to death
    And there were no mercy to act as leader and guide
    That would be a great crime.

4. And yet I am not so far from
    Joy or so close to vexation   35
    That I couldn't come back to her
    If she were to show me
    Her good sense and courtliness.
    How she could
    Overtake me completely   40
    If her humble, courtly,
    Honest, learned
    Body, full of joy and good repute,
    Were willing to forgive me!

5. I would be cured with even this much: 45
    That she lower herself
    Even to hear me out;
    For then,
    After seeing how my loss has punished me
    Mightn't she   50
    Ease up a bit?
    Because I once did something that hurt her,
    I have already put up with so much pain.
    I lost all the good things I had when I was with her
    And here I've been betrayed.   55

6. Therefore, I will be so courageous
    As to go beg at her feet,
    Humble, contrite, my hands joined together,
    That she give me
    One gift: pardon me or kill me!   60
    I'd be glad
    To let her kill me;
    But I don't think she'd do it
    Because it would make me so happy!
    All I know is that it is all up to her   65
    Whether I die or live on in sorrow.

7. To the lord who own Poitiers
I send word that he should not be upset
If, in his dealings with me, he is like one clearly sounded 'no'
That's worth a hundred enthusiastic 'yes's'.[1]

[1] The lord of Poitiers is Richard-the-Lionhearted and the references in the tornada are to Bertran de Born's senhal for Richard, "Oc-e-Non" ("Yes-and-No").

38. Gaucelm Faidit 167,52 (B/S, 180)
MSS: E 194, N^2 25, P 39 (lacking the beginning), R 1, p 3 (lacking the ending)
Base Text: E

When Gaucelm Faidit had given up addressing his songs to Lady Maria de Ventadorn through the wiles of Lady Audiart de Malamort, as you have heard, he remained for a long time saddened and suffering over the great trickery that he had been subjected to. But Lady Marguarita d'Albusso, the wife of Sir Rainaut, the viscount of Aubusson, brought back his joy in singing, for she said so many pleasing things to him and gave him so many loving glances that he fell in love with her and begged her for her love. And she, since he placed her in such a noble position and sang about her, received his prayers and gave them heed and promised him to give him pleasure in the rights of love.[1] Sir Gaucelm Faidit's entreaties went on for a long time, as did the love that he had for Lady Marguarita d'Albusso. He praised her greatly and begged her in word and deed and she, while recognizing that he and his praise of her were the reason for her being happy, had no love for him and never gave him pleasure in the rights of love. But one time, when he was leaving her, he kissed her on the neck and she allowed this, lovingly, and on that pleasure he lived for a long time in great happiness.

She, however, loved Sir Ugo de Lasigna, who was the son of Sir Ugo lo Bru, the count of La Marche, and he was a great friend of Sir Gaucelm. The lady was in the castle of Aubusson, where she was not able to see Sir Ugo de Lasigna or give pleasure; so she created for herself a fatal illness and vowed to go in prayer to My Lady Sainte Marie of Rocamadour. She had word sent to Sir Ugo de Lasigna that he should come to Uzerche, a town where Gaucelm Faidit lived; that he should come secretly, stay at Sir Gaucelm's inn, where she also would be staying; and that she would give him pleasure in the rights of love, and she told him the day that he should be there.[2] When Sir Ugo heard this news, he was happy and joyous; he came there on the day she had specified and dismounted at Sir Gaucelm Faidit's inn. Sir Gaucelm's wife welcomed him warmly upon seeing him, with great happiness and many assurances of secrecy, as he had requested. Then the lady came and dismounted at the same inn; and she found Sir Ugo de Lasigna in the inn, hiding in the room where she was to sleep. When she found him she was happy and joyous and she spent two days there. Then she went on to Rocamadour and he waited there until she returned. When she did, they had another two days, and each night they slept together with great happiness and pleasure in each other's company. Almost right after they left Sir Gaucelm returned, and his wife recounted the whole affair. Gaucelm, when he heard this, was in so much pain that he wanted to die, for he believed that she loved only him. And because it was in his own bed that she had slept, he was even more sad. For this reason, he composed a *mala chanso*[3] which begins like this:

If ever a man, on account of his fine heart...

as you will hear. And this was the last song which he composed.[4]

[1] Again, the razo author makes it quite clear that Gaucelm is tolerated for his ability to advance the lady in society, though Gaucelm seems consistently to misunderstand their arrangement.

[2] Two references here to "giving pleasure (in the rights of love)" establish that this expression is a way of referring to pleasure that is sexual.

[3] A mala chanso is a song which openly castigates a lady for unseemly behavior. Many more songs than are classified under this title in the razos actually fall into this category in at least a portion of their stanzas.

[4] This razo resembles in numerous ways razo 51 to Guillem de Saint Leidier's song 234, 16.

Song 167, 52   Gaucelm Faidit: "Si anc nuills hom, per aver fin
              coratge..."
              Source: Mouzat, 336.
              MSS: A 74, C 70, D 31, E 13, G 27, I 37, K 25, M
                  82, N 118, P 14, Q 58, R 45, S 95, T 145, V 32,
                  a 158, f 59.

1. If ever a man, on account of his fine heart,
   Or for having loved as he should, without falseness,
   Or for having suffered his damages without complaint,
   Received from His-Lord an honored destiny,[1]
   Then I should surely get   5
   Some sort of suitable pleasure.
   For I know how to put up with the good and the bad,
   Whichever comes my way, and I know just how to
   Do everything that My-Lord likes;
   Thus I cannot turn my heart away from her.   10

2. When it comes to fine love, I know how to follow the right
      road,
   So that I love My-Lord beyond all reason,
   And she can do with me anything that pleases her.
   I so fear saying something wrong
   That I don't ask her to kiss me or lie with me.   15
   Yet I know so well how to make myself valuable
   In the ways of loving, despite what whoever else is singing,
   That I dare to want and desire
   An honored day and pleasing evening
   And all the things that should be accorded to a lover.   20

3. Although I want it, I have no other guarantee of love,
   No gift, no grant, no sure word.
   But she is so frank and of such fine rank
   That worth and reputation, which stay on with her,
   Make it clear to everyone   25
   That Love has power over her.
   Where there is gay worth
   There should also be a place for mercy.
   That is all that appeases my concern over her
   And takes me from myself, so I do not despair.   30

145

4. But what is all this worth to me? For I haven't the vassalage
   Or the courage to allow me to dare speak my sorrow.
   I so fear her honor and high rank,
   Her gay youthfulness and her beautiful face
   That I get scared   35
   That she won't even bother to give a thought
   To the harm and suffering I get from this.
   If she wanted to retain me,
   I wouldn't care about being the King of May
   So long as I was with her.   40

5. I have heard it said, by a wise man without madness,
   That a man prays badly for things he doesn't need,
   And when he asks God to give him youthful lordly power.
   Regardless of whether that prayer is right or wrong,
   I have truly found love   45
   And, when I have it, I cannot be sad;
   For it is better to wait and hope for a rich gift
   From a true and noble lady
   Than it is to get one from a vile and detestable woman
   To whom one owes no thanks.   50

6. For I know one who is so frank in the way she behaves
   That she doesn't keep her honor under her belt,
   And it's her own fault if I say nasty things about her;
   For with no embarrassment, and right out in the open,
   She lets everybody see   55
   How hard she works at ruining her reputation.
   I don't think I could spend much time
   With a lady who tries her hand with so many others,
   For no one ever says anything good about her
   And I don't want that that task should fall to me!   60

7. Lady Maria, gay lady,
   You are not one of those,
   For you do nothing that displeases;
   Rather, everything about you pleases and must please.[2]

---

[1] The uses of 'honor'/'honored' in this song suggest the material gift as well as the translations 'honor, prestige, virtue.'

[2] The razo author has declared this to be Gaucelm's last song, composed in despair, and has taken pains to explain each reference and change in attitude to the prior plot. The last stanza and following tornada, however, can be seen to constitute a veiled threat to Lady Maria, a fact which would contradict somewhat his interpretation.

39. Gaucelm Faidit 167,33 (B/S, 185)
MS: N^2 25
Base Text: N^2 in Bertoni, 1915.

Gaucelm Faidit loved a lady from the bishopric of Gap and Embrun whose name was Lady Jordana d'Ebreun. She was a noble lady and strikingly beautiful, very courtly, graciously learned, generous with her wealth and desirous of honor and a fine reputation. Gaucelm served her and honored her greatly, praised her and had her welcomed among the most esteemed ladies. Lady Jordana lived most gaily and happily and she tried very hard to do and say the right things so that Sir Gaucelm would not be held a liar for the good things he had said about her. She was so highly considered by everyone, far and wide, that there was no nobleman in Viane or in all of Provence who could think himself worthy of the name if he hadn't seen her; nor was there any good lady in all those lands who did not envy her her beauty and fine reputation.[1] And what I am telling you here is the truth for I saw it and heard it.[2]

Now it was Lady Jordana's will to give Sir Gaucelm pleasure in love, so she invited him one evening into her room for a chat. She did so much and said so much to him that he left with great happiness. And while in this state of happiness, the Marquis de Monferrat undertook a crusade and made Gaucelm enlist in that crusade to cross the sea....Lady Jordana.[3] This is why Gaucelm composed this song:

The honored, rapturous evening
When, like a beautiful apparition,
My Good-Hope came...

Gaucelm used to call Lady Jordana "Good-Hope."

[1] Once again we find the lady's primary interest being the establishment of her reputation.

[2] One of the few occasions on which a razo author authenticates his tale with reference to first-hand information. See also razo 46 to Savaric de Malleo's song 432, 3.

[3] There is a gap in the text at this point. Gaucelm is supposed to have accompanied Boniface of Monferrat, the leader of the Fourth Crusade, overseas in 1202 (B/S,169; Egan, 38). Mouzat (36) believes that Gaucelm also participated in the Third Crusade in 1190 under Richard-the-Lionhearted.

Song 167, 33   Gaucelm Faidit: "L'onratz jauzens sers..."
               Source: Mouzat, 294.
               MSS: A 82, B 51, C 65, D^a 164, I 35, K 23, N 123, R 91, a 162.

1. The honored, rapturous evening
   When, like a beautiful apparition,
   My Good-Hope came
   To fulfill my desire
   Brings me back, with its sweet memory,   5
   To that feeling of pleasure
   And makes me compose songs
   When I thought I had given that up.
   For it is only right
   That I sing, gay and joyous,   10
   When she, whose lover I am,
   The noblest lady ever known,
   Wants me and my songs.

2. Her gracious and noble
   Courtly body, of such good breeding,   15
   Honest, precious and good,
   Humble and of high standing,

And her loving eyes
   Know so well how to lure me
   Toward her benevolence, 20
   From where I bow in the direction of Provence.
   They have raised me so high
   That I am rich and powerful;
   If only the delay leading to our pleasure
   Can be ended 25
   And that power doesn't fail us![1]

3. For in her there is
   Equitable learning,
   Valuable knowledge,
   A humble appearance, 30
   A most worthy reputation,
   And an honored and refined comportment.
   Through her I am ennobled and serve as the gay singer
   Who proclaims her merit.
   I praise her for the gifts 35
   And the delicious pleasures
   And the grief and sighs of anguish
   I saw her experience
   At our dreaded, painful parting.

4. This is why pardon is required: 40
   For I was once late, though hardly at all,
   Because I did not hurry
   In coming to her chambers.
   Thus, on my knees,
   I am her loyal petitioner 45
   That mercy will win her over
   And she will pardon my failing.
   Neither goods, nor sharing a bed,
   Nor praying nor building up my worth
   Can make me delay. 50
   May she never fear
   That I should waver in my desire for her.

5. However, if the travel
   I am undertaking as penance
   To the land where the true God 55
   Was truly born

Brings pain to her heart,
It should not last long;
For it is the opinion of all good men
That of all meritorious men, he is most esteemed   60
Who, healthy and happy,
Goes off to serve the glorious King
Who is the Savior.
For in the sky, and here down below,
The reward will be rich.   65

6. It is now time
To go to the place where God the Father,
Who died for us,
Will act as our guide
And guide to the companions   70
Who are our partners
In obedience;
Their faith,
Bodies and goods will be a help to me,
For his service is costly.   75
May he keep us in his presence
And may he find the destruction
Of the evil powers a sweet sight.

7. Lady Maria, you
Are so beautiful and noble   80
That there is no emperor
In the world who would not be
Honored by your gifts.[2]

---

[1] OR, in a sexual sense: "Her eyes have brought me so high/ That I'm rich and potent/ If only this joy can be consummated and my potency doesn't fail me!" The razo author does seem to have interpreted Gaucelm's visit to the lady's room in sexual terms.

[2] This song is really a crusading song which frames the departure for the crusade in terms of an adieu and a discussion of the *fin'aman* as loyal Christian servant. See Folquet de Marseille's song 155, 15 under razo 78 for a different example.

40. Gaucelm Faidit 167, 40 and 167, 15 (B/S, 187)
MS: P 39.
Base Text: P in Bertoni, 1915.

There was a long period during which Gaucelm Faidit turned his attentions to Lady Jordana d'Ebreu, a city which is located at the entry into Lombardia, just at the limit of Provence. She was a very beautiful lady: noble, attractive, learned and courtly. He composed his songs about her, honored and served her so much and begged her for her attentions so much that she fell in love with him and made of Gaucelm Faidit her knight and her lover. In his songs, they called each other "Good-Hope," as he says in one song that he composed about her, and which begins like this:

> It greatly irritates me.....
> ....
> And everything that exists is seeking its joy,
> And my fine heart breaks and grows bitter
> Because I am not there where I have my Good-Hope
> And without her I can feel no joy. (167, 40) [1]

And it happened that Count Anfos of Provence turned his attention to her and did for her many fine and meritorious things: he jousted and went to great expense for her love. The lady received him courteously, showed herself open to his attention, conversed and laughed with him. It was thus believed that the Count was her lover and it was recounted to Sir G(aucelm) Faidit that the Count had gotten from her all his pleasure and desire fulfilled. This is why he left her, in disgust, sadness and suffering, fleeing from the court and taking from her his singing and songs and the fine words that he had composed about her. So sad and mournful was he that he wanted to die and never again hear any man in the world speak of her. He was away from her like this for a long time, not wishing to be cheered or to sing or laugh.

Finally, when he learned for certain that what he had been told was not true and that it had in fact been the treacherous work of scandalmongers, he was greatly sorry for the false things he had said about love and the wicked words he had had for his lady, and he repented for his madness. Now convinced that what he had been told were lies, he wanted to return to the good graces of the lady and so he composed a song, which you will hear, in which he appeals to her and begs her to pardon his failing, saying that if she will pardon him and choose to love him again, he will forever be as loyal and obedient as the lion of Sir Golfier de las Tors.[2] He gave two reasons why she should pardon him. He wished to take up the cross and travel to Rome but couldn't rightly do so if he was at war or held a grudge against someone or if any other person had something against him and would not forgive him. It was also fitting that she should pardon him because God pardons good pardoners and would pardon her if she would pardon Gaucelm. And this is the song:

> Singing and amusement, joy, courting and conversation
> Learning, generosity and courtliness,
> Honor and good reputation and loyal loving
> Have been so demeaned by trickery and wickedness
> That in anger I have nearly given up hope;
> For out of a hundred ladies and suitors
> I don't see one woman or man who behaves as he should
> In the art of loving and who does not feign to have his interest
>   elsewhere;
> Nor can any man say what has happened to love:
> Look at how worth has been degraded! (167, 15)

Gaucelm Faidit called Sir Ugo lo Brun, the Count of la Marcha, "Beautiful-Sweet-Fine-Emerald" and called Sir Peire de Malamortz "Saintongier" and called the Viscount of Comborn "Supergay" and Lady Jordana d'Ebreun "Good-Hope" and Sir Raimon d'Agot "Lignaure."[3]

---

[1] The sole razo manuscript has a lacuna within this stanza. The missing lines, with numerous variations, are nonetheless present in other manuscripts which contain the song itself.

[2] A hero of the *Chanson d'Antioche* who is also mentioned in songs by Bertran de Born (80, 37), Guillem Magret (223, 7) and Uc de Pena (456, 1) (B/S, 191).

[3] According to Lejeune, 1939, "Lignaure" is a senhal also used by Guiraut de Borneilh to refer to the troubadour Raimbaut d'Aurenga.

Song 167, 40   Gaucelm Faidit: "Mout m'enoget ogan lo coindetz
                  mes..."
               Source: Mouzat, 287.
               MSS: A 75, C 67, D 34, M 83, R 45, S 115, a 135.

1. This year, the gracious month when the dark days brighten
   And sweeten is really irritating;
   And the nightingale, who used to be so courtly,
   Is now so villainous that he just about killed me.
   I hear his songs and and see that the world is turning green
   And that everything that exists is seeking its joy,   6
   But my fine heart just melts, dies and grows bitter
   Because I am not there where I have my Good-Hope
   And without her no joy can please me.

2. And yet, from here, where I am, I send my plea there,
      where she is,   10
   On my knees, bent in submission with my hands joined.
   I am so overwhelmed by the fire of love
   When I remember the joy with which she conquered me![1]
   Let it be known that wherever I may be
   I never look anywhere else but there, and can desire nothing
      else.   15
   I don't think I'll ever find another lady
   Who so controls me all day, morning and evening,
   That I could ever take my heart away from her.

3. I often remember the great honors and goods,
   And the lovely way she answered me as she sighed,   20
   And the sweet parting which holds my heart prisoner.
   Thus I should just die in her presence
   For I am already dying of the great love that grieves me.
   Am I not already dead when I am unable to see her?
   Yes I am; for Love charges at me and unseats me   25
   So that I can give my life no meaning
   And nothing but her has any power over me.

4. For my sake, she shouldn't have so much beauty;
   For when I look upon those clear-sighted eyes
   And that lovely appearance of hers that took me in,   30
   I can't do a thing but moan and sigh,

153

Tremble, shudder and die of pure envy
That I am not there to serve her as she goes to bed,
When she lays that gracious body to rest in joy and lets speak her desire for love.[2]
At that moment I often give way, and fall to the ground in a faint   35
From the desire that I feel but cannot show.

5. If it weren't for my lord, Count Geoffrey,[3]
Who keeps me on here in his courtly country,
I would never stay somewhere where I cannot see her all the time,
Not even for the honors and goods that I receive;   40
For my fine heart seeks grace nowhere else.
The count knows that someone who wages war with a lover
Cannot know a single thing about fine love
And that no lover should ever suffer damages from a friend.[4]
That is why I don't think he dares to retain my services.   45

---

[1] The 'joi' with which she conquers is translated by Mouzat as 'the jewel' (293). While this is another meaning for joi, such a translation raises the question as to whether all the many mentions of 'joi' in the troubadour corpus couldn't be similarly translated and understood in the erotic or economic sense of 'her jewel.' I have translated as 'joy' for the sake of consistency but would like to suggest that we hear the other as an ever-present double meaning.

[2] The lady "dompneja," i.e. literally 'courts ladies,' as she is going to bed. This is better translated as 'shows herself receptive to love' / 'flirts' or the like.

[3] Mouzat identifies the count as Geoffrey of Brittany, son of Henry II and brother of Richard-the-Lionhearted.

[4] Within these two lines, Gaucelm uses three different epithets that can all be translated 'lover': "amador," "drut" (with more physical overtones), and "amic."

Song 167, 15   Gaucelm Faidit: "Chant e deport, joi, dompnei e solatz..."
Source: Mouzat, 445.
MSS: A 79, C 71, D^a 163, G 28, I 34, K 23, M 72, N 113, D 10, Q 52, R 44, S 98, T 138, U 55, V 37, a 151, f 47, p 2.

1. Singing and amusement, joy, courting and conversation,
   Learning, generosity and courtliness,
   Honor, reputation, and loyal loving
   Have been so demeaned by trickery and wickedness
   That in anger I've almost given up hope;   5
   For out of a hundred ladies and suitors
   I don't see one man or woman who behaves as he should
   In the art of loving; nor, in all truth, is there one who isn't just pretending,
   Or who can tell you what has happened to love.
   Look at how worth has been degraded!   10

2. There are lovers and ladies who, if the subject comes up,
   Will hide their true feelings and tell you straight off
   That they are loyal, and love without cheating;
   And then, since each of them is shady and secretive,
   They will cheat here, there, and on every front.   15
   And those ladies who think that the more lovers they have
   The more their reputation is enhanced!
   May they get the rewards that they deserve!
   It's a disgrace and a dishonor to each of them
   When, having one lover, they go off looking elsewhere.   20

3. Just as beauty, good welcome, attractive demeanor,
   Refined conversation, good reputation and good company
   Are what best suit a lady,
   So is it best that she control her desires;
   For a body split in two halves isn't worth a thing   25
   And one that changes colors is not fine.
   Only one love should have hold of her.
   I don't mean to say that it reflects badly on a lady
   If a man courts her, or if she has admirers,
   But she should never bring relief to two different sites!   30

155

4. When friendship reigned loyally
   The world was good and without vulgarity
   But ever since love has turned into deceitfulness
   Youth has fallen from grace into ruin.
   And, since I want to tell you the truth, even I   35
   Have learned so much from false, cheating lovers
   That it isn't clear that I will ever recover.[1]
   I ran fleeing from the land where joy, repute and beauty reign
   As if they had once harmed me   39
   When it was they who cured me, exalted and advanced me.

5. If only it pleased her beautiful, honored body,
   Which so graciously retains me in a loyal bond of service,
   To soften enough to pardon me, since in other affairs
   She humbles herself; then I would be refined
   In her presence the way gold is refined in its furnace   45
   And riches and family standing couldn't harm me.
   For if she gets me out of my evil predicament, if she deigns to
       do this,
   I will be as faithful to her, without any sign of falseness,
   As was the lion to Golfier de Lastors,[2]
   When he saved him from his worst ennemies.   50

6. Lady, if this failing had been pardoned
   I would have crossed the sea from over in Lombardy;
   But I don't think I could legitimately make a pilgrimage
   Without having first cleared my name before you.   54
   This alone should induce you to want to reestablish peace.
   Since mercy and honor are within you,
   May my song, since nothing is holding it back,[3]
   Be off to beg you sincerely to remember
   That sweetness and sincerity become a noble heart,
   And that God pardons those who pardon.   60

7. Lady Maria, so great is the worth
   That resides and reigns within you, good lady,
   That I am amazed that any heart could sustain it.
   Every day your good deeds to troubadours
   Grow in number; hence your praises grow as well.   65

[1] OR: return (the sense in which the razo composer understood this passage).
[2] Golfier de Lastours is a hero from a legendary episode of the first crusade (Mouzat, 450). See note 2 to razo 40.
[3] OR: since it is not retained by, in service to, anyone else.

41. Gaucelm Faidit and Elias d'Uisel 167, 13 and 136, 2 (B/S, 192)
MS: H 46

Gaucelm Faidit went overseas and brought with him his wife, Lady Guillelma Monja, a woman who had once been a prostitute, and who was fatter than he was.[1] He thought he had had a son by her, a very unpleasant man in every way. He returned poor and with no prospects. Elias d'Uisel composed this stanza about him:

> The good pilgrim would be rich
> But he put his money into holiness.
> Over there he lived in great honor
> And for this Saladin had to suffer the damage;
> If it weren't for the big belly that hangs off him,
> The Turks would be paying dearly for his ardor.[2]
> He still says he'd like to go back there
> But he restrains himself so that his beautiful son will inherit.
> (136, 3)

> These words were composed by Sir Elias, who knew how to make them
> Better than Sir Gaucelm, who is fatter than a column.

Elias d'Uisel had a castle named Charlus, a lowly place which was in need of wheat and wine. When knights and good men came there, Elias gave them good entertainment and a warm welcome and instead of feasts he recited his songs and satires and poems. Sir Gaucelm responded to Sir

Elias, reminding him of his poverty and that of his castle, and he composed this stanza about it:

> He could certainly use some bread and wine
> At Casluz in its present state.
> Pity for the poor sinner
> Who is rich in jokes and laughter;
> For his great silver cups are his conversation,
> And his wheat and rye are his satires
> And his green and fur-lined clothing are his love songs.
> Let he who seeks a pleasant stay go straight to him! (167, 13)

Elias d'Uisel answered Gaucelm Faidit's stanza:

> Gaucelm, I myself will admit
> That I have no great amount of riches;
> And you are so noble that
> I have no desire to contradict you.
> If I am poor, you have a fortune,
> And Guillelma, the fine and worthy:
> She has no equal on this side of the sea
> In favors-for-fee and song-and-dance. (136, 2)

[1] "Soldadeira" has a double meaning here. A hired woman can be a prostitute or it could simply mean a woman who works and is paid for her (possibly dishonorable) work, i.e. as a poet and performer.

[2] "Ardimen" means both his ardor in battle and his appetite.

Song 167, 13 and 136, 2 :
  Gaucelm Faidit and Elias d'Uisel: "Manens fora.l francs
    pelegris..."
  Source: Mouzat, 478.
  MSS: D^a 210, H 46.

The above three stanzas, cited in the razo of manuscript H are complemeted by only one fragment of a stanza found in manuscript D^a:

In the judgement of his neighbors
Sir Elias is totally lying about the holdings
Of his half sister;
That's what Sir Ebles, her cousin, says.
No...
...for he spoke about fat, and he makes no sense.
We are both fat, but it seems to me that she gets like that
Out of pure hunger and I from eating so much.[1] (167, 13)

[1] OR: She is like that in good repute only...

42. Gui d'Uisel 194, 2 and 194, 19 (B/S, 205)
MS: P 48.

Before giving up, he fell in love with another lady from Provence whose name was Lady Gidas de Mondus, the niece of Guillem de Montpellier, the first cousin of the Queen of Aragon.[1] He loved her and served her for a long time, composed many good songs about her and put her in a position of high repute and praise. And during the time that he was beseeching her she said to him, "Gui d'Uisel, you are a noble man, even if you are a cleric and you are greatly praised and appreciated. And I wish you so much good that I cannot defend myself against my own desire to do anything that would please you. I am a very noble lady and I wish to get married. Therefore I want you to know that you can have me, as lover or wife, as you wish, and I leave it to you to decide in which capacity you wish to have me." Gui d'Uisel was very happy and asked his cousin, Sir Elias d'Uisel for advice in song. This is what he said:

Now tell me your opinion,
Sir Elias, of a fine lover
Who loves without a cheating heart
And is loved without any deception;
Which should he most desire
According to the right way of loving:

That he be His-Lord's lover or husband
If it happens that the choice is his to make? (194, 2)

    Sir Elias, his cousin, advised him that he should prefer to be her husband before being her lover. Sir Gui did not want to take her as his wife and he argued that he would rather be a lover than a husband. Because of this response from Sir Gui, the lady departed and took as her husband a knight from Catalogne whose name was Renardon and she gave Gui d'Uisel his leave, saying as she left that she would not take as a lover any man who was not a knight. For this reason, Gui d'Usel composed a mala chanso after he had composed the tenso. And the mala chanso which he then composed says:

> If you are really sending me away, evil lady,
> That is no reason for me to give up singing
> Or amusement; for that would make it appear
> That I am bothered by what really makes me happy.
> Once I was truly angry, but now I regret that;
> For I have learned, from your behavior,
> How easily my will can change.
> And that is why I now sing about what once made me cry.
>
> (194, 19)

[1] The identity of Na Gidas cannot be substantiated, though Guillaume VIII of Montpellier did rule from 1172-1202 and his daughter, Marie, married Pedro II of Aragon in 1204. It helps to keep in mind when reading Gui's razos and songs that his vida tells us that he was a clergyman who was eventually ordered by the Papal legate to give up singing (B/S, 204-207; Egan, 44).

Song 194, 2   Gui d'Uisel and Elias d'Uisel: "Ara·m digatz vostre semblan..."
                Source: Audiau, 69.
                MSS: A 180, C 393, D 145-505, G 98, I 159, K 145, N 273-435, Q 5, R 34-287, T 83, a[1] 564.

1. Now tell me your opinion,
    Sir Elias, of a fine lover
    Who loves without a cheating heart
    And is loved without any deception;
    Which should he most desire   5
    According to the right way of loving:
    That he be His-Lord's lover or husband
    If it happens that the choice is his to make?

2. Cousin, I have the heart of a fine lover
    And not at all that of a malicious cheater.   10
    This is why I believe it is a greater honor
    To have a beautiful and reputable lady
    All the time rather than for just one year.
    And I would take the role of the gallant husband,
    Who can spend all his days in comfort with His-Lord,   15
    For I have seen so many other types of courtships come to an
        end.

3. Anything that makes a man better himself
    Is better in my view, Sir Elias.
    And I consider a thing degraded
    Over which a man spends his days degrading himself.   20
    Through a lady, the good reputation of a man is enhanced
    While through a wife, a man loses his worth.[1]
    A man is admired for a love affair with a lady
    While a love affair with his wife brings a man ridicule.

4. Cousin, if ever you have loved, in whatever fashion,
    What you have just said is the height of folly.   26
    For it costs nothing for a hypocritical lover[2]
    To leave his lady after he has had his pleasure with her.
    I, on the other hand, want to stay on, kissing
    My-Lord, whom I love and adore.   30
    For I would then willingly go off into exile
    If ever I wasn't there when she wanted me.[3]

5. Sir Elias, if I refuse to take My-Lord
    As my wife, I do her no dishonor.
    The fact that I don't leave her is due more to fear   35
    And the great honor that she brings.[4]

       For if I should take her (as wife) and only then begin to
          court her
       There is no greater offense I could commit.
       And if ever I am vile or disrespectful toward her
       I have failed in the eyes of love, and courtship is then
          over.   40

6.   Cousin, you may rightfully consider me a cad
       If, being able to have for myself the lady I want
       Without any guardian, competitor or master,
       I should ever ask to have any other.
       A husband has his joy without suffering;   45
       A lover mixes his with pain.
       This is why I greatly prefer, regardless of the public outcry,
       To be a sensually satisfied husband rather than a lover in
          torment.

7.   I submit this to Lady Margarita,
       Sir Elias, as to the finest there is.   50
       May she judge this affair, and may I be dishonored
       If I do not love My-Lord better than her husband does.

8.   Cousin, I know her worth is such
       That she will be able to judge a plaint about love.
       And because her reputation is so fine and distinguished   55
       I know she'll say that you're wrong this time.[5]

[1] The topos of the knight who dishonors his own reputation by openly loving his wife is best known through Chrétien de Troye's treatment of it in *Erec et Enide*.

[2] OR: 'it is of little importance.' 'Cost' is preferable here only in that it highlights the economic language.

[3] This could be read as an erotic joke as well: the lover's 'failing' the lady being read as a case of impotence due to the extra demands of his other lovers.

[4] This could alternately be translated: "that I bring her," as in the French translations of J. Anglade, Lavaud and Nelli. The very ambiguity of the phrase underlines the fact that both lady and lover bring each other 'honor' in the exchange and that 'honor' can consist of material rewards as well as esteem.

[5] This final tornada, though excluded from many editions, is taken from manuscript A.

Song 194, 19

        Gui d'Uisel: "Si be.m partetz, mala dompna, de vos..."
        Source: Audiau, 30.
        MSS: A 111, B 108, C 218, D 50-172,D[c] 254, F[a] 20, G 58, I 90, J 6, K 74, L 112, M 205, N 202-308, O 25 (anonymous), Q 35, U 125,a[1] 256, f 59, R 145.

1. If you are really sending me away, evil lady,
That is no reason for me to give up singing
And amusement; for that would make it appear
That I am bothered by what really makes me happy.
Once I was truly angry, but now I regret that;   5
For I have learned, from your behavior,
How easily my will can change.
And that is why I now sing about what once made me cry.

2. Cry about it, I did; and my major motive (for composing this song)
Is that she not go off singing about it.   10
Regardless of what she is spreading, it is not a question
Of my shame and loss any more than it is of her honor and profit.
If she foolishly exchanged me for him,
She will only exhange him even more madly and more easily for someone else.   14
This is why I do not even hold this exchange against her
For she will go on making exchanges until finally she has changed her own heart.

3. Evil lady, I never thought that it would come to pass
That if I lost you I would hardly consider it a loss;

For your warm manner, about which you knew so much,
And your fine words and satisfying answers　　　　20
Made you, above all others, the most pleasing of women.
But now your madness has deprived you of those manners;
Your fine words have turned to double-talk[1]
And in no time you will lose your beauty.

4. Evil lady, you have made me angry　　　　25
   And harsh-speaking, a habit I shall not wish to continue,
   For I know very well that others will turn these songs against me
   And that my songs will be less highly esteemed because of it.
   But for so long I will have wanted
   Your desire, though I now regret it,　　　　30
   That I would find my heart going back to you.
   I do not know how to say reasonably that what you are doing is madness.

5. As long as a man does what he should, he is considered worthy;
   And as long as he stays away from treachery, he is considered loyal.
   It is for my own sake that I tell you that I used to praise you
   When your words were true and your deeds were good.　　　　36
   You must never say that I am lying about this
   Even though I no longer consider you worthy;
   For he who gives up on what he began in earnest
   Does not earn a good reputation for what has transpired.　　　40

6. It would be just, if not reasonable,
   For a man to keep it under wraps
   When a lady commits an evil deed, and that he continue to sing her praises;
   But this is no longer the time for such practices.
   Thus you had better refrain from committing offenses.　　　　45
   I am telling you this, but it applies to all women;
   For if you commit an evil act, it will no longer be kept secret.
   On the contrary, now we want to tell more of the truth.

7. Lady Margarita, beauty and youth
   Are yours; as are renown, courtliness and good sense;　　　　50

    And if I have said too much about that other lady, in my anger
        with her,
    About you I have spoken too little of the truth.

8. King of Aragon, it is in conquering, spending,
    And courting ladies that you conquer a worthy reputation.
    Keep this up as you have begun it;   55
    For if you don't, you will have lost all that you have been
        accorded.

[1] Note that one of the primary meanings of 'barat' is 'business deal, chicanery,' thus the word could here imply economic talk, as in "salesmen's gibberish, lies" (Levy, 41). The numerous uses of the word 'tornar' and 'camjar' (return, exchange) highlight this aspect of the love relation, as does the final tornada.

43. Gui d'Uisel 194, 9 and 295, 1 (B/S, 209)
MS: P 48.

You have by now heard who Gui d'Uisel was and from where he came, how he exchanged a tenso with his cousin, Sir Elias, about the choice his lady had given him, and which part he chose, and how the lady got angry about this and went off and married Bernardon de Catalogne. This is why Gui d'Uisel gave up singing and spent a long time in a state of sorrow and depression. And because he behaved like this, many people didn't like him, including both ladies and knights. To get him out of this brooding and resentful state, Lady Maria de Ventadorn provoked him in a tenso and it goes like this, as you will hear:

    Gui d'Uisel, I am very upset with you
    For you have given up on singing
    And I want you to get back to it.
    Since you know a lot about such things,
    I want you to tell me if, when a lover sincerely asks her to do so,
    A lady should do as much for her lover

165

As he does for her in matters of love,
According to the rights that he enjoys as lover.

This song can be found under Maria de Ventadorn, #45, below.

44. Peire d'Uisel 361,1 (B/S, 210)
MS: P 48.

After Gui d'Uisel had composed the mala chanson that I told you about and which begins like this:

If you are really sending me away, evil lady... (194, 19)

--in which he castigated what he used to praise, Sir Peire d'Usel, his cousin composed this stanza to reprimand him and sent it off to him:[1]

Brother Gui, I truly like your song,
The one which speaks badly of her, whom you used to praise;
Though you speak ill of her, her reputation will not suffer
For she should love a knight more than she loves you.
And if she foolishly made you a promise
She deliberately broke it.
For this she should be pardoned
Because she recognized her own folly.

Sir Gui d'Usel, you are well worth a worthy knight
In every pleasing manner
But it is not customary that a lady should love a cleric;
On the contrary, it is always criticized.

The verses cited in the razo are the only surviving portions of this song.

[1] The vida identifies Peire as the brother of Gui (B/S, 202). There is an error in the Egan translation on page 44. The two brothers are Ebles and Peire, not Ebles and Elias.

45. Maria de Ventadorn 295, 1 (B/S, 212)
MS: H 53

You have certainly heard about Lady Maria de Ventadorn, how she was the most highly reputed lady who ever lived in Lemozin, the one who did the most good and guarded herself against evil. Her intelligence always guided her, and folly never made her do crazy things.[1] God honored her with a beautiful body, pleasing and attractive on its own, without artifice.

Sir Gui d'Uisel had lost his lady, as you have heard in the song that goes like this:

If you are really sending me away, evil lady...(194, 19)

Because of this he lived for a long time in great sorrow and sadness. And it had been a long time since he had sung or composed. All the good ladies of that land were sad about this, and Lady Maria more than any of them, for Sir Gui d'Uisel used to praise her in all his songs. The Count of the Marche, he who was known as Sir Uc lo Brun, was her knight and she had brought him as much honor and love as a lady can bring to a knight.

One day when he was courting her they had a dispute, for the Count of the Marcha was saying that any fine lover, once his lady has given him her love and taken him as her knight and friend, should have as much authority and ability to give orders over her as she has over him, for as long as he remains true and loyal to her. And Lady Maria was defending the position that the lover should have no authority over her or authority to give her orders. Sir Gui d'Uisel was in the court of Lady Maria and she, in order to bring him back to singing and entertainment, composed a stanza in which she asked him if he agreed that the friend should have as much power over the Lady as the Lady has over him. It was for this reason that Lady Maria provoked him into joining the dispute and this is what she said:

Gui d'Uisel, I am very upset with you...

[1] This razo, though it begins with the formula "Ben avetz entendut" ("You have certainly heard"), does not have an accompanying vida. The opening suggests that such a vida once existed, though it could also be that the razo author is simply referring to the numerous references to Maria found in other troubadours. Maria was also sung of by Gaucelm Faidit and Pons de Capdoill and is mentioned by Savaric de Malleo (see razos 37-40, 47 and 57). She was married to Ebles V of Ventadorn (B/S, 214).

Song 194, 9 and 295, 1:
    Gui d'Uissel and Maria de Ventadorn: "Gui d'Ussel. be.m pesa de vos..."
    Source: Audiau, 73.
    MSS: A 185, C 389, D 149-520, E 220, H 53, R 78-647, T 83, a^1 548.
    Other English translations: Bogin, 99; Ferrante: in Stanton, 11.

1. Gui d'Ussel, I am very upset with you
   For you have given up singing
   And I want you to get back to it.
   Since you know a lot about such things,
   I want you to tell me if, when a lover sincerely asks her
       to do so,   5
   A lady should do as much for her lover
   As he does for her in matters of love,
   According to the rights that he enjoys as lover.

2. My lady Maria, I thought I had given up
   On composing tensos and singing   10
   But I can't just stand here and not sing
   In answer to your summons.

I can respond immediately concerning the lady
For she should do for her lover everything
That he does for her, without any regard for wealth or
   station;   15
For between two friends, one should not be more important
   than the other.

3. Gui, everything that a lover desires
   Should be asked for in mercy,
   And the lady must be the one to authorize him to have it;
   But she must be sure to choose the right moment.   20
   The lover should beseech her and follow her commands,
   And this applies equally to a friend or a lady.[1]
   A lady should do honor to her lover
   As she would to a friend, not a lord.

4. Lady, over here it is said amongst us[2]   25
   That when a lady wants to love someone
   She must honor her lover equally
   Since they are equally in love.[3]
   If it happens that she loves him more intensely
   Then she should make that clear through her words and
      actions;   30
   And if her heart is deceitful and cheating
   She should hide her folly behind a lovely exterior.

5. Gui d'Uisel, never with such reasoning
   Do lovers argue at the beginning!
   Instead, when they want something,   35
   They fall to their knees with their hands joined, and say:
   "Lady, if only you would agree to let me give you my undivided
      service
   As your liegeman" and so she takes him on.
   In the name of justice, I consider anyone who pretends to be a
      servant,
   Then claims to be an equal, a traitor.   40

6. Lady, it's a disgraceful point of view
   For any lady to maintain
   That she doesn't consider the man an equal
   With whom she has made of two bodies one!

You will either say that the lover should love her more
    faithfully,   45
An opinion which reflects badly on you,
Or you'll say that they are equals between themselves
And that that lover owes her nothing but what he does for love.

[1] Maria is distinguishing between "friends/amics" and "ladies/lords." It appears that the former are terms indicating a partner in a love affair and the latter are terms indicating people of superior status to whom things are given out of feudal obligation rather than desire.

[2] "Here," the usual place of the lover, as opposed to "there," the place of the lady, is in this passage associated with the entire male sex.

[3] The mentions of "honor" here are all to be read simultaneously as "esteem" and "material rewards."

46. Savaric de Malleo 432, 3 (B/S, 223)
MS: R 3.

I have certainly told you about Sir Savaric de Malleo, who he was and how he was the root of all the courtly behavior in the world. In all the good deeds than one can imagine in one good man, he was the undisputed master of them all.

And for a long time he loved and honored a noble lady from Gascogne, Lady Guillerma de Benaujatz, the wife of Sir P. de Gavaret, the Viscount of Bezaumes and Lord of San Macari and Lengo.[1] And I can state in all truth that never have so many good deeds been done for one lady. For a long time this lady repaid him with mad promises and fine messages and by giving him presents. Many times she made him come to her from Poitiers to Gascogne by land and by sea and once he had arrived she knew well how to mislead him with false reasonings for she never gave him pleasure in love. He was so in love with her that he did not recognize her conniving but his own friends made him understand that he was being tricked and showed him another lady from Gascogne, the Countess of the Manche and the wife of Sir Guiraut de Manchac, a young, beautiful and pleasant woman who desired to acquire a good reputation and to get to know Sir Savaric after all the good things she had heard about him. Upon seeing the lady, Sir Savaric approached her in a state of wonder and begged her for her love. The lady took him on as her knight on account of the great nobility that she saw in him and set a date on which he should return to her to get what he was asking for. He left her in a state of happiness, took his leave and returned to Poitiers.

It wasn't long before Lady Guillerma had learned about what had transpired and how Savaric had been given a date on which to return to get the pleasure he sought. This made her very sad and jealous for she had not succeeded in keeping him for herself. So she had letters and messages and greetings composed for her in the sweetest manner that she knew and was able to muster; and she sent them to Sir Savaric saying that on the very day that the Countess of the Manche had bid him to come to her, he should instead come in secrecy to see her at Benauges and have from her all his pleasure. And let it be known for a fact that I, Uc de San Sirc, who have written these razos, was the courier who went there and delivered those messages and letters to him.[2]

The Provost of Limoges was at the court of Savaric at that time. He was a noble and learned man and a good composer of songs. Sir Savaric, in deference to him, showed him all the facts and told him about what each party had said and promised him. Sir Savaric told the Provost to question him about this matter in a song and to engage him in a tenso over the question of which of the two ladies he should love on the specified day. So the Provost challenged him, saying:

Savaric, I ask you
To tell me in song...

---

[1] Benauges is a ruined castle that was once the principal fortress of the viscounty of Benauges, the capital of which was Cadillac. Peire de Gavarret, the husband and viscount, was himself a poet (B/S, 225).

[2] This is the only razo in which Uc de Saint Circ intervenes as an authorial presence and witness to the facts presented. How many of the razos he did compose is not clear though he seems to indicate that it is clearly more than one. In the vida to Bernart de Ventadorn

(B/S, 20; Egan, 11) he similarly identifies himself as the author of the text and indicates the source of his information. See discussion of Uc in the introduction to this volume.

Song 432,3   Savaric de Malleo and Prebost de Valensa: "Savaric, ie·us deman..."
Source: Kolsen, 14.
MSS: A 187, D 205, G 99, O 128, R 34.
Other English translations: Chaytor, 73.

1. Savaric, I ask you
To tell me in song
What you think about a worthy knight
Who for a long time
Has beseeched a lady   5
Who only scorns him.
Then, he turns his attentions to another, who becomes his friend
And gives him the day on which he should come to her
To have all his desire satisfied.
When the other lady finds out that this has truly happened
She sends him word that on that same day   11
She will give him the joy that he was seeking.
They are equal in reputation and appearance;
Choose which one he should go to.

2. Prebost, fine lovers   15
Don't go around having changes of heart;
They love loyally,
Although they may pretend
To turn their attentions elsewhere.
They would never, for such a reason, depart   20
From where they've already placed their love.
A man should never change his heart
Over an unrequited wait.
Rather he should hold out good hope
For the one who has kept herself so inaccessible.   25
Let him be firm and go to her
For I don't think she is tricking him

172

Since it's at her command that he will have returned.
3. Lord, she will really suffer the damages,
   That lady, for it is at her command 30
   That he finds her the right choice
   And is willing to go in on her promise;
   This is why he cherishes her and praises her.
   He will be displaying the sense of a child
   If he doesn't go to the one who was grateful to have him in her service 35
   And leave behind the one who was killing him.
   She never for a moment wanted to help him get ahead
   Or deigned to retain his entreaties.[1]
   But now when she sees that he could live
   Without her, she is dying of jealousy 40
   And sends him messages to return for no other reason
   Than that she doesn't want benefits to come to him from elsewhere.

4. A lady of fickle desires
   Doesn't really love at all,
   Prebost; nor does she realize 45
   That she could someday show good sense.
   For ladies never do
   What one wants them to until
   They know that they are loved without falseness.
   But the one who's not bound by love 50
   Wants to give everyone pleasure
   And quickly promises to lie with her lover.
   This is why it bothers me to think that he would go to the other,
   For she would go to bed with him, just like that.
   It's better that a man should die from loving 55
   Than have someone who'll be had by all.

5. Lord, ladies who are always
   Promising and putting off their gifts
   Destroy love.
   Someone who gives without hesitation 60
   Makes the gift greater and of more value.
   A gift given quickly is worth just as much as one
   That's always put off
   Until the right moment has gone by.

A gift is most valuable   65
At the moment that somebody wants it;
And here you are telling me that this thing
For which one should be most grateful is just madness!
She makes good sense, the lady who grants her gift
Before we start hearing all the noise.²   70

6. Prebost, the hard work
   And heavy, sorrowful pain
   And torment I've endured
   Would all turn to pleasure
   If my lady would just pass me a glove   75
   And send word
   That just once before I die I might see her.
   For at her call I would be off,
   Be it morning or evening.
   It's with her that I want to stay,   80
   She through whom I know it would come³
   If ever I were to get joy from love.
   But love enflames me and extinguishes her
   And I die as I endure it.

7. Lord, may Lady Guillelma of Benauga   85
   Decide on the truth of this, as it pleases her.
   And Lady Maria
   Of Ventadorn, I want her to be there,
   As well as the lady of Montferran.
   For these three are without deceit.   90

8. Prebost, they know so much about love
   That I will go by whatever they tell me.

---

¹ i.e. retain him in her service as a singer of her praises.
² OR: before one hears the rest of it (the songs), the noise (the criticism, rumors). This stanza is a remarkably clear discussion of love in terms of the marketplace.
³ Chaytor interprets this 'it' as being death.

47. Savaric de Malleo 432, 2 (B/S, 227)
MS: R 3.

Sir Savaric de Malleo had come to Benauges to see the Viscountess, Lady Guillerma, for he was courting her. He brought with him Sir Elias Rudel, the lord of Bergerac, and Sir Jaufre Rudel of Blaya.[1] All three of them were asking for her love, and prior to this visit she had retained each of them as her knight, though none of them knew this about the others.

All three were seated near her, one on one side, the other on the other side, and the third right in front of her. Each was gazing at her amorously. And she, as if she were the most ardent lady ever known, began to look at Sir Jaufre Rudel of Blaya amorously, for it was he who was directly in front of her. She took the hand of Sir Elias Rudel of Bregayrac and squeezed it lovingly; and she pressed on the foot of my lord Sir Savaric with her own foot, laughing and sighing. None knew the pleasure of the other until after they had left her, when Sir Jaufre Rudel told Sir Savaric how the lady had looked at him and Sir Elias told about her hand. When Sir Savaric heard how she had given a sign of pleasure to each of them, he was saddened and he did not speak of what had been done to him. Instead, he summoned Gaucelm Faidit and Sir Ugo de la Bacalayria and he asked them in a stanza to decide to which of the three she had given the greatest pleasure and love.

And the stanza that poses this question begins like this:

Gaucelm, three amorous games...

[1] Jaufre Rudel is the famous troubadour of the "faraway love." His vida can be found in B/S, 16 and Egan, 61. Further in the razo, Savaric summons Gaucelm Faidit and Uc de Bacalaria. Razos 37-41 concern Gaucelm's songs; Uc's vida can be found in B/S, 218 and Egan, 107.

Song 432, 2   Savaric de Malleo: "Gaucelm, tres jocs enamorat..."
               Source: Audiau, 203.

MSS: A 177, C 391, D 143-495, G 91, I 152, K 138,
L 80, M 264, N 278-445, O 82, Q 24.
Other English translations: Chaytor, 68.

1. Gaucelm, I want to share with you and Sir Ugo
   Three scenarios about love.
   Each of you will choose the best
   And leave me whichever one you want.
   A lady has three suitors.   5
   Their love holds such a force over her
   That when all three are before her
   To each of them she gives some sign of love.
   Upon one of them she looks lovingly;
   She lightly squeezes the hand of the other;   10
   And as to the third, she presses her foot on his, laughing.
   Since that's the situation, tell me:
   To which of them does she give the greatest sign of love?

2. My lord, Sir Savaric, you know perfectly well
   That the friend who is looked upon with charming eyes, 15
   Frankly, and without a bitter heart,
   Is the one who received the most gracious gift.
   Such sweetness springs from the heart:
   That is why it is one hundred times greater an honor.
   This is what I have to say about holding the hand: 20
   It does him no good and no harm,
   For ladies regularly accord
   Such a pleasure as part of their welcome.
   And as for the foot resting on the foot, I don't see
   That the lady was thereby showing him love   25
   Nor should it be taken as a sign of love.

3. Gaucelm, you're saying what you like
   But you're not making any sense.
   For from that look no good comes to the friend
   Whose position you are defending,   30
   And if he sees it that way it's crazy;
   For eyes can look at him and elsewhere
   But they have no other power.
   However, when a white hand, ungloved,

   Sweetly squeezes her friend, 35
   The love springs from the heart and the mind.
   Sir Savaric, you who share so graciously,
   Defend the courtly foot play
   For I will never do so.

4. Sir Ugo, since you leave me the best part, 40
   I will defend it with no argument.
   Thus I say that the placement
   Of the foot was a sign of fine friendship,
   Hidden from the scandal-mongers.
   And it seems clear that since the friend, 45
   Laughing and pressing, chose this way to give him aid,
   That her love is without deceit.
   Anyone who sees the taking of the hand
   As the sign of the greatest love is talking nonsense.
   As for Sir Gaucelm, it is not obvious to me 50
   That he would have accepted the look as the greatest sign
   If he really knew as much about love as he claims to.

5. Sir, you who denigrate the look
   Of the eyes and their lovely appearance,
   Don't you know that they are the messengers 55
   From the heart of the one who sends them?
   Eyes reveal to lovers
   What fear keeps hidden in their hearts,
   And thus they are responsible for the pleasures of love.
   Very often, while laughing and joking, 60
   A lady will bump her foot against any number of people's
   Without signifying anything more than that.
   And Sir Ugo is defending an error:
   Holding someone's hand means nothing
   And I don't believe it ever springs from love.[1] 65

6. Gaucelm, what you and the lord of Malleo
   Are saying is against love.
   It clearly supports my argument
   That the eyes you have chosen
   And defended as being the best sign of love 70
   Have deceived many suitors.
   And a lady with a wicked heart
   Could press on my feet for a year

And I wouldn't feel joy in my heart.
   When it comes to the hand, there's no contest: 75
   One squeeze is worth a hundred of the others,
   For if love didn't already bring pleasure to her heart
   She would never have extended to him her hand.

7. Gaucelm, you are beaten in this dispute,
   Both you and Ugo, without a doubt.   80
   I want My-Body-Guard, who conquered me,
   To deliver the judgement
   And Lady Maria, in whom good repute resides.

8. Lord, I'm not even close to being beaten
   And that will be made clear in the judgement.   85
   This is why I also want
   Lady Guillelma de Benauges to be there,
   With her loving and courtly speech.

9. Gaucelm, my argument is so strong
   That I overcome you both and defend myself.   90
   I know a lady with a gay and gracious body
   To whom this could be submitted for judgement
   But there is more to be gained from dealing with fewer than
         three.

[1] In denigrating the importance of the 'look' of love, Savaric and Uc are undermining one of the commonplaces of the courtly tradition, namely that the eyes are the conduit of love that leads to and from the heart and that they alone can reveal the lover's true wishes.

48. Uc de Saint Circ 457, 4 (B/S, 244)
    MS: P 49.

You have certainly heard who Sir Uc de Saint Circ was and where he came from. He loved a lady from Andutz whose name was Lady Clara.[1] She was clever and learned, pleasant and beautiful. She had a great desire for praise and to be heard about far and near and to have the friendship and intimacy of good ladies and noble men. Sir Uc knew about her desire and he knew just how to serve her in the way that she wanted, for there was not one good lady in that whole land with whom Uc was not able to arrange that Lady Clara should have her love and intimacy and who did not send her letters and greetings and presents in order to remain on good terms and pay her honor. Sir Uc was very good at writing responses to the letters of the ladies who had sent her their little gifts, as was called for. Lady Clara permitted Uc's beseechment and courting and she promised to give him pleasure in the rights of love. Sir Uc composed many good songs about her, beseeching her and praising her beauty and nobility. She rose in esteem on account of the songs that Sir Uc composed about her. Their love lasted for a long time and many times did they war and make peace along the way, as is the way of lovers in love.

She had one very beautiful neighbor whose name was Lady Ponsa. She was very courtly and learned but she was very envious of the reputation and honor that Lady Clara had acquired through Sir Uc's efforts. So she schemed and planned of a way to get Sir Uc away from Lady Clara and attract him to herself. She sent for Sir Uc and led him to believe that Lady Clara had another lover whom she loved more than him and promised to do and say whatever Sir Uc pleased. Sir Uc, like one who is neither firm enough nor loyal enough to any lady not to go off seeking attentions elsewhere, left Lady Clara and began to speak badly of her and to praise Lady Ponsa; and all on account of the evil things that Lady Ponsa had said about Lady Clara, her seductive demeanor, and her promises to give him whatever he pleased. Lady Clara was very upset and greatly angered by this but did not condemn Uc or speak badly of him in public.

Sir Uc was the friend of Lady Ponsa for a long time, waiting for the pleasures that she had promised him. But she came through on none of them, and every day the special attention she used to give him diminished. When Sir Uc realized that he had been tricked he was very saddened and angry. He went to see a friend of Lady Clara and explained to her the whole story behind his break with Lady Clara. He begged her, as earnestly as he knew how, to seek to establish peace between himself and Lady Clara and to return him to her forgiveness and good graces. She promised him that she would do all she could to help him. She recounted the whole story to Lady Clara and implored her so much that she did promise to establish peace with Sir Uc. They instructed Sir Uc that he should come to a conference with both of them, which he did, and he made his peace most amorously.[2]

> For this reason this song was composed which says:
>
> Never have I seen a time or season,
> Night or day, year or month
> Which brings me as much pleasure as now
> Or in which I have done myself more good,
> For I am delivered from an evil love
> Where Mercy could do me no good
> And am returned to the place where one should
> Find truth and honor
> And a loyal one-colored heart.

[1] Clara d'Anduza was herself a poet (trobairitz). One song has been conserved (115, 1). For fuller information see Paden, 1989, p. 230.

[2] This razo contains elements common to many others. For a similar tale, see razo 65 on Raimon de Miraval. Third party intervention in love spats occur in Guillem de Balaun (#58), Pons de Capdoill (#57) and Richart de Berbezill (#35). Homage sung to other ladies under false pretexts occurs also in Gaucelm Faidit (#37) and Pons de Capdoill (#57).

Song 457,4   Uc de Saint Circ: "Anc mais non vi temps ni sazo..."
Source: Jeanroy/Salverda de Grave, 68.
MSS: A 157, D 80-284, I 129, K 114, N^2 7, P.

1. Never have I seen a time or season,
   Night or day, year or month,
   Which pleased me as much as right now
   Or in which I have done myself more good.
   For now I am delivered from an evil love   5

Where Mercy could do me no good,
   And am returned to where I should be:
   Where one finds honesty and honor
   And a loyal, one-colored heart.[1]

2. And since my Lord has granted me a pardon   10
   And mercy has pleaded for me,
   If ever I do anything which displeases her,
   Mercy should never again defend me.
   And if one time I loved elsewhere
   This does not bother me; nor should it bother her,   15
   For I love her a thousand times more than I used to
   And learned there what folly one commits
   When he leaves a good lord.

3. I know very well that I am in no way worthy---
   Even if I would suffer a thousand times more evil   20
   Than I did, and would always have done for my lord
   Anything that would please her---
   That she should pardon me for her trouble.
   But a guilty man, when he humbles himself,
   Should find mercy if he acknowledges his guilt;   25
   For the repentent sinners
   Have the greatest joy in the heaven above us.

4. Never can I repay her
   For the joy, the pleasures and the goods
   That My-Lord gave and promised me;   30
   But for all of that, from where I now am,
   I bow down to where she is and I give adoration.
   And then I remember a thousand times a day
   Her words and deeds, her courtly ways,
   And the light-colored eyes, full of sweetness,   35
   That pull me sweetly toward her.

5. Though the other was false
   And cheated and misled me,
   I do not believe that this one would ever do the same.
   But because I know that there are so many seeking her   40
   Love, I live with the great fear
   That she loves elsewhere and I feel jealous.
   For he who possesses a castle

    On which many others have laid a claim
    Should be afraid of losing it.   45
6. Song, before going anywhere else,
    Take the path to Lady Azalais of Autier,
    For I want her to know how I am doing and where I stand with love
    And how I have parted ways with my mistake.

[1] OR: composes about...("trobar")

49. Uc de Saint Circ 457, 18 (B/S, 248)
MS: N^2 6.

Sir Uc de Saint Circ loved a lady from Treviso whose name was Lady Stazailla. He served and honored her with praise and renown and composed good songs about her and she gratefully accepted the love and prayers and attentions and said to him many pleasing things and promised him many pleasures. But she was the sort of lady who wants all men of high standing and worth to pay her court, so she accepted prayers and attentions from all of them and promised all of them pleasures to be done and said, and she did this with many men. Sir Uc was jealous about what he saw and heard and so he came to war with her and broke with her. But she was not a lady who feared criticism or gossip or negative stories about her. For a long time Uc carried on a war with her but she gave it little attention. Every day Uc expected her to seek peace and a treaty with him that would place him once again in a position such that he would compose a delightful song about her. When he saw that she was not about to come around to this stance, he composed a song about his explanation for what had happened and it goes like this:

    For a long time I waited...

Song 457, 18   Uc de Saint Circ: "Longamen ai atenduda..."
              Source: Jeanroy/Salverda de Grave, 50.
              MSS: A 156, B 95, C 224, D 79-280, D^c 257, F 23,
                   F^a 62, I 128, K 114, N^2 6, R 26-219, T 199, b 3.

1. For a long time I have waited
   For an appropriate subject
   About which to compose a pleasing song,
   But up to now it has not come to me.
   And if you want to know about the reason[1]   5
   I have for composing a true song,
   It will be divided into two parts:
   A joyous and a sad song,
   Praising the good I have had
   And mourning for what I have lost.   10

2. God helps those he loves
   And he loved me for a long time.
   He gave me a rich and sensual love
   For you, which I have now lost.
   Oh God, so pleasurable was   15
   The joy, and how much I relished it!
   What an agreeable life I had!
   But now that is over for me.
   I feel like I have fallen low from on high
   And my body (heart) is stripped of all rich joy.[2]   20

3. As to the honor that I received
   From your willing body,
   I now have a sad and mourning heart;
   For I see that the desire within you
   Which you had at the time   25
   That God was on my side is changing.
   Oh, this parting is so painful for me!
   And if love is finished
   Then I curse the fact that I ever saw your body
   And all the good that I knew there.[3]   30

4. It's a mad body which thinks and perceives
   That what disgraces it brings it merit;
   And for a madman, nothing is apparent.

I have seen such a one fall
Who had been greatly renowned   35
For her worth and appearance.
For she who is guided by madness
Thinks she is enriched
When she sees that her slightest actions
Turn into accusations and rumors.   40

5. Once a lady has fallen from esteem
   Due to blame over a failing,
   There is no coming back:
   Honor greets her from afar.
   For it is very difficult for a lady   45
   To find pardon for a true failing.
   Rather, they all run at her, screaming at her,
   And by the time the affair is forgotten
   The rumor has traveled so far
   That she has become a pariah.[4]   50

6. Lady, if you are angry
   With me, never will I defend myself
   Or turn from you, or run off;
   For never since I have known you
   Have I had any desire   55
   For any other, even if I should find
   No help or protection with you.
   For to me you are so pleasing
   That I do not want God to help me
   Or to give me joy and health, unless it be through you.[5]

7. He who seeks reason[6]   61
   In a place where justice is not known
   Is committing an error;
   And there where faults are criticized
   Honor should be recognized.   65
   But I have only lately come to know
   What hurts me and has been hurting me.

[1] In the original text, Uc says that he is waiting for a "razo" (line 2) and then says: "And if you want the razo why..." The word comes up again in the tornada: "Anybody who demands a razo."

This insistence on the word is provocative, since Uc is the only troubadour to have named himself as author within another razo (Savaric de Malleo, see above #42). It suggests how intimately the song and explanation were linked in Uc's own method of composition.

[2] The usual play on heart/body is made more evident here since Uc says his heart/body is "nut," "nude" of all rich joy.

[3] Again, the erotic meaning is suggested through the use of "conogut," which carries the sense of "know through physical intimacy."

[4] These two stanzas are among the clearest examples of a poet turning on the lady within a love song, and threatening to use his power as public spokesman to ruin her.

[5] If "salut" is translated "salvation" rather than "health," this thought becomes more openly blasphemous.

[6] As mentioned in note 1, the use of the word "razo" in this line is instructive. This untypical tornada could also be read as referring to the process of interpretation itself and the act of composing razos as supposedly reliable explanations for a poet's motivation.

50. Uc de Saint Circ and the Coms de Rodes 185, 3 and 457, 33 (B/S, 250)
MS: H 35

The Count of Rodes was very clever and very noble and he was a composer of songs. Sir Uc de Saint Circ composed this stanza about him:

My Lord Count, it is not worth your while to be upset
About me, nor to be worried,
For I have not in any way come to you begging
Or to ask for anything at all.
I have all that I need

And it is you I see in need of money.
This is why I have no reason in my heart to ask for anything
And would on the contrary be doing an act of mercy if I gave you a little something!

The Count responded with this stanza:

> Sir Uc de Saint Circ, I really must express my displeasure
> At seeing you again; you who were here earlier this year:
> Poor, naked and in need of everything.
> And it was I who brought you back to riches
> Though it cost me more than two archers
> Would have cost, or two knights.
> And yet I know perfectly well that if I were to give you a saddle horse, --
> God forbid!-- how well I know that you would take it![1]

---

[1] The verses cited in the razo are the only surviving portions of these two songs. They offer a rare glimpse of relations between a poet and patron once the economic relation is ended.

51. Guillem de Saint Leidier 234, 16 (B/S, 274)
MSS: E 206, P 45, R 1, Sg 171.
Base text: E

I have told you who Sir Guilem de Saint Leidier was and where he came from, who his lady was and how Sir Ugo Manescalc was his, and how all three called each other "Bertran": Sir Guilem, the marquise, and Sir Uc.[1] Sir Guilem had loved and honored the marquise for a long time. Their love had endured and they had always carried on the affair very graciously, without blame or madness, because they kept secret what should be kept secret and in confidence. Everyone was happy about their love on account of the many gracious deeds that were done and words spoken in the name of their love.

There was at that time a very highly reputed, very beautiful and learned lady in the Viennois, the Countess of Rossillon. All the noble men paid her great honor and reverence and Sir Guilem more than any of them. He greatly praised and esteemed her and was always willing to see her. So great a pleasure did he get from speaking with her that everyone thought that he was her knight. The lady was more willing to see him than any knight in the world and she took great pleasure in seeing him. And he took such pleasure in seeing her that he saw the marquise less often. The marquise became very jealous and thought that he really was the other lady's lover and all the people were saying the same thing.

She sent for Sir Ugo Manescalc and complained bitterly about Sir Guillelm saying that she wanted to take revenge on him: "And this is why I want to take you as my knight for I know you and I know I could never find another knight who would suit me more than you or the choice of whom could get him angrier! I would like to go on a pilgrimage to Saint-Antoine-en-Viennois and I want you to come with me. I want to go to the Saint Leidier inn, and sleep in his very own house, in his very own bedroom, in his very own bed. And in that bed I want you to sleep with me."[2]

When he had heard what the lady had to say, Sir Uc Manescalc was amazed and he said to the marquise: "My lady, you do me a great honor and give me the greatest pleasure that has ever been accorded to a knight. Here I am at your command." The lady got ready to go to Saint-Antoine-en-Viennois and set off with her ladies-in-waiting and many knights. She arrived at the inn at Saint Leidier and dismounted at Sir Guilem's inn. Sir Guilem was not in the castle but the lady was only more warmly welcomed, honored and served according to her every desire and pleasure. That night she took Sir Uc Manescalc to bed with her in Sir Guilem's own bed.

The news spread throughout the entire country and Sir Guilem was sad and disheartened beyond all measure. He did not, however, wish to appear resentful toward the marquise or his "Bertran"; nor did he wish to start a war or make it seem that he believed any of it. He therefore tried to serve the Countess of Rossillon and remove his heart from the marquise. He composed a song which says:

Since love is so forceful that it forces me to get involved...(234, 16) which is written down like this and which you will hear. Then, in the refrain, it says:

> Bertran, my friend, one would be right to criticize Bertran.
> If the lie were true, I'd do well to start again elsewhere...(234, 16: 43-44)

[1] The statement: "Sir Ugo Manescalc was his..." is not fully explained but this situation of the Bertrans may have been well known, for in the tornada to Guiraut de Borneill's song 242, 46, under razo 9, the two Bertrans are also mentioned. Guillem often refers to a Bertran in his songs.

[2] This situation is almost identical to the one outlined in razo 38 to Gaucelm Faidit's song 167, 52. Both texts are found in manuscripts E, P and R.

Song 234, 16   Guillem de Saint Leidier: "Pois tant mi forss'Amors que m'a faich entremetre..."
Source: Sakari, 154.
MSS: A 132, C 136, D 117, G 75, I 78, K 62, M 120, N 200, Q 41, R 41, Sg 100, a[1] 267, f 65.

1. Since love is so forceful that it forces me get involved
And dare to send my song to the noblest lady in the world,
And since I don't dare let my heart rush off elsewhere,
I had better put my keen intelligence to work.
If only she would deign to allow me to give myself over to her service,   5
She whose liege-man I am, even without having been given or promised a thing.[1]

2. I'd prefer to have her promise something and have the promise turn out to be false
Than to have had anyone else in the world grant me joy.
And if any other lady has set her sights on my love

May she turn her attentions to someone else, for I keep my firm
      will   10
   In the straight and fast lane that leads to a lady to whom I have
      not dared disclose--
   May the saints and the mass preserve me!--that my love has
      been committed to her.

3. I have so committed my love to her that I can't pull away
   Nor can any other lady in the world bring me great joy.   14
   I don't dare say any more than this or tell her anything more.
   But I say so many things with double-meanings in my songs
   So that she alone will understand that I cannot say another
      word
   For fear of the envious, who think they can steal her away from
      me.

4. She has so stolen my heart that I don't know where to turn.
   I can't leave her, yet I don't think I can ever reach her.   20
   But I beg for this: that she deign to take me on.
   May it not annoy her if I speak well of her, nor should she take
      it the wrong way.
   Thus I will put up with everything that comes my way
   And keep hoping that through her mercy she will retain my
      services.

5. I can't restrain myself or keep down the desire   25
   Which is born anew and grows each day; nor can I fight it.
   It makes me destroy my firm will through crazy quarrels.
   But no man can beat or restrain his own heart.
   What shall I do if I love her and can't break her down?
   I will languish in desire, for I cannot fight her.   30

6. No man can fight the fact that she is the noblest and most
      beautiful woman
   In the world and the best at doing
   All that behooves good reputation, for she does nothing
      improper.
   This is why her great worth must not be undermined.
   If ever love is abused or scorned somewhere   35
   All it needs to do is bring her to love and its prestige is
      reestablished.

7. I would be reestablished and put back on my feet if she would
    only deign to set
   A date when I could see her and she would make me forget
   The pain I suffer over her and which no one can know about,
   For there is no one who'd dare repeat with her what I've been
    through.[2]   40
   But I see her rich reputation take such a hold throughout the
    world
   That the choice is hers as to whom she wants and can take on.

8. Bertran, my friend, one would be right to criticize Bertran.
   If the lie were true I'd do well to start again elsewhere.[3]

[1] This song is constructed around root words and their prefixes. The rhyme words for the first stanza are, for example: "metre/entremetre/trametre/esdemetre/prometre." In addition, the final word (or some conjugated form of it) of one stanza is the first word of the next stanza. This makes for a very clever song and a particularly unsatisfying translation.

[2] OR: there is no one who'd dare criticize ("reprendre") what he'd found there.

[3] OR: you'd do well to start again elsewhere.

52. Guillem de Saint Leidier 234, 7 (B/S, 280)
MSS: E 207, P 46, R 1, Sg 172.

I have told you who Sir Guilem was and where he came from. He loved the Countess of Polonhac, whose name was Marqueza, as you have heard. She was learned and sophisticated. Sir Guilem de Saint Leidier had loved her and honored her for a long time and composed his songs about her but she did not want to take him as her knight or give him any pleasure in the rights of love. Rather, when things came to a head, the viscountess spoke to him thus: "Guilem, I would not take you on as my knight or attendant unless my husband the viscount asked me to, or ordered me to." When Sir Guilem de Saint Leidier heard the marquise's answer he was very sad and mournful and so he went off thinking of a way to arrange for the husband, the viscount, to ask the lady to take Guillem as her knight. He decided to compose a poem in the name of the husband in which the husband would implore the lady in Guillem's favor. The viscount, the husband of the lady, greatly enjoyed Guillem's songs and poems and sang very well. So Sir Guillem went and composed the song which says:

> Lady, I am sent here as a messenger
> And in these lyrics you will learn by whom...(234, 7)

When he had composed the song, he showed it to the Viscount of Polonhac, the husband of the lady, and told him about the reason for his having composed it: that one of his ladies had told him that she would not love him unless implored to by her husband. The viscount was very happy with the song when he heard it and knew the reason for its having been composed. He learned it most willingly and then, when he knew it well, he sang it to his wife. The lady heard the explanation[1] and remembered what she had said and promised to Guillem and she said to herself: "I can no longer defend myself against that one."[2]

After a good length of time, Sir Guillem came to see his lady and he showed her and explained to her how he had accomplished all her orders: how he had had her husband ask her to take him on and how she should now give credence to his prayers and those of her husband. And so the lady accepted him as a knight and attendant. The nature and course of their love I have spoken of in the previous razo.[3] And here is the song as you will hear it:[4]

> Lady, I am your messenger...

---

[1] The fact that the explanation for the composition is given at the time that the lady first hears the song supports the idea that the songs were accompanied by razos even in their early performances. Note that the lady hears her husband recite the razo with the song and only then remembers her earlier promise ("E la dona entendet ades la razo...").

[2] Another possible translation: "I can no longer forbid him access to me" or "I can no longer put him off." The question is whether the lady is at all willing to go along with this arrangement:

whether the promise was given to get rid of Guillem, or just to make it known to the husband so that she could not be blamed.

[3] As in note 1, the importance of the series of razos is stressed in order to place the events within a chronology traced out by the prose texts.

[4] The original states: And here is "lo vers..." Early troubadours, such as Guillem IX, Cercamon, Marcabru and Peire d'Alvergne call their compositions "vers." Guillem and Bernart de Ventadorn call their works "vers" and "cansos" (B/S, 283).

Song 234, 7   Guillem de Saint Leidier: "Dompna, ieu vos sui
                  messatgiers..."
               Source: Sakari, 96.
               MSS: A 133, B 112, C 132, D 118, G 75, I 79, K 63,
                  M 120, O 69, Q 41, R 41-144, Sg 101, V 117,
                  Ve. Ag. I 79, a^1 266.

1. Lady, I am sent here as a messenger
   And in these lyrics you will learn by whom.
   I greet you on behalf of
   Someone who is cheered and nourished by your joy.
   And keep this in mind: henceforth   5
   I shall be the true bearer of meaning
   Of this song, regardless of who is singing it.

2. I forbid you the love of all other knights
      But his.
   For he enjoys a good reputation; he was born under a
      lucky star   10
   And his exploits grow in prestige and are never-ending.
   If ever you should love someone,
   I beg you that your choice be him
   For there's nothing about him with which one could find fault.

3. His thoughts are so much with you   15
   That he flees all other sources of joy
   And no other desire but the one which holds him

In revery can lure him away.
  I think he's letting himself die through desiring.
  He suffers worse than any other prisoner 20
  Because he languishes in his thoughts rather than dying.

4. The love and desire which overpower him
   Have so tormented him that even when no one else is there
   He talks as if there were two people
   And when greatly agitated he will say to himself: 25
   "Oh, my heart, why do you kill me and betray me?
   You will be committing a false and frivolous act
   If you kill me like this through my own desire."

5. Don't ever take away his joy, his livelihood,
   And the good hope he maintains in silence 30
   For the sake of some aggravating scandal-mongers
   Through whose actions youth is demeaned and destroyed.
   And since your reputation, which surpasses all others,
   Never breaks or bends,
   Don't start now by deceiving him. 35

6. It's nothing but deceit, fickle-heartedness,
   And ignominy, about which there will be public outcry,
   That a lady friend should feign feelings or pull away from
   One who is truly fine in regard to her.
   Never has he hidden his feelings or mocked you; 40
   On the contrary, he is humble and agreeable
   To all. May he never suffer damages for having been so!

7. You know that well-known rebuke:
   "He who spreads pewter over gold
   Drives away joy and pleasant stay." 45
   If later things turn on him,
   And distress succeeds his former good,
   The rich joy which first came to him
   Overcomes the suffering and negates it.

8. I don't know which knight it is, 50
   But I beseech you on his behalf that
   What you had against him no longer irk you;
   And that for love of me this misunderstanding no longer stand.
   Rather let there be peace and accord.

> I am so completely your good counselor 55
> That you musn't fear a thing; and this is my command.[1]

9. Good song, if in mercy you conquer her for me
   I will be more firmly hers than ever before;
   For as surely as the sun does shine
   She is the finest lady nourished by this earth 60
   And the noblest and the most worthy.
   That is why I would rather turn my gaze
   To her land, for everything there shines for me.

10. I am nourished by that good thought alone
    And the desire is so overweening 65
    That I cannot serve any other love.[2]

---

[1] Up to this point it has been the song itself that is delivering the message for the anonymous poet, supposedly through the voice of the husband. Only in stanza nine does the point of view change, and the singer is identified with the poet. The insistence on the fact that it is the verse which speaks for itself, regardless of the medium of the human voice which speaks it, inspired the razo author to come up with the appealing scenario of the husband singing to his wife on behalf of her lover. This stance brings to the fore many of the issues raised by Paul Zumthor in his recent work on song in performance and the body as nexus of text and melody. Using Zumthor's framework, we might say that this song is a dialogue between two texts: one that was written or imagined and one that is performed. The song's insistence on its autonomy reminds us of Zumthor's observation that the performed song will always be other than what the author intended. The oral text escapes its written model (Zumthor, 1984).

[2] The tornada is not found in any of the manuscripts which contain the razo. It does, however, continue the imagery of "nourishing" which is found throughout the song.

53. Dalfi d'Alvergne and Robert, Bishop of Clermont 95,3 and 119, 4 (B/S, 286)
MS: H 46

Dalfi d'Alvergne was the lover of a lady from his castle whose name was Maurina. One day she asked the governor of Dalfi's estate for some lard and eggs to fry and he sent her one-half a bacon. The Bishop learned of this and composed this stanza in which he blamed the governor for not having given her the whole bacon, and Dalfi for having made him give her only one-half:

> For Christ's sake, if the servant were mine
> I'd give him a knife to the heart
> For he gave only a part of the bacon
> To her who asked him for it so graciously.
> He knew just what Dalfi wanted 5
> For had he put any more or less in that package
> He would have given him three (blows) to the cheek.
> But I can truly say
> That Maurina had little lard in which to fry the eggs.

The Bishop was the lover of a very beautiful lady, the wife of Sir Chantart de Caulec, who lived in Peschadoires.[1] Dalfi answered him with this stanza:

> The Bishop finds (writes) in his brief 10
> That cabbages are worth more than leeks (or pork)
> And, when it suits him, he goes fishing
> Very often at Pescadoiras
> For a good-looking fish that he catches there.
> The fish is gay and courtly 15
> But on one point he has gotten himself into trouble
> For he let himself be killed
> By the priest who only knows how to fry him (the bishop
>   or the fish).[2]

> If it weren't for Master Audefers,
> And he prevents me for saying any more, 20
> He'd (I'd) really know how to kill a crazy bishop.[3]

[1] Robert, the Bishop of Clermont from 1195-1227 and Archbishop of Lyon from 1227-1232. Dalfi was his cousin and the three songs of the Bishop that have been preserved are all directed against him. Dalfi was Count of Clermont and Montferrand from 1168-1234. (B/S, 288; Egan, 29)

[2] Dalfi responds to the Bishop's stanza with a stanza built on the same rhyme scheme, and full of word play. The lady is said to be married to Chantart de Caulec, and the word used for cabbage is "chaule." The couple lives in Pescadoiras, so the Bishop is said to go there to fish, "pescar," and the lady is likened to a good catch.

[3] The lyrics of the songs obviously refer to a private joke whose meaning is perhaps unfathomable. The razo author has tried to come up with a reasonable explanation but if we read the lyrics without the razo it is clearer that "giving someone the bacon" and "frying up some eggs" are erotic metaphors that have lasted into the blues songs of our own century. The "talen" of Dalfi in the first stanza: "Ben saup del Dalfi lo talen..." (l. 5) may be a joke about sexual preferences, thus explaining his not wanting to "share the bacon" with the lady. It would also explain his reference to the Bishop's preferring "cabbages to leeks" (women to men) and his later joke about the Bishop having been beaten to the pan by some anonymous priest. It may be of note that in the following song Dalfi's joglar is named Mauret and the lady requesting the bacon in this song is Maurina, again a case of possible conflation of identities.

The verses cited in the razo are the only surviving portions of the song.

54. Dalfi d'Alvergne and Bertran de la Tor: 92,1 and 119, 5 (B/S, 289)
MS: H 47

Dalfi composed this stanza about Sir Bertram de la Tor and sent it to him through his joglar, Mauret, during the period when Bertram had given up on valor and generosity:[1]

Mauret, Bertran has given up
(As rich and powerful as he is)
On valor, for which he was once so honored,
And on traveling into other countries.
Instead he stays at la Tor   5
Raising falcons and hawks
And thinks he is celebrating Easter or Christmas
When he has twenty people gathered in his home.

Bertram responded to Dalfi in this stanza:

Mauret, it pleases the Dalfi   10
That they tell me I'm bad;
And the well-known reproach is true:
"Like lord, like household."
I was good as long as I had a good lord
Whom I pleased and kept in honor.   15
Now, Mauret, since he is worthless
Even if I were good, he would still see it as bad.

[1] This portion of the song is the only known composition by Bertran de la Tor, a lord from the Tour d'Auvergne mentioned by the troubadour, Elias de Barjols, as one of the twelve lords from whom he would like to borrow a quality for his composite ideal knight (B/S, 290).

The verses cited in this razo are the only surviving portions of the song.

55. Dalfi d'Alvergne and Peire Pelisier: 119,1 and 353,1 (B/S, 291)

MS: H 46.

Peire Pelisier was from Martel, from one of the Viscount of Torrena's towns. He was an esteemed bourgeois, noble, generous and courtly. Through his courage and intelligence his reputation grew so greatly that the viscount made him the governor of all his lands. Dalfi d'Alvergne was at that time the lover of Lady Comtor, the daughter of the viscount, a woman with a great reputation for beauty and nobility. Peire Pelisier served him every time that he came to him, giving him anything he desired and lending him his money. However, when Peire Pelisier wanted to recover his money, Dalfi did not want to pay him, refused to give him recompense for the services he had performed and stopped seeing the lady; he no longer went to the land where she lived and sent her no messages or letters. This is why Peire Pelisier composed this stanza:

> I ask the Dalfi to stay in his home,
> To eat his full, and be careful not to grow thin
> For no one knows any worse way to avoid his friend
> When he has taken from him his capital and his interest.
> The messages and correspondence have stopped   5
> And I have not seen a card or letter for a long time.
> No man is worse at accomplishing what he says;
> But he is young and will mend his ways.

Dalfi answered Peire Pelisier vilely and unjustly:

> Courtly commoner, you have brought to ruin
> Everything your father left you at his death.   10
> Do you really expect to get rich off me now,
> In spite of God, who made you a natural born fool?
> Never, by my faith, will you get anything from me.
> Go ask travelers and pilgrims!
> For now you seek rewards blindly   15
> And you always sing about it, about him who gives you nothing in return.[1]

[1] This is an interesting example of a response to a satire in which a lord is castigated for being insufficiently generous. Many songs concern such references and thus appear to serve as a kind of blackmail: either give generously or I'll ruin your reputation. It is rare to have a response from the poet/patron in which he acknowledges that this is indeed the case.

The stanzas included in the razo are the only known portions of the song.

56. Dalfi d'Alvergne and Richard-the-Lionhearted: 119,8 and 420,1 (B/S, 294)
MSS: I 185, K 171.
Base text: I

When peace was established between the King of France and King Richard, there was an exchange made between Alvergne and Quercy, for Alvergne belonged to King Richard and Quercy to the King of France and at the end of the transaction Alvergne belonged to the King of France and Quercy to Sir Richard. Dalfi and his cousin, the Count of Gis, being a lord from Alvergne and a count, were very sad and angry about this for the King of France was too close a neighbor. They also knew that he was stingy and avaricious and had a reputation for being a bad lord. And so he was, for as soon as he took control of that land he bought a fortified castle in Alvergne called Nonette and he took Issoire, a rich town, from Dalfi.

Shortly after Sir Richard went back to war with the King of France he came for a meeting with the Dalfi and the Count Guion, the Dalfi's cousin. He reminded them of the wrongs that the King of France had committed and how he had treated them. He told them that if they wanted to be of service to him and declare themselves against the King of France that he would give them knights and archers and money whenever they asked for it. Believing Sir Richard, they went to war against the King of France for all the wrongs he had done them.

As soon as King Richard found out that the two counts from Alvergne, Dalfi and count Gui, had declared themselves as being against the King of France, he made peace with the King, abandoned Dalfi and the count, and returned to England. The King of France raised a great army and entered into Alvergne. He set on fire and flame all the lands of Dalfi and the count and took over their towns and cities and castles. Since they realized they could not defend themselves against the king of France, they made a five-month's peace with him and arranged for Count Gui to go to England to find out whether Sir Richard would help them as he had sworn and promised. Count Gui went off to England with ten knights. Sir Richard saw him begrudgingly, received him inhospitably, and treated him with no respect; nor did he give him any knights, mercenaries, archers or money. He (Gui) returned in shame, poor and sorrowful.

As soon as he returned to Alvergne, Dalfi and the Count Gis went to the King of France and made peace with him. Just as their treaty with the

King was concluded, the truce between the King of France and Richard came to an end. The King of France assembled his great army, entered into King Richard's lands, took over the cities, and burned towns and castles. When Richard heard the news he came immediately from across the sea to the site. As soon as he had arrived, he sent word to Dalfi and Count Guion that the truce was ended, saying that they should prove themselves and come to his aid by going to war against the King of France. But they did nothing for him.

King Richard, when he heard that they did not want to help him in his war, composed a sirventes about Dalfi and the Count Guion which reminded them of the oath that Dalfi and the Count had made to him and how they had abandoned him when they found out the treasury of Chinon was spent and because they knew that the French King was good at arms and Sir Richard was worthless. He said that Dalfi used to be generous and spendthrifty but that he had become cheap from building fortified castles. He also wanted to know if Dalfi thought it was fine about Issoire, which the King of France had taken from him, or if he would take vengeance and hire some soldiers. The sirventes begins like this:

> Dalfi, I want to clear up a few things
> With you and Count Guion
> Who have...(420, 1)

Dalfi responded to King Richard in another sirventes, answering all the points that Sir Richard had attacked, showing that he was right and that Sir Richard was wrong, and accusing Sir Richard of wrong-doing for what he had done to himself and Count Guion and in many other affairs where he had been guilty of wrong-doing. Dalfi's sirventes begins like this:

> King, since you sing about me
> You have made me (found) a singer...

Song 420, 1   King Richard-the-Lionhearted: "Dalfins, jeus voill deraisner..."
Source: Rochegude, 13.
MSS: A 203, B 119, D 135-462, I 185, K 170, R 23-197 (anonymous),

1. Dalfi, I want to clear up a few things
   With you and Count Guion,
   For during this year
   You were good fighters
   And swore allegiance to me;   5
   And you had such faith in me,
   Like Sir Aengris had in Rainart.[1]
   Now you seem like two grey hens.

2. You gave up helping me
   Over the manifestation of a reward   10
   And because you knew that
   There was no money or riches in Chinon.
   You want a rich king,
   Good at arms, who keeps his word,
   And since I'm a cheap coward,   15
   You turn around and support the other side.

3. I still want to ask you
   About Issoire: whether it's all right with you,
   Or if you're going to take vengeance
   And go hire mercenaries.   20
   But there's one thing I'll assure you of:
   If you were to break the law
   You would find in Richard
   An excellent warrior for the banner of his land.

4. In the beginning I saw you   25
   As generous, living in a great home.
   Then you found a reason
   To erect a fortified castle
   And you gave up on gifts and pleasure,
   Holding court and going to tournaments.   30
   But reputation doesn't matter
   When Frenchmen are like Lombards.[2]

5. Go, sirventes, I am sending you
   To Auvergne;
   And tell the two counts for me   35
   That if from now on they cause any trouble, God help them!

6. Why sing when a valet betrays his word
   And a servant boy respects no law?
   But from now on, each of them had better watch his step
   Or he'll get the worst of it as his share.   40

[1] Reference to Isengrin, the wolf in the *Roman de Renard* poems.

[2] References to Lombards usually carry the positive connotation of rich and prosperous, and possibly the negative one of being those who act only for profit and commit the sin of usury. See another reference under Na Lombarda (#67). This is one of several references to the fact that great expenditures for fortresses have impoverished many nobles and changed the economic balance of the area. See another in stanza 6 of Giraut de Borneilh's song 242, 46 under razo 9.

[3] This song is the only one of this collection originally written in French rather than in the usual Occitan.

Song 119, 8   Dalfi d'Alvergne: "Reis puois de mi chantatz..."
               Sources: Rochegude, 84; MS. A; de Labereyre, 48.
               MSS: A 203, B 120, D 135-463, I 185, K 171, R 23-198 (anonymous).

1. King, since you sing about me,
   You have made me (found) a singer.
   But you scare me:
   That's why I am forced now to turn to you.
   I may be addressing you pleasantly,   5
   But I do have many things with which to reproach you.
   If, from now on, you are going to abandon your fiefs
   Don't go ordering me to reclaim my own.

2. I may not be a crowned king,
   Or a man of great riches   10
   Who could defend my inheritance

Against my powerful lord;
   But you!--whom the wicked Turks
   Feared more than a lion,
   King and duke, Count of Angers,   15
   You allow him to hold Gisors!

3. I never was your sworn man,
   And I recognized my madness.
   You gave my cousin Guion
   So many horses, worth thousands,   20
   And so many heavy sterlings
   That his companions say
   That he will follow your stirrups forever,
   Provided that God keeps you just as generous.

4. I used to be of some importance to you   25
   And it seemed to me when you gave me that order
   That you were leaving me with nothing
   For you really left me in the lurch.
   But God has made me so valorous
   That anywhere between Le Puy and Aubusson   30
   I am among my own men;
   For I am no serf or Jew.

5. Worthy and honorable lord
   Who helped me out elsewhere,
   If you didn't seem so fickle   35
   I would have returned to you.
   But our temporary king
   Is giving back Issoire and giving up Usson!
   Getting them back brings me great pleasure
   For I have had to put up with his attacks down here. 40

6. I am very desirous
   To have you and your love;
   For the Count of Angoulême, to whom you gave so much land,
   Is very handsomely paid for his services.
   For, like the generous baron you are,   45
   You gave him Telveirra and its domain
   Because he never stood in your way;
   That's what a pilgrim told me.

7. King, from now on you will see me show my excellence;
   For there is a lady who summons me,   50
   And to whom I so completely belong,
   That all her commands are my happiness.[1]

[1] This would be a good example of a song in which the lady figure, the one who is praised, is very likely a stand-in for the real patron, Richard.

57. Pons de Capdoill 375: 14, 18, 20 (B/S, 314)
    MSS: E 205, P 47, R 3, Sg 182, b 15.
    Base Text: E

As you have just heard, Pons de Capdoill loved Lady Alazais de Mercuer, the wife of a great count of Alvergne, and the daughter of Sir Bernart d'Anduza, and he was much loved by her.[1] Their love was greatly celebrated by all the high-born people and because of it there were many fine courtly festivals, jousts, entertainments and beautiful songs.

Pons, in spite of his being held in such honor by her and all their happiness, had a desire, like a mad lover who doesn't recognize happiness or can't accept it, to test whether she loved him; for he didn't believe with his own eyes the pleasing pleasures and honored honors that she gave him and said to him. So he decided, in his mad heart, to pretend to love another lady, Lady Audiart, the wife of the Lord of Marseille. He got the idea that if his lady was hurt by his leaving her that he could then know that she did love him, and that if she was pleased by his leaving it would be clear that she did not love him. And so he began to move away from Lady Alazais, like a madman who doesn't repent until it's too late, and to turn his attentions to Lady Audiart and to speak well of her. This is what he said about her:

   I would not want the empire of Germany
   If my eyes couldn't see Lady Audiart;

> And I am not saying too much if I dress gayly, and undress,
> And give her thanks, for my company pleased her...(375, 14)[2]

When Lady Alazais saw that Pons de Capdoill had left her and turned to Lady Audiart, after all the love and honor she had given him, she was highly insulted and never again spoke of him to anyone or asked about him; and if someone else spoke of him she she would not answer. She went on living amidst great pomp and courtly ceremony.

Pons de Capdoill went throughout Provence for a long time, paying court to ladies and fleeing Lady Alazais' honors. But when he saw and learned that she didn't show any anger over his parting and never sent him messengers or letters, he realized the evil he had done. He began to return to her land and to give up on the foolish test he had concocted. He sent her messengers and letters but she did not want to hear them or listen to them. He began to feel sad and mournful and he sent her letters and humble verses full of entreaties to her that she allow him to appear before her to explain the background to the situation[3] and to beg for her mercy and say that she should take revenge on him if he had offended her. But she didn't want to hear about mercy or explanations; and so he composed this song which says:

> Like one who has no lack of supporters...(375, 20)

This song was of no avail with the lady and so he composed another which says:

> He who makes a big mistake
> Due to foolish thinking
> Should suffer the damages...(375, 18)

This one did him no good either in convincing Lady Alazais to take him back or in making her believe that he had left her to see whether she would be happy or not after he had gone. So he went to see Lady Maria de Ventadorn and my lady the Countess of Montferrand and the Viscountess of Aubusson and brought them all to Mercuer to beg for her mercy and ask her to forgive him. Lady Alazais gave in for love of these ladies. Pons de Capdoill was the happiest man in the world and said that he would never again feign anything just to test his lady.

The songs that deal with the background to this story are written here, as you shall hear.

[1] Capdoill is today Saint-Julien-Chapteuil, in the arrondissement of Le Puy. Bernart d'Anduze VII is a lord mentioned in songs by G. Faidit, G. de Balaun and Uc Brunet. Mercuor is probably in the arrondissement of Brioude (B/S, 313; Egan, 86).
[2] This partial song is preserved only in the text of this razo.
[3] The text reads: "razonar soa razo."

Song 375, 18 Pons de Capdoill: "Qui per nesi cuidar..."
 Source: von Napolski, 57.
 MSS: A 57, C 120, D 114, I 75, K 59, R 12, a 219, b^1 6, b^2 16.
 Other English translations: Blackburn, 216.

1. He who makes a big mistake
 Due to foolish thinking
 Should suffer the damages.
 And if my lady begins to look badly upon me
 Or banish me from her sight   5
 Then it's only right; for I committed
 Such an act of madness that I should die
 Of grief and lamentation.

2. If I have behaved like a madman
 Through over-loving   10
 And trying to prove myself to My-Lord,
 Then her heart would fill with joy
 If the firm resolve that I harbor
 To serve her were to leave me.
 I'm quite sure that that would please her   15
 For I foolishly tried it out.

3. Thus I force myself to compose songs
 Despite my ignorant mind and heart,
 For when I think I'm showing pride
 Nothing comes of it;   20
 And when my heart shows humility
 That does me no good either.

Neither pride nor courtliness
Bring me any joy from her.

4. But I can't take my 25
Heart and desire anywhere else
And if she'll only deign to pardon me
I'll pay her back with my grace and gratitude
And I'll do so forever;
For no one could make me take my heart 30
From the rich spot it now occupies,
Not even if he killed me.

5. This is why I don't bother doubting
Her rich and just-right body.
Nor will I have to leave her 35
On account of the rumors, for each one of them is lying,
And I am certainly the one to know that.
There's nothing better a man could have
For love-making
Than gay conversation.[1] 40

6. Lady, the noblest I know,
I love you better, without any deceit,
Than Tristan did his friend;
And I get no benefit from doing so.

[1] OR: She could find no better man for love-making, except for his gay conversation.

Song 375, 20   Pons de Capdoill: "Si com sellui c'a pro de valledors..."
Source: von Napolski, 65.
MSS: A 59, B 37, C 107 (A. de Mareuil), D 111, D^c
251, G 79, H 48 (anonymous), I 73, K 57, M 128,
N 212-325 (anon.), (A. de Mareuil), O 24, P 36,
Q 109 (Girardus), R 12-87, (A. de Mareuil), S 207-
133, T 119, U 98, b^2 16, f 56.

1. Like one who has many supporters,
   But they are not there for him in his hour of need
   And he will never be so loved again,
   So is My-Lord not there for me; for she is aware that love
   Of her makes me die a slow and painful death.   5
   And if there's anything else she could do to offend me,
   She'd do it! I think any baron who abandons someone
   Whom he sees is already beaten, is worth less because of it.

2. I know this much: that it's cause for damage and dishonor
   When someone doesn't come to the aid of the powerless. 10
   No weak castle, once attacked,
   Can hold out for long without help;
   And if the lord to whom it belongs doesn't defend it,
   The loss will be attributed to him for a long time to come.
   My lady too will be in the wrong if she loses me now   15
   And doesn't help me when I am begging for her mercy.

3. She can't really lose me to the point where I could love
     elsewhere;
   However I did go away from her for a long time
   And pretended that everything had changed
   In order to see if my mad act would please her.   20
   And I did prove that if I really were to turn my interest
   To another lady, her heart would not be so thrilled
   About my leaving her. But none of this means a thing,
   For my heart can never leave her.[1]

4. Beautiful lady, I deserve your help   25
   For never has anyone so tormented, miserable and mistreated
   Been able to endure his punishment so nobly and in such silence.
   And since this suffering is my delight and my pleasure,
   For God's sake, and because it will make you look good,
   Have some pity on me.   30
   I am your liege-man, and if you want to do me some good,
   You will thus be performing an act of courtliness and mercy.

5. Your beautiful eyes, your fresh complexion,
   Your rich reputation, your fine beauty
   Make me find in you a pleasure more cruel.   35
   I don't need to be made into the mirror
   In which you see your body, beautiful and noble,

    Frank and joyous, loving and pleasant,
    For that shows too much pride; and for someone who maintains his
    Reputation, pride is not shown to his lord and is not appropriate.[2]   40

6. My Most-Loyal, if I saw you more often
   I'd be better off and so would you.
   For I could advise you, and you me:
   After all, nobody knows anything about his own good.

[1] OR: my heart can never get away from itself.

[2] The pronoun is "lo sieus" rather than "la soa," indicating that the object of possession is masculine, as in the lord rather than the lady.

58. Guillem de Balaun 208, 1 (B/S, 321)
MSS: H 18, R 3.
Base Text: Translation based on H with additional elements from R being indicated in italics within the translation.

Guillem de Balaun was a noble lord from the Montpelier area, a skillful *knight*, very learned, and a good composer of songs. He fell in love with a noble lady from the bishopric of Gevaudan whose name was Lady Guilelma of Jaujac, the wife of Peire, the lord of Jaujac. He loved her greatly and served and honored her through singing and telling tales about her. And the lady loved him so much that she did and said all that he wanted according to the rights of love.

    Sir Guillem had a companion named Peire de Barjac, who was valiant and worthy, good and handsome. He loved a young and beautiful lady from the castle of Jaujac whose name was Vierneta. She had taken him on as her knight and he had from her all that he desired.[1]

Both Guilem de Balaun and Peire de Barjac were their ladies' lovers. But it happened that Peire de Barjac got angry with his lady so she sent him away disgracefully and he left her more sad and mournful than he had ever been. Guillem de Balaun comforted him and told him not to despair for he would make peace between them upon his return to Jaujac.

It was a long time before he returned there, but as soon as Guillem de Balaun arrived at Jaujac he made peace between Lady Vierneta and Sir Peire de Barjac. This gave Peire happiness greater than any he had ever had. Guillem de Balaun was amazed at this and especially when he heard that Peire de Barjac said that never had any joy made him so happy, not even when he conquered his lady for the first time. Therefore, Guillem de Balaun decided that he wanted to find out if the joy of recovering a lady's love is as great as the joy at the first conquest. He pretended to be very angry with Lady Guillelma and so it was that he did not send her messages or talk about her or want to hear others talk about her or travel any more into the land where she lived.

She sent him her messenger with passionate love letters, wondering why it had been so long since he had come to see her and why he had not even sent any messages. And he, like a mad lover, did not want to hear or listen to her messenger or her letters and had him dismissed disgracefully from his castle. The messenger returned to Lady Guillelma sad and mournful and told her about what had happened.

She was very sad about this and ordered a knight from her castle who knew about their relationship to go to Sir Guillem de Balaun and ask him why he was angry with her; if she had said or done anything that displeased him ; and to tell him that she wished to make amends according to Guillem's explanation of the events and his wishes. The knight went to Balaun and Sir Guillem saw him but received him very badly. When the knight had told him what Guilelma had sent him to say, Guillem responded that he would not tell her the reason for the rift. He said that she knew perfectly well that it was one which allowed for no amends and which could not be pardoned. The knight returned and told Lady Guillelma what Sir Guillem had said. The lady was in despair over this and said that she would never again send him messages or beseechments or explanations. And the lady remained for a long time in a state of sadness.

There came a day when Sir Guillem began to reflect on how he had lost, through his own madness, great joy and great happiness. He got on his horse and went to Jaujac where he stayed in the home of a townsman rather than in the castle, saying that he was on a pilgrimage.

Lady Guillelma had heard that he was in the town. During the night, when all were in bed, Lady Guilelma left the castle with one lady and a maid and came to the lodging where Guillem was sleeping. She called for the lady of the inn and had herself admitted to the room where Guillem was sleeping. She came to his bed and threw herself to her knees before him. She lowered her head-dress to kiss him, begging his pardon for the wrong that she had not committed. And Guillem did not want to take her back or pardon the wrong he had suffered at her hands. Beating her and slapping her, he chased her from his sight. The lady went back then to her own bed, saddened, afflicted and mournful, with her heart set that she would never again see him or speak to him and she repented for what Love had made her do.

He too was left saddened over what his madness had made him do. He got up by and by and made his way to the castle and had it announced that he wished to see Lady Guillelma because he wanted to show her and tell her about the mad deeds he had committed and why, and because he wished to ask for her pardon over this madness. The lady did not wish to see him or hear him. She had him dismissed and thrown out of the castle *disgracefully*. He left then like a madman, a crazy man, moaning and crying and sighing while the lady repented over the humility that she had shown him.

Guillem de Balaun was in this state for at least a year, during which time the lady never consented to see him or listen to anyone who wished to speak to her about him. This is why he composed the poem of desperation which says:

My song moves, seeking mercy, toward you...

Sir Bernart d'Andusa, the most honored noble baron of that land and the friend of Guillem and Guillelma, *learned about the affair, climbed on his horse and came to Balaun. He spoke to Sir Guillem and told him what he could do to get to see his lady. Sir Guilllem told him the whole story and about the madness that had come over him. Sir Bernart, upon hearing this explanation, thought it a huge joke and said that he would arrange a peace between them. Guillem was very happy when he heard that Bernart was willing to act as an intermediary.*

So Bernart left him and went to Jaujac where he told the lady all about Guillem's side of the story and how sad and miserable he was over the madness that had come into his head. He told her that it was all a joke done as an experiment. The lady answered that she was ashamed of herself for having humiliated herself before him. Sir Bernart told her that it was up to her to pardon him first, for she was in the right and Sir Guillem was in the wrong. He gave her the written poem and begged her as nicely as he could or knew how to pardon him *in the name of God and mercy*; and he told her to take her revenge first, *whenever it should please her.*

The lady responded that since he wished it, she would pardon Guillem, provided that he pull out the fingernail from his little finger for the wrong he had done her and that he bring it to her *with a song in which he blames himself for the mad deeds he committed.*

When Bernart d'Andusa *saw that he could do no better than that, he took his leave and* returned to Sir Guillem to tell him about the lady's vengeance and the pardon she would grant him. *When Sir Guillem heard about the pardon he had arranged,* he was the happiest man in the world and he thanked him for having gotten so much from the lady. He *immediately sent for a master,* had his finger tied up and the nail pulled out, *on account of which he suffered great pain.*

He *composed his poem,* climbed on his horse and came to Jaujac with Sir Bernart to see Lady Guillelma. *She came out to meet them.* Both men threw themselves at her feet. *Sir Guillem begged her on bended knee for mercy and pardon,* and he presented her with his fingernail. *She felt pity for him and, taking his hand, brought him to his feet.* She took him back and forgave him his unthinking madness. All three entered into her bedroom and there she pardoned him as she kissed and embraced him. He took out his song and she listened to it happily. Since then they have loved each other much more than they had ever before.

It is only right that when a man who has great happiness goes seeking unhappiness that he should find it, just as Guillem de Balaun did. For this is how a madman learns how to reform for what he has done, by suffering the punishment.

And here you will find some of his works.

¹ B/S note that the geographical information in this razo is so precise that it could only have been composed by someone who knew the region well (B/S, 332).

Song 208, 1   Guillem de Balaun: "Lo vers mou merceyan ves vos..."
  Source: Boutière, 243.
  MSS: C 367, Dᵃ 191-688, H 19, I 111, K 96, R 33-280, e 162.

1. My song moves, seeking mercy, toward you,
   Lady, though it's not that I expect that
   Mercy for me should overcome you,
   So serious is my crime.
   That is why, though I perish, I do not complain.   5
   It's that I've lost my very self as well as
   You that leads me to despair;
   If I now lose my words, I won't be able to go on.

2. My condition is so critical
   That I don't know how to handle it;   10
   For a prayer that no one hears
   Is worth little to a destitute man.
   That's why it's only right that an accursed man should complain.
   And since I hear that God never performs a miracle
   For a cowardly man   15
   I pray without hope of reward.

3. Lady, although you do not accord me a pardon,
   I shall not desist both from giving myself to you
   And especially from honoring you,
   For prayers conquer both the good and the bad.   20
   And if ever pity should bend your resolve
   Enough to forgive an admitted crime,
   Something that I neither hope for nor think of,
   And I should ever falter again, may I never rise from the mud!

4. Alas! How I regret that I was irritable   25
   The day she lowered her veil for me,

Sought me out like a true lover, and made her amends
By offering something of which I should be desirous.
She begged me, offering such excellent terms
That since then, I have often felt great sadness in my heart.
I would consider myself a redeemed man   31
If she'd even greet me like a stranger.

5. Unfortunately, that other season is on its way
And I fear it, for it makes me pay so dearly.
That's why I really have to learn   35
Why it is that I live in such a state of need.
Rich joy like that never comes my way;
Nor do I know from where it will ever come.
If only I had known before!
But now I know what I'm complaining about.   40

6. I know perfectly well that I failed her utterly.
I'm not someone who'd try to defend a guilty action;
I really deserve nothing more than to be hanged!
Emperor, if I were the first one,
It would only be right that my companions not grow
    in number.   45
But if all those guilty of crimes were put to death,
And none of them were accorded any mercy,
There'd be no one left, big or small.

7. If you really want my death, and it will do you some good,
There'll be no one defending me before you   50
And you won't get any larger revenue.
He who is powerful gets a lot out of
Someone to whom he extends a generous heart
And it behooves him to show him mercy;
For one doesn't expect mercy   55
In a land where power is lacking.

8. Lady, too late did I recognize
My mad reasoning, if my case means nothing to you.

59. Peire Vidal 364: 2, 36, 37, 48 (B/S, 356).
MS: H 22[1]

I told you at the beginning of his songs who Peire Vidal was and what he was like. So I now want to tell you that he fell in love with a lady, Alasais de Rocamartina, the wife of Sir Baraill, the lord of Marseille, with whom Peire shared the name, 'Rainer.'[2]

Sir Barail loved him more than any man in the world and took more pleasure from his songs and antics than anyone else; and he was happy about the courting of his wife for he saw it all as an amusement. Lady Alasais also saw it as an amusement so she permitted Peire's beseechments and courting in return for the beautiful songs he composed about her and the amusement that he provided her. And he stayed with him at court, dressed him like himself, and armed him.

One day Peire learned that Sir Baral had gotten up and left his bedroom and that the lady was still in her bed, sleeping. He came into the bedroom where she was sleeping, came over to the bed, took her in his arms and kissed and embraced her. She woke up, saw it was Peire Vidal and began to scream. Ladies and maidens came running and Peire began to flee in an attempt to get out of there. The lady called for her husband, Sir Barail, and began to tell him how the madman, Peire Vidal, had kissed her, and said that she wanted him put to death. Sir Bairal began to reproach her and tell her that she should not hold it against him as Peire was mad.

Peire Vidal was afraid and left that land. Lady Alasais made every effort to do him harm and would have, had she been able to find him. Because of the state of fear in which he lived, he went overseas, as he tells us:

> It is very clear that she wants me
> To leave her land
> When she makes me cross the sea;
> Hence, the accusation... (364, 2: 16-19)

He stayed there for a long time and composed many good songs in which he recalled the kiss he had stolen from his lady, as he tells us:

> I would be better rewarded than any man ever born
> If the stolen kiss were simply given to me
> Or even granted me as my right... (364, 48: 25-27)

In another spot he says this:

> Love beats me well with the sticks I gather
> For one time, in her royal keep,
> I stole from her a kiss which I remember still... (364, 36: 13-15)

And in another spot, he says this:

> For I served with a true heart
> As much as I could, without reserve,
> And I never got any other recompense
> Except for a little piece of cord.
> Well, I did get one: for one morning
> I slipped into her chamber
> And kissed her, like a bandit,
> On the mouth and the chin... (364, 2: 21-28)

When the barons of Provence, Baralz and Sir Uc del Baus saw this, they so begged the lady that she sent for Peire.[3] Having gotten over her anger, she sent him letters and greetings telling him to come back, to return to Provence. He got right on a ship and came straight to Provence, to Sir Uc del Baus. Sir Barals, when he heard that Peire Vidal was in Baux, got on his horse and went to get Peire and bring him to Marseille. Lady Alasais received him with great happiness and she let him kiss her, as he says here:

> After a long wait, I
> have finally gotten, in great sweetness,
> The kiss that the force of love
> Made me steal from My-Lord.
> For now she deigns to grant it to me... (364, 37: 14-18)

---

[1] This is one version of this tale, as recounted in manuscript H. See the following razo for the other manuscripts' version.

[2] The practice of sharing one name between a poet and a patron, or two poets, is common and is also referred to in razo 51 on

Guillem de Saint Leidier, in razo 67 on Raimon de Miraval, in razo 12 on Bertran de Born, and in razo 8 on Giraut de Borneilh. See S. Stronski, *Folquet*, 36. Raimon Barral was the viscount of Marseille. He repudiated his wife, Azalaïs, in 1191. Both are mentioned by other poets, particularly Folquet de Marseille. See razos 75-77 (B/S, 355 and 360).

[3] Uc del Baus, the prince of Orange, was married to Barrale, the daughter of En Barral and Azalaïs. He is not mentioned by name in Vidal's songs but may be referred to under the senhal Gazanhat ("The Acquired One") (B/S, 355).

60. Peire Vidal 364: 2, 36, 37, 48 (B/S, 361)
MSS: E 194, N^2 20, P 42, R 2, e 10.

Base Text: E

Peire Vidal, as I have told you, fell in love with all the excellent ladies and believed that they all really loved him in true love.

He was in love with Lady Alazais, the wife of Sir Barral, lord of Marseille, the one who loved Peire Vidal more than any man on earth for his excellent poetic skills and for the amazing and crazy things that Peire did and said. They called each other 'Rainier.' Peire had private access to the court and bedroom of Sir Barral, and in this was more privileged than any man in the world.

Sir Barral knew perfectly well that Peire Vidal was paying court to his wife and he saw this as an amusement, as did all who knew about it. He got much happiness from the crazy things Peire did and said; and the lady, too, saw it as an amusement, as did all the ladies to whom Peire paid court. Each of them said pleasing things to him and promised him all that he pleased and asked for, and he was so well advised that he believed it all! When Peire Vidal quarreled with her, Sir Barrals immediately arranged for peace and made the lady promise to grant Peire anything he wanted.

One day, Peire Vidal learned that Sir Barral had gotten up and that the lady was alone in her bedroom. Peire Vidal entered her room, came over to the Lady Alazais' bed and found her there, sleeping. He knelt before her and kissed her on the lips. She felt the kiss and thought that it was Lord Barral, her husband, and she woke up laughing. Then she looked and saw that it was the madman Peire Vidal and began to scream and make a lot of noise. Her maidens came from all over the house when they heard the commotion, asking themselves: "What is going on?" Peire Vidal left the room in flight. The lady summoned Sir Barral and accused Peire Vidal of having kissed her. Crying all the while, she begged him to take revenge. Sir Barral, like the honorable and just man that he was, took the whole thing as a joke. He began to laugh and reproach his wife for having made such a scene over what the madman had done. But he wasn't able to convince her not to go around telling everyone what had happened and not to seek out Peire Vidal so as to do him harm; and she made many threats against him.

Peire Vidal, for fear of what was going on, got on a ship and went to Genoa and he stayed there until he was able to cross the sea with King Richard. He did this because he was greatly afraid that Lady Alazais wanted to take his life. He spent a long time there and composed many beautiful songs in which he reminisced about the kiss he had stolen. And in one song, "Ajostar e lasar," he says that he never got any reward from her:

> Except for a little piece of cord.
> Well, I did get one: for one morning
> I slipped into her chamber
> And kissed her, like a bandit,
> On the mouth and the chin... (364, 2: 24-28)

In another spot he says:

> I would be better rewarded than any man ever born
> If the stolen kiss were simply given to me,
> And granted me as my right... (364, 48: 25-27)

And in another song he says:

> Love beats me well with the sticks I gather;
> For one time, in her royal keep,
> I stole from her a kiss which I remember still.

Oh! What a worthless life he leads, who cannot see what he
loves... (364, 36: 13-16)

He spent a long time overseas for he did not dare return to Provence.
Sir Barral, who loved him well, as you have heard, so begged his wife
that she forgave the theft of the kiss and granted him one as a gift. Sir
Barral sent for Peire Vidal and had him sent word of his wife's forgiveness
and good wishes. Peire, with great happiness, then came to Marseille and
was received with great happiness by Sir Barral and Lady Alazais. She
granted him the kiss that he had stolen from her as a gift. Peire Vidal
therefore wrote this song which says:

Since I have come back to Provence... (364, 37: 1)

Song 364, 2   Peire Vidal: "Ajostar e lassar..."
               Source: D'Arco Silvio Avalle, 33.
               MSS: A 95, C 37, D 26, H 7, I 41, K 28, L 141, M
                  5, N 90, R 65, T 256, c 59, e 1.
               Other English translations: Goldin, 254.

1. I can so smoothly link and meld
   Words and melodies
   That when I have a good subject
   No man gets near my heel
   In the noble and precious art of composing songs.   5
   But now the beautiful lady to whom I belong
   Is killing me so,
   As if I had shown her some slight
   Or betrayed her.
   When I first saw her she struck me   10
   In my miserable heart.
   I am always working for her benefit
   And all she does is hurt me.
   She wishes me evil and I don't know why
   Except that I love her more than she loves me.   15

2. It is very evident that she wants me
   To leave her land

When she makes me cross the sea,
And it is for this that I reproach her.
There is no hope left; 20
I served her with a true heart
As much as I could, without reserve,
But I never got any other recompense
Except for a little piece of cord.
Well, I did get one: for one morning 25
I slipped into her chamber
And kissed her, like a bandit,
On the mouth and the chin.
So that is what I got and nothing more
And I am a dead man if she holds back on the rest. 30

3. She has been making me sigh and weep
For a long time now.
I would rather be happy and sing
If that were what she wanted,
But she has the heart of a dragon. 35
She says evil things to me and laughs
With the others around her
And looks at me with the eyes of a lion.
Because of that mistake
She has made me into a pilgrim, 40
Except that no pilgrim in search of prayer
Has ever been so roughly treated.
And, to be perfectly honest,
A man has to look out for his own welfare
Before some evil lord starts mistreating him. 45

4. She sets me aflame and makes me burn
The way fire works on coal.
When I look at her, I see her eyes
And face so pure
That I know no recompense 50
That could change my mind or make me give up
On loving her. Oh, barons!
How Love holds us in
The prison that conquered Solomon,
And David too, 55
And the mighty Samson;
And how she held them in bondage;

For they were not released
Until the moment of death. Therefore, since it now has me,
I shall stay that way, forever at its mercy.   60

5. She leaves me hoping and dreaming
   Like a Breton[1]
   Yet never did my loving and honoring her
   Get her into trouble.
   Rather, God forgive me,   65
   I parted from one who
   Would have given me a gift so rich
   That the king of Aragon
   Would have been honored by it. So why then
   Did I go into exile? I swear to you   70
   That when I hear good things being said about her
   Utter joy tells me[2]
   That I should compose a song about her.
   And then again, since I love her so and believe in her,
   I should never find in her any sign of bad faith.   75

6. Since I can at no time pause
   Or put an end to my wandering,
   I want to return
   As quickly as possible,
   And go in secret to the land between   80
   Arles and Toulouse; for I'd rather have
   A little parcel of land back there
   Than own Le Daron
   Or Le Toron
   Or Ibelin.[3] But vile,   85
   Despicable, lying flatterers
   Have started up a quarrel with me
   And gotten me sent away from Lo Peiro,
   And Sir Drogoman won't listen to me or see me
   Because he is sending my dear Friend away.[4]   90

7. To my friend Folco,[5]
   That is where I send my song;
   May he sing it for me in a choice spot,
   A place where joy comes and goes.

8. May God send bad luck to whomever   95
   Was so evil as to get the Count of Avignon
   Angry with me.
   That's why Lady Vierna won't see me.[6]

9. I pledge myself to Tripoli;
   For when other barons   100
   Are chasing away their good reputation, he holds on to his
   And does not let it get away from him. [7]

[1] The plight of the Bretons, who hope endlessly for the return of King Arthur, is likened to that of the poet (D'Arco Silvio Avalle, 40).

[2] Some have taken "Gaug Entier" (Utter-Joy) to be a senhal for the lady in this passage.

[3] These are all sights in Palestine. Lo Peiro, mentioned in line 88, is the area around Saint-Sernin in Toulouse (D'Arco Silvio D'Avalle, 42; Goldin, 260).

[4] D'Arco Silvio Avalle identifies "Drogoman" as Guilhem VIII of Montpellier. The friend being sent away is Eudossia of Constantinople, who had been repudiated by her husband, Guilhem (Avalle, 42).

[5] "Folco" is the poet Folquet de Marseille. He also speaks about the repudiation of Eudossia in his songs (Avalle, 43). See razos 75-77.

[6] The Count of Avignon at this time was Raimon V of Toulouse, whom Peire elsewhere refers to as "Castiat," "The Reformed One" (Avalle, 43). "Tripol" is Raimon II, cousin of Raimon V of Toulouse, who played an important role in Jerusalem at the time that Peire would have been there.

[7] Note how this song conflates political events and personnages (the repudiation of Eudossia, the Crusades) with the personal love story of exile in such a way that we see how closely they really are linked. None of the tornadas, however, appears in the manuscripts containing the razo.

Song 364, 36   Peire Vidal: "Plus que.l paubres, quan jai el ric ostal..."
Source: D'Arco Silvio Avalle, 317.
MSS: A 101, B 63, C 34, D 25, D^c 249, E 25, F 17, H 23, I 41, J 4, K 29, M 51, P 3, Q 72, R 64, S 11, T 247, a^1 116, c 74, e 25, f 58.
Other English translations: Blackburn, 105.

1. More than the poor man who sleeps in the rich man's house
   And doesn't complain, in spite of his great sorrow,
   For fear that it might irritate the lord,
   I don't dare complain of my mortal pain.
   It's only natural I should suffer since she   5
   Whom I want and desire more than anything scorns me.
   At least I don't dare ask her for mercy
   Because I'm so afraid she'd be annoyed with me.

2. Like one who stares open-mouthed at the stained glass
   Because it looks so beautiful in the bright light,   10
   I feel such sweetness in my heart when I look at her
   That, seeing her like that, I forget myself.
   Love beats me well with the sticks I gather;
   For one time, in her royal keep,
   I stole from her a kiss which I remember still.   15
   Oh! What a worthless life he leads, who cannot see what he loves.

3. So help me, God, my beautiful lady
   Is committing a criminal sin, for she doesn't give me any help.
   She knows that I have my heart and love invested in her
   And care nothing about any other means of
        earning wages.   20
   Why then does she call for me and give me such welcome
   When she doesn't intend to ease what's causing my pain?
   Does she think that by doing so she can make me leave her?
   No, I must do what I do for it comes with love.

4. It's fitting that any true lord should put up with   25
   The wrongs and the rights, the good sense and the madness.
   It's very hard for a man to win property in a war
   After he's been exiled, against his will, from his own land.

223

I will truly be in exile if I stray from her love.
   I will never do that for I love her even more than
      I used to. 30
   I will be considered vile if I give up on love;
   No, I must put up with what I've always put up with.

5. My lady took me into her service in such a way
   That if she hurts me, she will never be treated any the worse
      by me.
   Her pleasure gives me such pleasure 35
   That I forget my own, and care nothing for it.
   There is no day on which her love doesn't burn into my heart
   And that is why I feel such joy when my eyes see her.
   When my body considers all her virtues
   There is no other thing in the world that I hope for,
      or desire. 40

6. Do you know why I feel such an intense love for her?
   Because I've never seen anyone more fine and beautiful
   Or so good; and so it's fitting that I have great wealth,
   For I am the friend of a lady whose worth is so great!
   If ever I see her undress, with me in her presence, 45
   I'll be better off than the Lord of Excideuil[1]
   For he maintains his reputation when others lose theirs
   And I don't know any more, except that Geoffrey has just as
      much!

7. Things look bad for the four kings of Spain[2]
   For they don't want to make peace
      amongst themselves. 50
   In every other way they are greatly esteemed,
   Clever, honest, courtly and true.
   If only they could spruce up their bell
   And turn over a new leaf with these wars, directing them
   Against those people who don't believe in our laws, 55
   Until the day when all of Spain is of one faith.

8. Beautiful-Reformed-One, my lord, it is over you that I suffer[3]
   For I don't see you; and My-Lord, Lady Vierna,
   Whom I love in good faith, doesn't come to me.

9. I am telling the truth, as I always did: 60
   He who makes a good start but then gives up
   Would have done better never to start a thing.

[1] This Lord of Excideuil has often been identified as Richard-the-Lionhearted, and 'Geoffrey' in the final line as Geoffrey of Brittany, his brother. Geoffrey, however, had been dead for seven years when this song was written, and Lewent (1946) has identified both men with literary figures: Gui d'Eissidolh, hero of a now-lost chivalric romance, and Jaufre, the eponymous hero of the Provençal Arthurian romance. See a similar reference to Gui d'Excideuil in stanza 7 of Raimbaut de Vaqueiras' song 392, 20 under razo 70.

[2] These kings have been identified as Alfonse VIII of Castille, Alfonse II of Aragon, Alfonso IX or Ferndinand II of Leon, and Sancho of Novarra (Avalle, 324).

[3] "Castiatz" (Reformed-One) is Raimon V of Toulouse, a frequent patron of the poet. None of the tornadas appears in the manuscripts containing the razo.

Song 364, 37   Peire Vidal: "Pus tornatz sui em Proensa..."
               Source: D'Arco Silvio Avalle, 367.
               MSS: A 95, B 60, C 35, D 22-73, E 23, G 42, H 23,
                    I 41, J 3, K 29, M 52, N 97-116, P 21, Q 70,
                    R 63-530, S 7-5, T 255, U 100, b^1 5, c 60, e 9.

1. Since I am back in Provence
   And my lady likes it that way,
   I must compose a gay song,
   If only as a gift to return a favor.
   A man conquers gifts and good deeds and honor   5
   From a lord
   Who knows how to appreciate him
   By giving service and honoring him.
   That's why I have to give this all I've got.

2. One who complains about a long wait   10
   Is making a big mistake.

The Bretons still have Arthur
   In whom they placed their faith!
   And I, by virtue of a long wait,
   Have conquered with utmost sweetness   15
   The kiss that the force of love
   Made me steal from my lady,
   And which she now deigns to grant me.

3. And since I was never untrue to her
   I have my hopes up   20
   That my pains will end up benefitting me
   Now that the good times are beginning so nobly.
   Other lovers can all take heart
   From my example;
   For through my extraordinary effort   25
   I now get bright fire from cold snow
   And sweet fresh water from the sea.

4. Without having sinned, I took my penance;
   Without any wrong-doing, I sought her forgiveness.
   And from nothing at all I got a noble gift   30
   And from anger, kindly thoughts,
   And complete joy from weeping
   And sweet savor from the bitter,
   And through fear I have learned courage
   And I know how to win for losing   35
   And to triumph when beaten.

5. Otherwise I would get no relief;
   But since she knows that I am conquered,
   My lady's reasoning is such that
   She wants me, having been conquered, to conquer her.   40
   Thus I must subjugate
   Her noble rank with true humility.
   But since I can find no one capable of[1]
   Helping me in her regard
   I can only beg for her mercy and pray.   45

6. Since I have now totally abandoned myself
   To her protection,
   She should never say no to any request;
   For I am hers completely,

To buy or to give away. 50
   Any man who says that I am turning my attentions elsewhere
   Is acting in madness;
   I would rather fail completely with her
   Than conquer joy with someone else.

7. Beautiful-Rainier, on my faith,[2] 55
   I don't know of your equal or partner,
   For all worthy barons
   Rank below you in worth.
   And since God made you without equal
   And gave you me as your servant 60
   I will serve you with praise
   And in any other way, whenever I can,
   If you wish it, Beautiful-Rainier that you are!

[1] OR: Since I cannot compose anything good enough to... (double meaning of the verb "trobar").
[2] "Rainier" is Raimon Barral, the Viscount of Marseille.

Song 364, 48   Peire Vidal: "Tant me platz jois e solatz..."
               Source: D'Arco Silvio Avalle, 44.
               MSS: A 97, C 37, D 24-81, D^c 248, H 25, I 41,
                     K 29, M 54, N 92, Q 74, R 47-395, c 62, e 31.

1. To see the joy and refinement
   Of honored men is such a pleasure for me:
   That's why I am composing this song right on the spot,
   Good king, and I pray that you will learn it.
   And if you ask me: 5
   "Why do you sing so much?"
   It's because it annoys the dreary
   And brings joy to the contented ones.

2. You should know that if I were loved
   You would hear even more perfect 10

And prized little songs
   Than now, when I am being mistreated.
   I can compose marvelous
   Words and golden melodies.
   But friendship is of no use to me right now;   15
   And I am only singing for profit.[1]

3. Slender body, so well brought-up,
   Have mercy on me; I urge you
   To show pity
   For I am distressed and tormented.   20
   Oh lady, look upon
   My body and do not kill me
   For it will be a crime, a sin, a case of deception,
   If I do die, despairing.

4. I would be better rewarded than any man ever born   25
   If the stolen kiss were simply given to me
   Or even granted me as my right.
   But I don't want you asking
   Where all my gratitude is,
   For you could very easily hurt me that way.   30
   Cupidity often brings down
   Those of the finest upbringing.

5. Since beauty can make even the reasonable man
   Rash, it is stupid
   Not to keep oneself hidden.   35
   But, having spoken to My-Lord,
   I get so bewitched
   That I cannot move from her side.
   Either I'm just an unmasked jealous old fool
   Or a man who's completely in love.   40

6. With a little pair of loaded dice,
   Cowardliness, the source of avarice,
   Has cheated us.
   Sir Rainier, don't stop
   Acting in a such a way   45
   That you'll reap the benefits as long as you live.
   For a rich young man who is cheap
   Is worth less than a dead man already in the ground.

7. Lady Vierna, I want my Reformed-One
   To make peace with me,   50
   For I have come back to Provence
   To die like a hare in his den.

8. Snow and ice, why don't you stop?
   Summer is already on its way. Beautiful meadows,
   Why won't you turn green?   55
   Because I am more in love with
   The lady I burn for
   Than our emperor is.
   I know this much: he lost   59
   Seven hundred coins, and never even got hold of the dice.[2]

---

[1] Peire distinguishes between professionally competent compositions and expressions of love. See Uc de Saint Circ's vida for a similar distinction (B/S, 240 and Egan, 110).

[2] The final stanza is not included in the manuscripts containing the razo. Avalle identifies the emperor with Peire, whose vida tells us that he once had people call him "Emperor" while under the crazy notion that he was to inherit the empire of Constantinople from his wife's father (B/S, 352-54).

61. Peire Vidal 364, 16 (B/S, 368)
    MSS: E 196, N^2 21, P 42, R 2, e 13.
    Base Text: E

Peire Vidal deeply mourned the death of the good Count Raimon of Toulouse and felt great sadness.[1] He dressed in black, tied back the tails and ears of all his horses, and had the hair shaved from his own and all his servants' heads. But their beards and fingernails were not cut back. For a very long time he went about like a man crazed with grief.

It happened that at the same time that he was going about grieving, King Anfos of Aragon came to Provence. He brought with him Blascol Romieus, Sir Guarcia Romieus, Sir Martis del Canet, Sir Miquel de Luzia, Sir Sas d'Antillon, Sir Guillem d'Alcalla, Sir Albert de Castelveill, Sir Raimon Gauseran de Pinons, Sir Guilem Raimon de Moncada, Sir Arnaut de Castelbon, and Sir Raimon de Cerveira.[2] They found Peire Vidal sad and grieving and dressed like a man crazed with grief. The king began to beg him, as did all the other barons who were his special friends, to leave behind his sorrow. They told him he should cheer up and sing and that he should compose a song that they would bring back to Aragon with them. So much did the king and his barons press him that he told them he would cheer up and renounce the state of mourning in which he had been living and that he would compose a song and do what the king wanted.

He loved the Loba of Pueinautier and Lady Estefania, who was from Cerdegne. And now he was in love again, with Lady Raimbauda of Biol, the wife of Sir Guilem of Rostanh, the lord of Beuil. Beuil is in Provence, in the mountains between Lombardy and Provence. The Loba was from the Carcases and Peire Vidal called himself "Lop" (wolf) in her honor and the arms he carried were decorated with wolves.[3] In the Cabaretz mountains, he had the hunters and shepherds with their mastiffs and greyhounds hunt for him as they do wolves. So the shepherds hunted him down with their dogs and they beat him so badly that he was taken for dead and carried back to the lodging of Loba of Pueinautier.[4]

When she realized that it was Peire Vidal that this had happened to, she was greatly amused by the crazy thing that Peire had done and she and her husband both laughed about it. They welcomed him in great happiness and her husband had him taken away and placed in an isolated spot and treated him the best that he could or knew how. He sent for the doctor and made sure he was given medical attention for as long as he needed until he was cured.

And since I began by telling you that Peire Vidal had promised the king and his barons to sing and compose songs, it was when he was cured that the king had clothing and arms made for himself and for Peire. Peire fixed himself up quite nobly and composed this song, the very one you will hear, which says:

I had given up on singing
Over the grief and sorrow... (364, 16: 1-2)

[1] The good Count is Raimon V of Toulouse, to whom Peire often referred as "Castiat." Avalle notes that the song was actually composed before, not after Raimon's death, and that the razo presents a very different picture from that of the song (B/S, 372; Avalle, 59).

[2] Avalle does note that despite other discrepancies between the song and razo, King Alphonse II did travel to Provence after the death of Raimon V and that all of the mentioned notables are historic personnages whose names can be found in contemporary documents (Avalle, 52).

[3] The "Loba" (wolf) is mentioned in three of Peire's songs and in razo 65 on Raimon de Miraval.

[4] The Loba is from the region of Carcassonne. The mountains of Cabaretz are identified as the present-day mountains of Cabardes.

Song 364, 16   Peire Vidal: " De chantar m'era laissatz..."
                Source: D'Arco Silvio Avalle, 57.
                MSS: A 97, C 38, D 24, E 24, H 27, I 44, K 31, N 99, Q 71, R 16, T 252, a^1 119, e 13.

1. I had given up singing
   Over the grief and sorrow
   That the count, my lord, has caused me.
   But since I see that it would please the good king,
   I will compose a quick song   5
   For Guilhelm and Sir Blascols Romieus
   To bring to Aragon,
   If they find the tune good and light.

2. And if I sing like someone who has been forced,
   Since it would please My-Lord,   10
   Please don't think less of
   My song; for my heart has turned
   From the lady from whom I never got any profit
   And this leaves me banished from hope.
   Leaving her is so painful for me   15
   That nobody but God knows of what I speak.

3. I am cheated and tricked
   Like a good servant
   When that which should bring one honor
   Is considered to be madness.   20
   The only recompense I can expect to get from all of this is
   That of a man who serves with spite.
   But if ever again I serve him
   I will think less of myself than of a Jew.[1]

4. I have given myself to the sort of lady   25
   Who lives on joy and love,
   Worth and esteem,
   In whom beauty is refined
   Like gold in burning coal.
   Because my prayers please her,   30
   It seems like all the world is mine
   And kings are tending my fiefs.

5. Above all emperors,
   I am crowned with fine joy,
   For I have fallen in love   35
   With the daughter of a count
   And I get more out of a little cord
   That Lady Raimbauda gives me
   Than King Richard gets from Poitiers,
   Tours or Angers.   40

6. Even though you call me a wolf
   I don't consider that a disgrace;
   Nor if shepherds beat me
   Or go off hunting for me.
   I love the trees and the bushes   45
   More than any house or palace
   And my path to her, through wind, ice and snow
   Will be undertaken with joy.

7. Beautiful-sable, for you I love
   Sault, Usson and Alion.[2]   50
   But since my view was brief,
   Here I am, mournful and suffering.

8. The-Wolf says that I am hers,
   And she has every right and privilege to say so,
   For I more truly belong to her   55
   Than to anyone else, or even myself.³

¹ This is not the only anti-Semitic remark in the razo songs. See also razo 25 to Bertran de Born and Guillelm de Berguedan's songs 80, 35 and 210, 10 and Dalfi d'Alvergne's song 119, 8 under razo 56.
² Beautiful-Sable (Bels Sembelis) is unidentified except for the razo's statement that this is Peire's code name for Stephania of Son.
³ This final tornada is not included in any of the razo manuscripts.

62/72   Peire Vidal 364, 47

The song is falsely attributed to Raimbaut de Vaqueiras in a razo dedicated to his songs. It can be found with other songs by Raimbaut under razo 72.

63/65   Peire Vidal 364, 21 and Raimon de Miraval 406: 4, 27, 38.

Peire's song is cited along with other songs by Raimon de Miraval in razo 65/63. Song 364, 21 can be found among the other songs following that razo.

64. Raimon de Miraval 406: 12, 15, 28, 38 and Uc de Mataplana 454, 1 (B/S, 379)
MS: H 20.

I told you above, in the other "raison" (razo), about Sir Raimon de Miraval; and you have heard who he was, where he came from, and how he continually turned his attentions to the finest and noblest ladies of those lands, as he tells us:

> My lady should not complain
> If I throw myself at her mercy
> For I don't have the heart to lower my sights
> Or seek a love beneath my station;
> I have always wanted the very best
> Inside and outside of my home... (406, 12: 46-51)

And he built their reputations and brought praise to them from the finest people.

There were among those ladies some who treated him well and others who treated him badly, as he tells us:

> So many times I have given in to madness
> And so many times come back to joy and sweetness...
> (406, 15: 23-24)

He was certainly cheated by some of them, whom he, once having been deceived, then deceived:

> But, while putting up with my damages,
> I found a way to deceive her even as she was deceiving me,
> And thus to stay at peace with her... (406, 38: 18-20)

He was very displeased with the fact that it was said that he had never gotten any benefits from ladies, and he argued against those who said he had never gotten anything, as he tells us:

> Now they are saying behind my back
> That I have never gotten any profit out of love.
> They are lying: for I have had goods and pleasures from love

And I've also put up with set-backs and deceit... (406, 28: 21-24)

He never wanted to cheat on fine or loyal ladies, regardless of the pains they made him suffer; instead, he was able to reap a profit from the harm they did him. But he never wanted anything that wouldn't be good for them.

And so he fell in love with a noble young lady from Albi named Aimengarda de Castras. She was beautiful, courtly, attractive, learned, and well-spoken.

He loved her, honored and praised her greatly, in song and in speech, and he brought her great renown among the noble folk. For a long time he had begged her to give him pleasure in love according to the rights of love. She told him that she would not give him pleasure in love just for the sake of love but that if he would only leave his wife, she would take him as her husband.

When Raimon de Miraval heard that she wanted him as her husband, he was overjoyed and returned to his castle. He tried to think of a reason for leaving his wife, whose name was Caudairenga, named after her father, Caudeira. She was beautiful and attractive and she knew how to compose verses and dances. Sir Guilelm Breimon, a noble, good and handsome knight, was courting her. Sir Raimon de Miraval found as an excuse for leaving his wife that it was not good to have two troubadours in the same house. He told her that he was sending her back to her parents and that she should return to her own home. When she learned what her husband had in mind, she sent for Guilelm Bremon. He came at once and Raimon de Miraval gave her into his hands. Guilelm went off with her and took her as his wife.

Meanwhile, the lady Raimon had been courting, Lady Aimengarda, took as her husband a noble baron from that region whose name was Olivier de Saisac.[1] Thus Miraval ended up sad and grieving, over the lady he had lost and his wife.

The news spread throughout the land, far and wide, and came to the attention of a noble baron from Catalogne named Sir Uget de Mataplana, a very just man, a good composer of songs and a close friend of Miraval. And so he wrote this sirventes which says:

A desire to compose a sirventes has come over me... (454, 1: 1)

[1] Most of the persons named in the text have not been positively identified by editors. B/S note that Olivier could be the brother of Bernard of Saissac, a patron mentioned by Raimon Vidal and Miraval himself (406, 1). The Saissac castle was taken by Simon of Montfort during the early stages of the Albigensian Crusade. Uc de Mataplana, mentioned in the next paragraph, died in 1213 from injuries incurred during the battle of Muret, one of the most infamous incidents of that same war. He was one of the favorites of Pedro II of Aragon, to whom this first song, 406, 12, is addressed (stanza 7). Raimon is asking for his assistance in the war against the French crusaders.

Song 406, 12 Raimon de Miraval: " Bel m'es q'ieu chant e coindei..."
Source: Topsfield, 301.
MSS: A 43, C 75, D 95-329, E 34, F 25, H 15, I 69, K 54, L 106, M 111, N 217-336, P 31, Q 62, R 83-708, S 138-86, U 95, V 46, a^1 318, f 40.
Other English translations: Switten, 161.

1. It pleases me to sing and be refined
   For the air is sweet and the season gay
   And in the orchards and garden hedges
   I hear the cooing and chattering
   Of the tiny birds, amidst   5
   The green, the white and the multi-colored.
   So it is right that someone who wishes
   Love to help him out should
   Begin to behave like a lover.

2. I am not anyone's lover but I do court ladies;   10
   I don't fear suffering or a heavy burden;
   I don't complain easily or get angry;[1]
   And I don't lose heart when confronted with arrogance.
   Fear, however, makes me mute.
   I don't dare show her,   15
   This elegant lady, or tell her about my heart,

For I have kept it hidden from her
   Since first I discerned the esteem in which she is held.

3. Even without having implored her mercy or been granted a
      thing
   I have entered into a state of great anguish.   20
   If I do announce her great worth publicly
   How could it seem believable?
   For never yet has any lady born of a mother
   Acquired so esteemed a reputation
   That it could stand up to hers.   25
   I know many who are considered of great value
   And hers has surpassed the best of them.

4. She is very willing to be courted in a refined manner
   And joy and pleasant conversation delight her.
   She doesn't like wicked men   30
   Who turn away from them or behave like fools.
   The valiant are always welcome, however,
   And she shows them so much favor
   That each of them praises her more
   When away from her   35
   Than if they had been sold into her service.

5. I don't think that the beauty of any other lady
   Can compare to hers,
   For the rosebud at its birth
   Is no fresher than she: 40
   A lovely body, well-developed,
   A mouth and eyes to light up the world.
   Beauty gave her all that she had;
   She put all of her virtue into this one
   So that nothing was left behind.   45

6. My lady should not complain
   If I throw myself at her mercy,
   For I don't have the heart to lower my sights
   Or seek a love beneath my station.
   I have always wanted the very best   50
   Inside and outside of my home
   And I don't go around talking about her everywhere.

>   For I have never expected any more from her
>   Than that she greet me and welcome me graciously.
>
> 7. Song, go for me and tell the king,   55
>   Who is guided, clothed and nourished by joy,
>   That there is nothing crooked in him:
>   The way I'd like to see him is the way I see him.
>   If only he could recover Montagut
>   And return home to Carcassonne!   60
>   Then he will be the emperor of high esteem
>   And the French, on this side, and the Muslims on the other,
>   Will all fear his shield.[2]
>
> 8. Lady, you have always helped me,
>   For as long as I have been singing about you;   65
>   And I didn't think I would compose a song
>   Until I could return to you the fief
>   Of Miraval, which I have lost.
>
> 9. But the king has promised me
>   That I will get it back before long,   70
>   And my Audiart will get Beaucaire.
>   Only then will ladies and lovers be able to
>   Return to the joy that they have lost.[3]

For further information see razo 67 below, which is dedicated solely to this song.

---

[1] OR: "Crazy rumors don't upset me" ("Fol brut no m'irais"). This is the reading from manuscript H, the only one containing this razo. This song is commented on by another razo found in manuscripts E, P, and R (see below). In manuscript E the line also reads "Ni per fol bruit..."

[2] The song appears to have been written to and for King Pedro II of Aragon, shortly before the battle of Muret in 1213. Topsfield hypothesizes that the song was written in praise of a lady at Pedro's court in order to flatter him (Topsfield, 309). The personnages of the lady and the king appear to be intertwined throughout the praise

sections of the song. Razo 62 explains further the role Raimon played in bringing Pedro to Toulouse, where he perished with his army before the walls of Muret.

[3] Audiart, the frequent patron of Raimon, has been identified as Raimon VI of Toulouse. Beaucaire is one of the lands in the arrondissement of Nîmes that Raimon VI had lost to the French army.

Song 406, 15   Raimon de Miraval: "Ben aia.l messagiers..."
Source: Topsfield, 272.
MSS: A 44, C 82, D 98-345, D^c 252, E 42, H 16, I 68, K 52, M 116, N 218-339, R 83-709, U 95, a^1 317, b^2 21.
Other English translations: Switten, 175.

1. To the messenger, I wish him well,
   And to the lady who sent him to me
   I offer a thousand thanks
   If ever my happiness returns.
   I, however, am so overwhelmed by the   5
   Terrible set-backs I've had
   That I can scarcely believe that any lady could have it in her heart
   To love me or wish to bring me honor.

2. For by my many skillful services
   I had conquered such joy   10
   That I thought I could be hers,
   If only I were entirely true to her.
   I wouldn't believe that great wealth or superior reputation
   Could ever do me harm,
   For I had set my sights on a lady of such worth   15
   That it didn't matter if her beauty and riches weren't up to par.

3. Such was the situation between us that scandal-mongerers
   Didn't bother to try to intervene,
   Though they caused me many problems

When I was still an eager young lover, 20
I believed back then that an entire empire
Couldn't keep my lady from me;
So many times I have given in to madness
And so many times come back to joy and sweetness.

4. That's why I put myself last, 25
Behind all the others
So that no Roland or Olivier
Could take my land away
And no Orestain or Ogier
Would even think of taking my place.[1] 30
I am thought to be a man of such good taste
That whatever I want is considered by others to be the best.

5. I really thought my lady
Was different from what she is,
And that that first pleasure 35
Would be with her forever.
Her crazy thoughts are full of lies
And her bad faith has caught up with her.
May God diminish what little prestige she has
For she turned my once firm heart into a troubled one.[2] 40

6. At first I was her saddle-horse
And then I became her pack-horse
But now the harness is so much bigger
And the satchels weigh too much!
Since the compensation is forever shrinking 45
And it seems the labor is ever increasing
She won't have me around any more to be her servant.
May God allow me to find a better situation elsewhere.

7. A lady who turns her praise into blame
Cannot have even the tower of Miraval. 50

8. May God save my Audiart and his lands[3]
For everyone's value is increased by virtue of his value.

This song is also commented upon in razo 66.

[1] Orestains may be a reference to one of Charlemagne's men in the *Pseudo-Turpin* cycle. He is variously referred to as Arastagnus, Arastang or Arastannus. In the *Gesta Karoli Magni ad Carcassonam et Narbonam* he is referred to as Torestagnus or Torestan. Olivier and Roland are the heroic warriors of the *Chanson de Roland*. Bertran de Born refers to the same four heros in his song 80, 6a: "A totz dic..." (Topsfield, 278).

[2] At this point the song takes on the characteristics of a mala chanso, a song of deprecation of the lady.

[3] Topsfield also translates "honor" in this instance as "land," rather than "honor," though there is no more reason here than anywhere else in the troubadours' songs to think that the term means exclusively one or the other: land or honor, rather than both.

Song 406, 28   Raimon de Miraval: "Entre dos volers sui pensius..."
                Source: Topsfield, 224.
                MSS: A 43, B 30, C 81, D 98-344, D^c 252, E 42, H 16, I 69, K 53, L 136, M 113, N 216-333, R 83-707, S 213-137, T 181, U 92, V 44, a^1 316, f 67.
                Other English translations: Switten, 203.

1. I am torn between two desires:
   My heart tells me not to sing any more
   But Love doesn't want me to give up
   As long as I'm alive on this earth.
   I would have good reason   5
   Not to compose songs any more,
   But I continue to sing because love and youth
   Restore everything that good sense and moderation take away.

2. If ever I strove
   To be upstanding, courtly and gay,   10
   It is now time that I give it all I've got,
   With charming words and deeds;
   For I have a feeling about a certain lady
   That no one lacking in manners

    Can ever qualify for her esteemed and valuable prize   15
    No matter how rich and powerful and handsome he is.

3. For a long time I have been loyal
   To such a lordly authority;
   No torment, no suffering, no fear,
   No bad treatment has ever driven me away.   20
   That's why they are saying behind my back
   That I have never gotten any profit out of love.
   They are lying; for I've had goods and pleasure from love
   And I've also put up with set-backs and deceit.

4. I feel ashamed for any good lady   25
   When she does something which lowers her reputation.
   Should I become a villainous fault-finder
   Just because an unworthy lady is betraying me?[1]
   No, because it would please her
   If I were to make her the subject of rumors.   30
   Worthless women don't suffer from having been caught cheating;
   Jokes and arguments about them only raise their self-esteem.

5. Let other people's reputation decline
   While the honor of My-Lord grows and climbs;
   For just as the rose and the gladiolus   35
   Become more beautiful when the summer returns,
   The season in which my lady knows to increase her beauty
   With lovely manners and charming ways
   Lasts all year long.
   Thus her conduct and reputation increase in value.   40

6. Because of her I love fountains and rivers,
   Woods, orchards, fields and gardens,
   Ladies, the valorous and cowardly,
   And the wise, crazy and stupid ones
   From that noble land   45
   She lives in and the lands around it.
   My thoughts are so turned in that direction
   That I don't believe there exists any other land or people.

7. Lady Alazais de Boisanso
   Makes her already good reputation better.   50

May anyone who is ever ungracious to her lose God,
For she is following up so well on a beautiful beginning.

8. A new love commands me
To serve her in such a way
That in Miraval shall be founded a home 55
For the goods of love and all true promises.[2]

This song is also discussed in razo 66.

[1] I follow Switten here in translating "domneta" as "unworthy" (204). Note that Raimon again veers into the mala chanso mode at this point, supposedly to contrast the new lady's behavior with that of the old one.

[2] This final tornada is not included in manuscript H, the only one containing the razo.

Song 406, 38   Raimon de Miraval: "S'ieu en chantar soven..."
　　　　　　　Source: Topsfield, 150.
　　　　　　　MSS: A 45, B 31, C 78, D 95-330, E 38, I 68,
　　　　　　　　　K 53, N 219-342, R 83-706, b[1] 6.

1. If I don't often feel like singing,
Or give it much attention,
Do not think that it is because
I am lacking in skill, subject matter
Or amorous desire. 5
The thing I most want to do
Is to have joy and song;
And I have so many things to sing about
That I could go on singing for quite some time.
But I don't want you to know everything I know. 10

2. For a long time now I have loved
Someone with whom no pleasure

Or service I've provided
   Has done me any good at all.
   None of my prayers or songs,   15
   Or my hiding and fearing,
   Have kept me from being deceived.
   But, while putting up with my damages,
   I found a way to deceive her even as she was deceiving me,
   And thus to stay at peace with her.   20

3. Otherwise it wouldn't look good for me,
   Since the sight of her failing
   Had already been noted,
   To keep seeking her betterment
   Until a state of equal availability   25
   Was reached for both parties.
   She acted on her own desires
   So I'm out pursuing mine.
   This is a more equitable deal[1]
   Than if I were to leave her in anger.   30

4. Any lover who takes any other
   Vengeance on His-Lord
   Doesn't know what it is to go to bed together.
   Nasty rumors and arguments
   Can make an otherwise discreet man too free with his tongue.
   Besides, it's not being sincere   36
   When a lady pretends
   To want to be courted
   By someone who will never be intimate with her,
   And then considers him to have been been duly paid. 40

5. When I present myself
   At my chosen spot
   My behavior is
   Neither falsely flattering nor deceptive.
   Why, I am more fearful than a young boy   45
   When I'm there, in the presence of her power.
   May God grant me this much
   When I find a worthy lady:
   That having gone through all that trouble for her
   I find the prize honorable!   50

6. Down here in Minerva
   The Marquise
   Raises on high everything that speaks of youth
   And noble, worthy reputation;
   So much so that there are few among us   55
   Whose own value doesn't rise.
   If, however, I say this with some fear
   It is because I may be courting enemies;
   And just because there is no favor granted me over there
   Doesn't mean I should be attracting enemies over here. 60

7. More-than-a-Friend, wherever I may go,
   You are the top of my song
   And the master of Miraval,
   But I don't want you to lose the ring.[2]

This song is also discussed in razo 65/63.

[1] This song is riddled with references to markets, value and exchange. This line reads: "Et es plus adreitz lo mercatz...": And the market/the deal/the exchange rate...". See also such expressions as "ben pagatz" (well-paid/satisfied) in line 40.

[2] This song is not contained in manuscript H, the only one in which the razo is found. We must assume that the author knew the song from elsewhere or that he had another manuscript before him even as he prepared the razos for H. It could also be that the razo was composed (written or recited) well before the compilation of the manuscript and that the scribe is simply setting down the entire text as he heard it, regardless of whether he knows the song.

Song 454, 1   Uc de Mataplana: "D'un sirventes m'es pres talens..."
               Source: Topsfield, 334 (based on P. Andraud).
               MSS: A 205, D 137-470, H 20, R 101-850.

1. A desire to compose a sirventes has come over me:
   My good sense shows me the subject and dictates it;
   And when I've finished, I will take the direct route
   To Miraval, running all the way

    To Sir Raimon, who is causing me some grief,   5
    For he is doing such dishonor
    To the practice of courtship, something he has always been
        proud of.
    Where he once stayed on the straight path
    Of the courtly lover, he is now having a change of heart.

2. In him there are now signs of   10
    The wise man's reproach:
    No man sees as well in himself
    The faults that he sees in others.
    For he used to put all his hope
    In joy and happiness,   15
    But now he's changed for the worse.
    He has put his talents to such a use
    That he can never deny that it's villainy.

3. For on account of her good behavior
    And the lovely songs she composes,   20
    He has sent away his courtly wife.
    It certainly seems like his resolve is up for sale.[1]
    He has left behind
    All hope of being anyone's lover
    For he wouldn't do these outrageous things   25
    That make all courtly people wish for his downfall
    If he were more interested in courtship and refined pleasures.

4. A husband who likes youth
    Must put up with certain behavior so that
    Those around him will put up with him.[2]   30
    But his opinion on all this has changed,
    And because he committed such a dishonorable deed,
    He is striving to reach an agreement with her.
    If he really wants her and likes the idea of getting her back
    Let him do a lot more about it   35
    So that she might put up with a lover who composes from the
        heart.

5. When he finally gets back with her
    Then his house will be joyful again,
    Provided that he doesn't criticize her
    For composing songs and pleasing lyrics;   40

And that he doesn't always doubt her;
And that he doesn't get all upset
If his house is often the site of courting;
For such a situation would be good for
Those of us who are courtly, and disastrous for the jealous
    types.   45

6. Lady Caudairenga, my lady, be aware
That I am bothered by all the rumors,
But there you are, close by your loyal heart.[3]

[1] OR: His attentions are now like paid servants/mercenaries.

[2] "Youth"/"joven" is one of those words that is charged with meaning in the lyrics but which has never been satisfactorily deciphered. "Youth" would seem to be a prerequisite for the participation in fin'amors. This may mean that there is an age limitation to these activities, though this is unlikely. It is more likely that it means an attitude toward received ideas, or an inferior status before elders.

[3] Uc de Mataplana was a patron of the troubadours as well as a poet himself. He was one of the favorites of Pedro II of Aragon and was killed during the battle of Muret. Raimon Vidal de Besalu made him the hero of his tale, *So fo el temps*, (B/S, 383), though Riquer (1972, p. 455-60) says he was fleeing from Muret, deserting his sovereign, Pedro II of Aragon, when he was killed (cited in Meneghetti, 192).

65./63.   Raimon de Miraval 406: 4, 27, 38; and Peire
             Vidal 364; 21 (B/S, 384)
            MSS: E 200, P 40, R 1.
            Base Text: E

You have certainly heard about Sir Raimon de Miraval, who he was and where he came from, in the razo that is written before his songs. For this reason I do not wish to talk about what I have already told you.[1]

But he loved a lady from the region of Carcassonne whose name was Lady Loba de Pennautier, the daughter of Sir R. de Pennautier, and she was the wife of a rich and powerful knight of Cabaret and the co-owner of the castle of Cabaret.[2]

La Loba was highly attractive, beautiful, courtly, learned and desirous of honor and repute. All the noble men and noble barons from that land and elsewhere who saw her paid her court, including the Count de Foix, Sir Olivier de Saissac, Sir Peire Roger of Mirepoix, Sir Aimeric de Montréal, and Sir Peire Vidal, who composed many beautiful songs about her.

Sir Raimon de Miraval truly loved her above all others, and he composed his songs about her and advanced her reputation and standing, in song and in speech, as would one who knows how to do this better than any knight in the world; and he did so in lovely stories with beautiful words. Loba accepted his beseechments and his attentions and promised to give him pleasure because of the exalted reputation which he had acquired for her and because he knew better how to make or break a lady's standing than any other man. She accepted his service and sealed the arrangement with a kiss. But she did not love him; nor did she ever say or do pleasing things to him except as a trick. She loved the Count de Foix, so much so that she had taken him as her lover. Their love and love affair were the talk of the whole country of Carcassonne and because of it she fell from her position of esteem and honor and lost her friends of both sexes and all because they considered a lady who would take as her lover a high-born baron as good as dead.

When Miraval heard the news about the awful thing she had done and the evil things that were being said about her, and learned that Peire Vidal had written a mala chanso about her which begins: "I was for a long time... " and in which he says in one stanza:

> My heart is resolutely against her
> For the evil that she has done.
> For she has thrown me over
> For a red-headed count.

> It is only too clear what Loba is
> When she takes up with a count
> And leaves in her wake an emperor
> Who has spread her praises
> Throughout the world.
> But he who lies does not tell the truth... (364, 21: 41-50)

he (Miraval) was sadder than all the rest and felt like saying evil things about her and ruining her. Then he realized it would be better to try to trick her like she had tricked him rather than just leave her in anger. So he began to go about defending her, covering up and making excuses for the whole affair with the Count of Foix.

Loba heard that Miraval was defending her and justifying the evil she had done in spite of the great sadness it had caused him. Miraval's defense made her happy for she had been more afraid of him than of all the others. She summoned him and, in tears, thanked him profusely for his support and defense. And so she said to him: "Miraval, if ever I had renown and merit and honor and friends of both sexes and was listened to and talked about, near and far, and had wisdom and courtliness, it was all due to your efforts; I owe it all to you. And as to why I have not done all that you wanted in the rights of love, it was not love of another that held me back each night. On the contrary, it was something you said in one of your songs which held me back, the one that says: Love makes me sing and rejoice:

> A good lady should not abandon loving
> And if she goes so far as to give in to love
> She musn't move too fast or make someone wait too long
> For all things are worth less when out of season..." (406, 4: 15-18)

"I wanted to give you so much pleasure as an honorable and just act[3], so that you would hold it dearer. I did not want to hurry, for it had been only two years and five months since I took you on with a kiss, as you said in your song:

> It's been two years and five months
> Since I took you into my service..." (406, 27: 49-50)[4]

"Now I see that you do not intend to abandon me over the false accusations and lies with which my enemies of both sexes dishonor me. This is why I want to tell you that since you are supporting me against all these people, I renounce everyone else in favor of you. I grant you my heart and body, with and about which you can do and say whatever you want. I place myself entirely in you, in your power and in your hands. I beg you only to defend me against my enemies of both sexes." Miraval accepted Loba's gift with great happiness and for a long time he had from her whatever he wished.[5]

But, before all this, he had fallen in love with the Marquise of Minerve, whose name was Gent Esquia of Minerve, a young, gay and noble lady, the wife of the Count of Minerve. She had never lied or cheated or been cheated upon or betrayed. It was for this lady that Miraval left Loba. And Miraval composed this song based on all of this and the song goes like this:

> If I don't often feel like singing
> Or give it much attention,
> Do not think that it is because
> I am lacking in skill, subject matter... (406, 38: 1-4)

That song is written here.[6]

[1] It is curious that the razo so explicitly states that the other informational text (presumably the vida) should be found in front of the songs when in all three of the manuscripts the vidas and razos are clustered together, separate from the songs. This clearly indicates that at least in these manuscripts the texts have been preserved from some other source and that the later manuscripts (here E, P and R) are merely collections which do not pretend to follow the performance practice of having vidas precede songs.

[2] This is the same Loba for whom Peire Vidal dressed as a wolf and submitted to a beating by shepherds. See razo 57 above.

[3] The text uses the word 'razo' here, as in: "I wanted to give you so much pleasure, like an honorable razo."

[4] The song actually reads: "Since she took me into her service."

[5] This passage is as close as one gets to an admission of sexual fulfillment between poet and patron. Note that the terms are still loaded in favor of the poet "getting" and "taking" what he desires, as if sexual favors were yet another commodity.

[6] Several of the figures mentioned in the razo have been tentatively identified. The Count of Foix, Raimon-Roger de Foix was famous in his time for his depraved morals, according to

Andraud (107). Peire Rogier de Mirapoix is not the troubadour of the same name. Gent Esquia de Minerve is addressed as a woman here. In fact, the lord of one of the fortresses of Minerve was named Esquieu, so the poet could be referring either to him or to his wife in using the feminized form of the name. (B/S, 391)

Song 406, 4   Raimon de Miraval: "Amors me fai chantar et esbaudir..."
Source: Topsfield, 173.
MSS: A 49, C 77, D 97-340, E 39, I 71, K 55, R 86-730, b^2 21.

1. Love makes me sing and feel happy;
Then it takes away my enjoyment with the worry that it brings me
And turns all my pleasure into worry!
Therefore, if my song isn't exceptionally good
I shouldn't be criticized for it.   5
Yet I've decided to sing a song of my own free will
About those who seek love, about lovers, and about their lady friends.

2. But I don't at all intend to permit ladies to do
What they are rightfully reproached for doing,
For there are some who don't even want to listen   10
At the moment that their love is most sought after;
Then, when youth steals away his beauty,
They end up taking the worst of the lot, the one they disdained,
Like the Lombard did with the figs.[1]

3. A good lady should not abandon loving;   15
And if she goes so far as to give in to love,
She musn't move too fast, or make someone wait too long,
For all things are worth less when out of season.
But know how to hide the truth!
For those who could be trusted confidants in other affairs 20
Could be obstacles when it comes to love.

4. The beauty I most love must never think
   That I am lecturing her, or criticizing her or telling her what to do,
   For she knows so well when to step back and what to do and say
   That I wouldn't bother adding anything to what she already knows. 25
   And since she enjoys keeping me hidden,
   I, for the same three reasons that all lovers are loved,
   Could do her a lot of good; tell her that for me.

5. If ever I have done anything which caused my lady to get angry,
   May God never forgive her if she pardons me; 30
   For I don't want to deceive her or betray her
   Or defend what she is blaming.
   Anything that she honors will be honored by me
   And anything she welcomes, I welcome,
   And so I have wars and enemies. 35

6. Good lady, out of all those I have courted
   I want you before all other ladies
   To have my songs and keep Miraval as your vassal.

7. More-than-a-Friend, although your heart is angry with me,
   I have saved Miraval for your use 40
   And I end up with enemies so that you can have it.[2]

8. Cloak of reason, merit, beauty
   And youth, I see you so nobly honored
   That there are many ladies here angry about it.

---

[1] This reference is unclear, though it may refer to a fabliau-like tale about Lombards (synonymous with bankers, or the rich, in much of the literature of the period) being rich and cheap and ending up with the worst figs in the bunch. It also likely refers to the hand gesture common in Italy, "to make the fig," a reference to female genitalia. See Topsfield 177.

[2] These last two tornadas are found only in mss. I and K, i.e., in manuscripts that do not contain the razo to this song. They seem to

refer, once again, to political alliances more than to affairs of the heart.

Song 406: 27   Raimon de Miraval: "Enquer non a guaire..."
                Source: Topsfield, 156.
                MSS: C 83, H 56.

1. It was my opinion[1]
   Until just recently
   That I would not be happy enough this year
   To go in for singing.
   But I can't keep myself   5
   From setting out my complaint in a new song,
   For the many-colored branches
   And each of the birds I hear singing
   Consoles my heart
   From the harm that has been directed at me   10
   By My-Lord, the most beautiful in the world,
   For whom I am dying of desire.
   Alas! How lovingly she looked at me
   When first I approached her!
   But now she's changing on me,   15
   Just when she should be bringing me along;
   And I, like a true lover,
   Beg for her mercy and endure the pain.

2. If I have acted as I should toward her,
   Honest and submissive,   20
   And don't even wish to admit what harm I've suffered,
   Why does she take away from me
   What good she used to grant me
   And go on putting distance between her lovely presence and
       myself?
   I can find no other site   25
   That attracts me,
   For she makes me look down upon
   Any other against whom I have sinned.
   Thus, if she wants to undo me
   Just let her see if I turn against her.   30

253

I won't become her enemy even for that.
I'll spend all my time going about invoking her name
And bemoaning my past joy
Which I have now lost by her own sweet command.
And still no one can reproach me, 35
For I have never deceived her, here or there.

3. Messenger, my beautiful Brother,
For the sake of your father's soul
Go to my lady and tell her in song
That I am no traitor to her, 40
No false lover, no cheating man
Who goes around turning this way and that.
No, I'm good at enduring pain,
Not at cheating,
And I don't go around bragging about a good deed done. 45
I am like the prudent thief,
Quiet and discreet,
So that no one can find out what I'm after.
It's been two years and five months
Since she first took me into her service; 50
She must have done it without offering the kiss.
But now they go around whispering and laughing,
Saying it's about time she made her intentions clear to me;
Otherwise I'll leave her service once and for all.

4. Lial, henceforth I hold onto my song 55
And Miraval thanks to my Cloak,
But I sigh because I am not there before it.
I have such a great desire to see it
But I shall not put off for a moment
Setting off to see my Audiart.[2] 60

---

[1] This song is preserved in only two manuscripts, neither of which contains the razo.

[2] As for the senhals, Fraire, Lial and Mantel, Bertran de Born used "Brother" (Fraire) to refer to Guillem de Berguedan; it is also used by Peire Vidal and Raimbaut d'Aurenga. (Stronski, *Folquet de Marseilles*, 31; Hoepffner, *Peire Vidal*, 60; and Topsfield, 160.) Audiart is Raimon's usual senhal for Raimon VI of Toulouse.

Mantel and Lial are not definitively identified; Topsfield considers them ladies about whom Raimon sang.

Song 406, 38 can be found under razo 63/65 above.

Song 364, 21 Peire de Vidal: "Estat ai en gran sazo..."
Source: D'Arco Silvio Avalle, 94.
MSS: C 39, D^a 163-567, H 26, M 51, Q 75, R 47-392, S 15-9, e 47.
Other English translations: Blackburn, 118.

1. For a long time I have been
Miserable and worried,
But now I am more sprightly
Than any bird or fish
Since my lady sent me   5
A message saying she might take me back
In the capacity of lover.
Oh! What sweet pleasure
That brings me: that she would deign to permit me
To return to a state of good hope.   10

2. For I cannot be happy,
Even if God were to forgive me,
Until I hurry back
To the sweet prison
Into which her beauty placed me.   15
She is of a courtly demeanor,
Full of joy and sweetness.
This is why I want
No earthly treasures or goods
As much as I want to fulfill her every desire.   20

3. The effect upon me is so good and beautiful
When I look upon her face

   And lovely, loving eyes,
   That I don't even know where I am.
   She has caught me and taken me;   25
   Won me over and captured me,
   And I cannot turn my eyes
   Or love in any other direction.
   All it takes is to look at her
   For my whole being to rejoice.   30

4. Lady, in the name of God on his throne
   May you give me your friendship,
   Consideration, mercy,
   Prayers, and good faith,
   Since I give myself to you,   35
   Humble and with an open heart.
   If you do, it will be to your honor;
   For I am greatly afraid
   That desire, from whom I can't take much more,
   Will overcome me entirely.   40

5. I now have such anger in my heart
   Against one who was never evil before;
   For she has abandoned me
   For a red-headed count,
   And it seems to me that she really is a wolf.   45
   She is rushing off with a count
   And leaving behind an emperor[1]
   Who has sung her praises
   So that all the world would know them.
   But anyone who lies does not tell the truth.[2]   50

6. May God save the honored marquis
   And his beautiful sister[3]
   For with her true love
   She was able to conquer me graciously
   And keep me even more graciously in her service.   55

7. Daughter of a king, it is good that you caught me
   For I gave up a false love,
   Earned more on account of it,
   And learned how to make myself more valuable,
   And how to please and speak of pleasure.   60

[1] The Emperor is Peire himself. See note 1 to song 364, 48, under razo 56, above.
[2] Ms. R, the only razo manuscript containing this song, gives this line as: "Anyone who tells the truth isn't telling a lie."
[3] The marquis is Bonifacio I of Montferrat. His sister is Azalais, about whom Raimbaut de Vaqueiras also sang. Razo 71 to Raimbaut's song 391, 2 says that Azalais permitted Peire Vidal to sing of her. The "daughter of a king" mentioned in the final tornada is not easily identified. For various hypotheses, see Avalle, 97.

Song 406, 38 can be found under razo 64.
Song 364, 21 can be found under razo 63/65.

66. Raimon de Miraval 406: 8, 28 and 15.
(B/S, 392)
MSS: E 202-203, P 40, R 2.

You have heard about Sir Raimon de Miraval and how he found out how to deceive la Loba and stay on with her in peace. But now I will tell you about how Lady Alazais of Boissezo tricked him and how later her neighbor, Lady Esmenjarda of Castres, the one they called 'The Beauty of Albi', did so as well. They were both from the bishopric of Albi. Lady Alazais was from a castle named Lombers and was the wife of Sir Bernart de Boissezo. Lady Aimenguarda was from a city called Castres. She was the wife of a rich vavassor who was quite old.[1]

Raimon de Miraval fell in love with Lady Alazais de Boissezo, a young, noble, and beautiful lady, highly desirous of renown, honor and praise. And because she knew that Sir Miraval was more able to bring her renown and honor than any man on earth, she was very happy when she saw that he was in love with her. She showed him all the right signs and said to him all the pleasing things that a lady should say and do to a knight; and he brought her esteem through song and stories, as well as he could and knew how. He composed many beautiful songs about her, praising her reputation, her merit and her courtliness. He brought her to such a position of honor that all the noble barons of that country began to pay her court: the Viscount of Beziers, the Count of Toulouse, and King Peire of Aragon, to whom Miraval had so praised her that he fell in love with her without ever having seen her. He (the king) had sent her his messengers with letters and presents and he himself was dying to see her. Miraval went to great lengths to arrange for the king to come and see her and composed a stanza about it in one of his songs which says: "Now with the force of the cold..."

> If the king is courting at Lombers
> Joy will forever more be with him;
> And though he is already exceptionally sharp,
> This time he'll get two for the price of one:
> For the courtesy and joy
> Of the beautiful Lady Alazais,
> Her fresh coloring and blond hair
> Make the whole world rejoice. (406, 8: 41-48)

So the king came to Albi and to Lombers to see Lady Alazais. Sir Miraval came along with the king, who asked him to make him look good and help him with Lady Alazais. The king was singled-out and honored and was seen by Lady Alazais as he wished. And as soon as he was seated beside her, he asked for her love and she answered immediately that he could do anything he wished. So that night the king got everything he wanted from her. And by the next day the story was known throughout the castle and by everyone at the king's court. And Sir Miraval, who had expected to be rich with joy from his beseechments to the king, heard the news. He was sad and mournful and went away, leaving the king. He complained for a long time about the evil the lady had done and the crime that the king had committed against him. He composed this song about this whole affair and it says:

> I am torn between two desires...(406, 28:1)

and it is written here.

I have told you about how Lady Alazais de Boissezo tricked Miraval, betrayed him and thus killed herself.[2] Now I wish to tell you how Lady Aimenjarda de Castres, she who was known as the Beauty of Albi, as I told you in another spot, tricked and betrayed him.

Lady Aimenjarda de Castres knew that Lady Alazais de Boisazo had tricked and betrayed him so she sent for Miraval and he came. She told him she was sorry about what was being said about Lady Alazais and sorry also about his pain over her shameful deed. She said that she had the heart and will to make amends to him with her own self for the evil that Lady Alazais had done to him. He was easy to trick once he had seen the signs of love that she was showing him and heard the tempting words with which she presented the offer of reparation for the damage that he had suffered. He answered that he would be very willing to accept amends from her for the damages inflicted on him by Lady Alazais. So she went and took him on as her knight and servant.

Sir Miraval began to praise her and thank her and advance her reputation, honor, nobility, beauty and youth. The lady had intelligence, wisdom and courtesy and knew how to reward her male and female friends. Sir Oliver de Saissac, a noble baron from that land, was courting her and she was telling him to take her as his wife. When Sir Miraval saw that he had succeeded in advancing her honor and reputation, he wanted to get his reward, so he begged her to give him pleasure in the rights of love. She answered that she would not give him love for the sake of sensual satisfaction alone; that she would first want to make him her husband so that their love could never come apart or be broken and that he would have to leave his wife, whose name was Lady Caudairenca.

Miraval was very happy when he heard that she wanted to have him as her husband. He returned to his castle and told his wife that he didn't want to have a wife who knew how to compose songs; that one troubadour was enough in a household. He told her to pack up and go to her father's house for he would no longer keep her as his wife. She, meanwhile, was courting a knight whose name was Guilem Bremon, and it was about him that she composed her dances. When she heard what Miraval was telling her, she pretended to be very angry and she said she wished to send for her family and friends. She then sent for Sir Guilem Bremon, telling him to come and get her, for she wanted to take him as her husband. Guilem Bremon was very happy when he heard the news. He gathered his knights, climbed upon his horse and came straight to the castle of Miraval and dismounted at the gate. Lady Caudairenca found out that he was there and told Sir Miraval that her family and friends had come for her and that she wished to leave with them. Miraval was very happy and his wife even more so. The lady got ready to leave and Miraval led her outside where he found Guilem Bremon and his companions. He gave them a fine welcome. When the lady was ready to mount her horse, she told Miraval that since it was his wish to leave her, that he should give her over as wife to Sir Guilem Bremon. Miraval said he would gladly do what she wished. Sir Guilem stepped forward and took the marriage ring. Sir Miraval gave him the lady as his wife and Guilem then took her away.

After Miraval had sent his wife away, he went to Lady Aimenjarda and told her that he had obeyed her order by leaving his wife and marrying her to another man; and that she should now do and say what she had promised him. The lady told him that he had done well and that he should now go to his castle to get ready to welcome her there and that he should be ready to come for her, as she would be calling for him soon.

Miraval went off and completed his preparations to go and bring her to his castle and have a big wedding celebration. But she sent for Sir Olivier de Saissac and he came straightaway. She told him that she had the heart and will to do anything he wanted and to take him as her husband. He was the happiest man in the world. And they arranged things in such a way that that very evening he took her to his castle and the next day they were married. And they had a big wedding and held great court.

The news reached Sir Miraval that the lady had taken Sir Olivier de Saissac as her husband. He was sad and mournful that she had made him give up his wife and had promised him to take him as her husband and that he had made all the arrangements for their wedding. He was also still suffering over what Lady Alazais de Boisazo had done with the King of Aragon. He lost all his joy and happiness, his affability, and his desire to sing and compose songs; and for two years he was like a lost man and many troubadour knights made fun of him on account of the lies that the ladies had made up about him.

But one noble young lady, whose name was Lady Bruneisens de Cabaret, the wife of Sir Peire Rotgier de Cabaret, and who was desirous of honor and reputation, sent for him with warm and comforting words, beseeching him to be happy again through love of her. She told him that he should know that she would come to see him if he didn't come to see her, and that she would show him so much love that he would know for sure that she had no desire to trick him. It is for that reason that he composed this song, which you will hear:

To the messenger, I wish him well... (406, 15).

[1] Most of the characters here have been identified in the previous texts by and about Raimon de Miraval. Alazais de Boissezon is not mentioned in any contemporary documents but is mentioned in several of Raimon's songs. Bruneissen de Cabaret, the final lady mentioned in this razo, is unknown as well.

[2] That is, she destroyed her own reputation in the all-important public sphere. Presumably Raimon de Miraval would get his revenge by writing a mala chanso which would expose her perfidy to the community and make of her a pariah. In general, this is one of the most telling of the razos as concerns the role that the troubadour played for his lady. Even though these episodes are clearly fictionalized accounts of inferences taken from the songs, the razo author has added details about the poet/patron relationship which are intended to make the treachery of the ladies seem plausible. It is therefore likely that this structure is itself intended to seem normal if it has been added to lend credence to the details of the scenes of betrayal.

Song 406, 8   Raimon de Miraval: "Er ab la forsa dels freys..."
Source: Topsfield 232.
MSS: A 45, C 85, D 97-337, D^c 253, E 37, I 70, K 54, L 144, N 220-343, R 87-736, a^1 320.
Other English translations: Switten, 153.

1. Now, when all the world trembles and creaks
   Under the force of the cold,
   Courtship, refined conversation and songs
   About every lovely pleasure are more valued
   Than during the season when leaves and flowers bloom.   5
   It seems to me that anyone who is noble and gay,
   In spite of the weather and the world,
   Must have an abundance of goodness in his heart.

2. In love there are many laws
   And on all sides they lead to   10
   Wrong-doing, wars and treaties.
   Quickly it comes and quickly it goes;
   It is quickly appeased and quick to take offense.

Anyone who is true to it
   Sighs often and deeply   15
   And must serve and hide his many sorrows.

3. So far it has never tormented me that much,
   But now it has found me with someone
   Who inspires fear and anxiety,
   Grieves me, tortures me and destroys me.   20
   And still, for all of that, I do not give up on the idea
   That I shouldn't take my desiring heart
   From there, the source of my terror,
   Where desires most destroy me.

4. The great beauty one sees   25
   In the beautiful lady whose vassal I am,
   And her rich reputation, which grows by the day,
   Have taken away my desire to court anyone else.
   But one sweet look attracted me
   To that beautiful lady, with whom I need never fear   30
   Hunger, cold or lack of sleep;
   If only she had the heart to give me the answer I'm waiting for.

5. Although it's ridiculous,
   My good hope leads me on;
   And even if she were to say worse things to me   35
   I wouldn't want to go back there from where I flee.
   Since it has now come to the test,
   She has the power to bring me up or down;[1]
   And I won't run away from her,--I don't even want to know
      where I could go--
   Even if she shaves me or shears me.   40

6. If the king is courting at Lombers,
   Joy will forever more be with him;
   And though he is already exceptionally sharp,
   This time he'll get two for the price of one:
   For the courtliness and joy   45
   Of the beautiful Lady Alazais
   And her fresh coloring and blond hair
   Make all the world rejoice.

7. Lady, I am so true to you
   That I want Miraval to help you   50
   In all your courtly affairs.
   But I don't dare say who you are or where you come from.²

8. I am gay on account of my Audiart
   For all people enthusiastically³
   Prize Count Raimon   55
   More than any other count in the world.

¹ This passage is ambiguous and seems to imply that the poet wants to be brought back up to his former prestige, i.e. reestablished. His images of rising up and lowering, shaving ("ras") and shearing ("ton") seem to refer to the Biblical tale of Samson and Delilah. They are also highly suggestive of castration and this passage could easily have been interpreted comically.
² Of the manuscripts that contain the razo, this first tornada is only found in R. The second one is not in any of the razo manuscripts.
³ The text given by Topsfield, based on manuscript C, reads: "ad eslays", i.e. enthusiastically, without any hesitation. Topsfield notes that this may be a case of word play, suggesting the lady's name, Alazais.

Songs 406, 28 and 15 can be found under razo 64, above.

67. Raimon de Miraval 406, 12 (B/S, 404).
    MSS: E 203, P 41, R 2.
    Base Text: E.

When the Count of Toulouse had been disinherited by the Church and by the French and had lost Argensa and Belcaire; and the French had taken Saint-Gilles and the area around Albi and Carcassonne; and Beziers had been destroyed, and the Viscount of Beziers was dead, and all the good people from that land had been killed or had fled to Toulouse; Miraval was with the Count of Toulouse, the one with whom he shared the name "Audiartz." He lived in a state of great sorrow because all the good people for whom the count had served as master and lord, both ladies and knights, were now dead and dispossessed. Moreover, he had lost his wife, as you will hear; his lady had cheated and tricked him; and he had lost his castle.[1]

And it so happened that the King of Aragon came to Toulouse to speak to the count and to see his sisters, Lady Elienor and Lady Sancha. He greatly comforted his sisters and the count and his godson and the good people of Toulouse and he promised the count that he would get back Belcaire and Carcassonne for him, and for Miraval, his castle; and that he would do what he could to see that the good people recover the joy that they had lost.[2]

Sir Miraval was overjoyed with the king's promise to himself and to the count to return all that they had lost with the coming of summer. He had previously resolved to compose no songs until he had recovered the castle of Miraval that he had lost, but because he had fallen in love with Lady Elienor, the count's wife and the finest and most beautiful woman in the world, to whom he had not yet shown any signs of his love, he composed this song which says:

It pleases me to sing and be refined
For the air is sweet and the season gay..., (406, 12: 1-2)

which you will now hear for it is written here.

When he had finished the song, he sent it to the king in Aragon. This is why the king returned with a thousand knights to come to the aid of the count of Toulouse--to keep his promise to recover the land that the count had lost. And this is how it came to pass that the king was killed by the French before the walls of Muret and all his thousand knights with him, for not one of them escaped.[3]

[1] Argensa, Beaucaire and Saint-Gilles are in the arrondissement of Nîmes. See notes to the previous razo for information on the principals. The Viscount of Bézier's death is also mentioned in razo 4 to Arnaut de Mareuil's song 30, 19.

² Elienor was the sister of Pedro II and was married to Raimon VI of Toulouse. Her sister, Sancha, married Raimon VII.

³ The razo author attributes great power to Raimon's songs and B/S consider this a sign of naïveté. While the statement is no doubt exaggerated, it does indicate that the author considered the songs to have played an important role in the political arena. Perdigon's vida includes a very similar exposition of the events surrounding the king's death at Muret (B/S, 407 and 408; Egan, 83).

Song 406, 12 can be found under razo 64, above.

68. Lombarda and Bernard N'Arnaut 54, 1 and 288, 1
 (B/S, 416)
 MS: H 43.

Lady Lombarda was a noble, beautiful, attractive and learned lady from Toulouse. She knew how to compose songs and she used to compose beautiful verses about love. Because of this, Bernart N'Arnaut, the brother of the Count of Armagnac, heard talk of her goodness and nobility, and so he came to Toulouse to see her. He was on intimate terms with her, asked her for her love and was her close friend. He wrote these verses about her and sent them to her at her home. Then he got on his horse, without first seeing her, and went off to his own land:

1. I would like to be "Lombard" for Lady Lombarda
 For Alamanda doesn't please me as much and neither
  does Giscarda.
 With her lovely eyes she looks at me so sweetly
 That it seems like she is giving me her love; but she
  makes me wait too long;
 For she holds back on her beautiful glance 5
 And my own pleasure

    And keeps for herself her lovely smile
    And no one can get them away from her.

2. Sir Jordan, I leave you Allemagne (Germany)[1]
  France and Poitiers, Normandy and Brittany;   10
  So you should leave me, without any dispute,
  Lombardia, Livorno and Lomagna.
    And if you can help me
    I will help you ten times over
    With her who distances herself   15
    From anything hinting of bad repute.[2]

3.   Mirror of Merit,
    You have consolation.
    May this love in which you hold me
    Never be broken for the sake of someone unworthy.[3]

Lady Lombarda was greatly amazed when she heard that Bernart Arnaut had gone off without seeing her and she sent him this poem:

4. For Bernard I would like to take the name Bernarda, 21
  And for Sir Arnaut I'd be called Lady Arnauda.[4]
  And I thank you very much, sir, for being so kind as to name me
  With two such ladies.
    I want you to tell me   25
    Which one you like better
    Without keeping anything covered or hidden;
    And about this mirror in which you see yourself.

5. For the mirror and the state of not-seeing bring such discord
  To my accord (togetherness) that it's a wonder I don't disaccord
    completely (come apart);   30
  But when I record (remember) what my name records (signifies)
  It is with full accord that my thoughts reaccord (come back
    together).
    It is your heart/body that worries me.
    Where have you put it?
    For I see no house or hut   35
    These, you silence.

[1] This song is full of word-play, as I have tried to indicate within the translation. Allemagne is here a reference both to a place and to the lady's name, Alamanda, in the first stanza; just as Lombarda's name is used to indicate a lady, a place (Lombardia), and a source of wealth ("Lombard" being a standard reference to bankers). These are the only verses known to have been written by Bernart but he is mentioned by Raimon Vidal in *Abrils issia* as one of the protectors of the troubadours. This is also the only song known to have been written by Lombarda, whose vida says she is from Toulouse. B/S identify Alamanda as the lady sung of by Guiraut de Borneilh. Giscarda is mentioned by Bertran de Born in songs 80, 1; 80, 10; and 80, 12 (See B/S, 419).

[2] The bad repute in question is both the potential lover's and her own.

[3] The "vila" (unworthy one) in question refers to "vilain," a common man, and to the feminine form of "vil," meaning a disgraced woman. Bernart is implicating Lombarda's own behavior in the contract (mirror) that he has established with her, as well as referring to the intrusion of a third and unworthy party.

[4] These lines can be translated in two opposite ways, which both paradoxically come down to the same thing. Either Lombarda *will* take on her pretendants' names or she won't ("nom" meaning either "not for me" or "name"). In either case, she responds to Bernart's opening line by categorically refusing him access to her name, which also implies access to her fortune and body. (See Sankovich, 1989: 190.)

The verses from song 54, 1 and 288,1 cited in this razo are the only source for this song. Other English translations can be found in Bogin, 114 and Sankovich, 1989: 188.

69. Almuc de Castelnou and Iseut de Capio 20,2 and 253, 1 (B/S, 422)
MS: H 45.

Lady Iseut of Capieu begged Lady Almue(i)s of Castelnou to pardon her knight, Sir Gigo of Tornen, who had committed a grave offense against her and did not repent or even ask for pardon:

Please, Lady Almues,
I wish to address to you this plea:
That mercy for him put an end
To your anger and bad feeling;
For he sighs and moans,
Dies languishing and complains,
Begs humbly for your pardon.
I make a pledge to you on his behalf:
That even though you wish to end it with him,
He will be much more careful about ever committing an offense.
(253, 1)

Lady Almus, who loved Sir Gigo de Torna, was greatly saddened, because he wasn't asking for pardon for his offense. This verse tells how she answered Lady Iseuz:

Lady Iseuz, if I knew
That he was sorry for the deceitfulness
He has shown toward me in such great measure
It would only be right to show him
Mercy; but I say this isn't the case,
For he does not turn from his wrong-doing
Nor repent for his offense;
I no longer have any choice.
But if you make him repent
You will easily be able to convert me.[1]

[1] These verses are the only ones known to have been written by both of these trobairitz. Almucs has been identified as the wife of Guigue de Châteauneuf-de-Randon (B/S, 424).

The verses of song 20, 2 and 253, 1 found in this razo are the only source for this song. Another English translation can be found in Bogin, 92.

70. Raimbaut de Vaqueiras 392, 20 and 392, 24
   (B/S, 451)
   MS: P 43.

Rambautz de Vaqeras was from a castle called Vacheras. He was the son of a poor knight whose name was Peirol and who was thought to be crazy.[1]

Rambaut became a jongleur and was for a long time with the Prince of Orange, whose name was Sir Guillelm de Baux. He was good at singing and at composing verses and sirventes. And the Prince of Orange rewarded him with great goods and honor, advanced his reputation, and made sure that he was known and esteemed by all the noble folk.

He then went to Montferrat, to the marquis, Bonifacis. He spent a lot of time with him and rose so much further in the arts of arms and poetry that he was greatly esteemed at the court. The marquis made him a knight and his companion at arms and dress because of the valor he knew he had within him.[2]

He (Raimbaut) then fell in love with the marquis' sister, whose name was Lady Biatrix, the wife of Enric of Carretto. He composed many beautiful songs about her and called her "Beautiful Knight."[3]

And this is why he called her by that name: fate had it that Sir Rambaut was able to see lady Biatrix whenever he wished, through a narrow window, provided that she was in her bedroom; and no one could see him doing so.

One day the marquis came back from hunting. He went into the bedroom, put his sword beside the bed, and went back out. Lady Biatrix stayed in the bedroom. She took off her dress and remained in her underdress. She took the sword and put it on in the manner of a knight. She took it out of its sheath; raised it up high; then took it in her hand and brought it down to her arm over one shoulder and then the other. Then she replaced it in its sheath, took it off and put it back in its place beside the bed.

Sir Ranbauz de Vaqera saw all that I have just told you through the narrow window. And this is why he called her from then on "Beautiful knight" in his songs, as he does in the first stanza of this song which begins like this:

> *I never thought I'd see the day*
> *When Love would so control me*
> *That a lady could hold me*
> *Entirely in her power;*
> *For in the old days I could be haughty*
> *To match their haughtiness.*
> *But now the youth and beauty,*
> *The noble, pleasing body*
> *And the gay and charming words*
> *Of my Beautiful-Knight*
> *Have tamed my wild spirit.*
> *And since a hard heart submits*
> *To love in a a precious place,*
> *It knows better how to love a lady*
> *Than a humble man, too much in love,*
> *And desirous of them all.* (392, 20: 1-16)

It was believed that she loved him in the true sense of love. And he spent a long time with the marquis and had much good fortune while in his company.

When the marquis went to Romania he brought with him Sir Ranbaut de Vaqera.

He (Raimbaut) suffered great sadness over this departure on account of his love for his lady, who stayed behind with us.[4] *He would willingly have stayed behind as well. But because of his love for the marquis and for all the honor that he had brought him, he did not dare refuse to go. And so he left with him. At all times he did his best to excel at war and in the use of arms and all other praiseworthy acts. He acquired great honors and wealth. But in spite of all this, he did not forget his sadness, as he says in the fourth stanza of this song which begins:*

> *Neither winter nor spring delights me...* (392, 24: 1)

and in another stanza which says:

> *What then do conquest and riches avail me?*
> *I thought of myself as being far wealthier*
> *When I was loved; was a fine lover;*

And was nourished by the love I shared with Sir Engles.
I loved even just one pleasure from those days
More than the great riches and courts over here.
For now, when my powers are expanding,
I feel a great sadness within myself
Because my beloved Beautiful Knight
And joy are far away and out of sight.
And my consolation will die out without them
This is why my anguish is growing greater and ever stronger...
                                            (392, 24: 37-48)

This is how he lived, Rambaut de Vazera, just as you have heard, and displayed a more pleasant demeanor than what his heart really inspired.

He had a large estate that the marquis had given him in the kingdom of Salonica and it is there that he died.

[1] The first portion of this text is essentially the vida text that is found in ten other manuscripts. The razo portion begins with the interpolation (the italicized portion) found only in manuscript P.
[2] See razo 60 to Peire Vidal's songs 364: 2, 36, 37 and 48 for another instance in which this terminology is used to indicate that the poet had become the most intimate of the lord's companions.
[3] This entire sequence can be read as an allegory for the sexual and political drama of the triangular poet-patron-lady relation.
[4] This collective "us" is an unusual inclusion of the troubadour within the social group under discussion. As in razo 46 to Savaric de Malleo, it implies that the razo author is an eye witness to these events.

Song 392, 20　　Raimbaut de Vaqueiras: "Ja non cujei vezer..."
　　　　　　　　Source: Linskill, 174.
　　　　　　　　MSS: A 161, B 99, C 129, D 105-363, D^c 251, G 54, I 76, K 60, M 108, Q 48, R 62-518, S 131-82, Sg 54, 17, U 75, a^1 336, O 73 (anonymous).
　　　　　　　　Other English translations: Linskill, 178.

1. I never thought I'd see the day
   When love would so control me,
   That a lady could hold me
   Entirely in her power;
   For in the old days I could be haughty   5
   To match their haughtiness.
   But now the youth and beauty,
   The noble, pleasing body,
   And the gay and charming words
   Of my Beautiful-Knight   10
   Have tamed my wild spirit.
   And since a hard heart submits
   To love in a precious place,
   It knows better how to love a lady
   Than a humble man, too much in love,   15
   And desirous of them all.[1]

2. My lady alone can have me,
   And never any other,
   Because she is the noblest of all
   And she knows how to increase her worth.   20
   She is just as I want her to be:
   There is nothing to add or take away.
   She's lovely, gay and pleasing,
   Beautiful and gracious,
   And of undiminished reputation.   25
   She's wise when she needs to be
   And crazy when appropriate
   And there's nothing that she lacks.
   With deeds and grants
   She makes all men esteem her   30
   And the most worthy praise her,
   For they see in her even more qualities to praise.

3. If she decides to retain my services
   Just as she promised she would,
   I'll be pleased that love took me over.   35
   But she makes me wait too long
   For I am suffering from the desire
   That shows forth from her beautiful eyes
   And precious laughter.
   If she were to give me her noble body,   40

The thing for which I've been asking her consent,
   My conquest would far surpass
   The adventures of Gawain.²
   I remain at her mercy
   Since first she granted me permission   45
   To implore her
   And love her in secret
   And sing of her in my songs.

4. May God allow me to conquer her
   And may justice and faith stay with me,   50
   For I am entirely in her control
   And can't hold out much longer against her.
   When a lord welcomes a vassal
   Into his domain
   And the vassal shows him obedience,   55
   It doesn't take much effort for the lord to vanquish him!
   Thus, if My-Lord conquers me
   While I am offering my fine and true heart
   To her, or if she breaks
   My promise, she will gain nothing   60
   From my loss.
   But she will be blamed
   If I give her my service with no recompense
   And then she is pleased by my demise.

5. Lady, this makes me fear   65
   That the joy I've aimed for will fail me,
   For I have set my sights so high
   That I am now afraid of falling low.
   But I don't dress or undress
   With any sign of bad-tempered conduct.   70
   Secretly and fearfully,
   Humbly and patiently,
   I am yours, and my heart is not fickle.
   As the proverb says:
   "An honorable gift can redeem any wrong."   75
   This is why I am with you:
   For evil, stingy lords
   Bring their vassals down with them
   And the generous one furthers with his gifts
   Both himself and his companions.   80

6. With conversation and riches
   You are generous, excellent lady;
   There is nothing missing from you but mercy
   And it's mercy that I am asking you for.
   The fruit that we gather from the tree   85
   Appears right next to the leaf and flower;
   And mercy, when sought with simple honesty,
   Appears just as quickly
   Where there is already merit and good sense.
   A man could have gone and tamed   90
   A wild sparrow-hawk
   In the time that I've been complaining to you
   That I can find no mercy.
   How could God have fashioned
   Such beautiful features   95
   For a place where there was no mercy?

7. It's my misfortune that
   Your gracious and noble body so pleased me,
   For I am losing countless goods from other ladies.
   And this is why I have to leave them:[3]   100
   It's for you that I must leave them behind,
   Like Sir Gui d'Excideuil,
   Who, when the memory
   Of the loving queen came back to him,
   Lost the fairy in the orchard.[4]   105
   I go on,
   Waiting, crying, and moaning
   Over you; and I worry and complain
   About how I might conquer you,
   And how I should win you;   110
   For I'm losing out on others, on account of you,
   Others who would have brought me joy.

8. Good and worthy lady,
   Courtly and knowledgeable,
   Don't believe scandal-mongers   115
   Or jealous men who speak
   Against me, for it's with you that I will stay.
   I don't lament to others
   And cannot love any other lady;
   But I do want to serve them and honor them all   120

On account of you,
Who are the most beautiful and the most esteemed.

9. Worthy Lady Biatrix,
You are beautiful and pleasing,
And the ladies and knights,   125
And anyone else who stays by you,
Give you their undivided esteem.
You know how to say and give
To each of them his due,
And to save the best honors for the best of them.   130
If I speak well of you,
I have many companions in doing so!

---

[1] These lines could easily have been interpreted in a more erotic sense by reading "body" instead of "heart," thus implying that since the "hard" man knows how to give in before a "precious place", it makes him a better lover than a too humble man who does nothing but desire, i.e. the typical troubadour stance.

[2] Gauvain was one of the most respected knights of the Round Table in the Arthurian romances.

[3] This stanza is an excellent example of the way in which a troubadour might see his function in economic terms.

[4] Gui d'Esiduoill was the hero of a romance which has not survived, according to Linskill (see also Lewent, 1946).

Song 392, 24   Raimbaut de Vaqueiras: "No m'agrad'iverns ni pascors..."
Source: Linskill, 242.
MSS: A 163, B 100, C 124, D^a 181-644, D^c 252, I 77, K 61, M 105, N^2 10, R 61-514, S 133-83, Sg 50, T 188, U 78, a^1 338.
Other English translations: Goldin, 268; Linskill, 245.

1. Neither winter nor spring delights me,
Nor the sunshine, nor the oak leaves,

For my advancement seems like a loss of ground
   And all my greatest joys like sorrow.
   All my pleasures are pain 5
   And my hopes are but despair.
   Love and courtship used to
   Keep me gayer than water keeps a fish,
   But since I split with love,
   Like a ruined man in exile, 10
   Any other life seems like death to me
   And any other joy an affliction.

2. Since the flower of love is missing,
   Along with its sweet fruit, seed and ear,
   From which I got such joy and pleasant instruction; 15
   And honors and renown were mine in abundance,
   And I knew how to fit in with the most valorous,
   I am now plunged from high to low.
   Fear doesn't seem like folly to me:
   Never was a flame put out more quickly 20
   Than I was smothered and relinquished,
   Banished in word and deed,
   The day when the affliction hit;
   For its effects do not diminish, no matter how hard I struggle.

3. Fine armed men and excellent deliverers of blows, 25
   Sieges, catapults and pikes,
   Breaking through walls, old and new,
   Taking battles and towers,
   This I see and hear; and still I can't find
   A thing that can help my cause before love. 30
   I go off in my finest array, looking for
   Wars, skirmishes and tournaments
   And am enriched when I emerge the victor.
   But since the joy of love has eluded me
   All the world isn't worth a little garden to me[1] 35
   And my song no longer brings me any comfort.

4. What then do conquest and riches avail me?
   I thought of myself as being far wealthier
   When I was loved; was myself a fine lover;
   And was nourished by the love I shared with Sir Engles.[2]
   I loved even just one of the pleasures from those days 41

More than the great riches and lands I have here.
For now, when my powers keep growing,
I feel a great sadness within myself
Because my beloved Beautiful-Knight   45
And joy are far away and out of sight,
And my consolation will die out without them:
This is why my anguish grows greater and ever stronger.

5. My valor does not, however, command me
   To bring joy to my enemies   50
   By giving up my praise and renown,
   No matter how sad and angry I am.
   I can still give and withstand blows
   And even in anguish I know how to look joyous
   Here among the Latins and Greeks.   55
   The marquis, who fitted me with this sword,
   Is battling the Wallachians and Drogobites,
   And never since the world was created
   Has any people fought any harder than we,
   Whom God has mercifully delivered.³   60

6. For this the marquis is honored and exalted,
   As are the man from Champagne and Count Henry;
   Sicar, Montos and Salonica
   And Constantinople are saved,
   For those men know how to hold on to a piece of land; 65
   And any man can put that to the test, for it's the truth.
   Never before has any people attained
   Honor so great that it could match theirs.
   Our empire has been won by
   Good vassals, worthy and courageous,   70
   And may God send us reinforcements
   So that we may fulfill our destiny.⁴

7. Alexander never led such an honored expedition,
   Nor did Charlemagne or King Louis.
   Not even the excellent Sir Aimeric,⁵   75
   Or Roland with his warriors,
   Could have conquered with such ease
   An empire so rich with power
   As we have; thus the commandments of our Faith prosper.
   We have created emperors, dukes and kings, 80

Set up armed fortresses
Near the Turks and the Arabs
And opened up the roadways and ports
From Brindisi to the Straits of Saint George.

8. Through our efforts, Damascus will be invaded,   85
Jerusalem conquered,
And the kingdom of Syria liberated;
For the Turks find all this in their prophecies.

9. As for those despicable, lying pilgrims
Who deserted us here on the battlefield,   90
Anyone who supports them in his court is doing wrong,
For each is worth less living than dead.

10. Beautiful, sweet-mannered Englishman, honest, courageous,
Courtly, learned and distinguished,
You are the comfort to all my joys,   95
And since I must live without you, I just do my best.[6]

---

[1] A garden being the traditional site for courting, or a metonymical figure for the body of the lady.

[2] The persons referred to by the two senhals Bel-Cavalier and N'Engles (Beautiful-Knight and Englishman) have not been clearly identified, though hypotheses abound. Linskill concludes that Bel-Cavalier was used to refer to a highly placed lady at the court of Montferrat and that Englishman refers to Raimbaut's patron, Boniface of Montferrat. De Bartholomaeis acknowledges that Englishman refers to Boniface but says that in line 40 Raimon is referring to a lady. The razo author himself was anxious to show in the interpolated portion of the razo above that Bel-Cavalier is a lady rather than a man. I would maintain that the gender confusion is, as is often the case in these lyrics, intentional (see Linskill, 250).

[3] These are skirmishes in which Boniface participated during the fourth crusade. The Wallachians are the Wallacho-Bulgarians who had invaded the Latin empire in the East. The Drogobites were a Rumanian people inhabiting Macedonia (see Linskill, 250).

[4] The references are to figures participating in the fourth crusade and include Guillaume of Champlitte and Count Henry of Flanders. See Linskill, 250, for more complete information.

[5] Aimeric refers to Aimeri of Narbonne, father of Guillaume of Orange, whose exploits were the subject of the twelfth-century epic *Foucon de Candie* (Linskill, 251).

[6] Manuscript P is the only one which contains the razo but it does not contain the full song, only the fragments cited within the prose text.

71. Raimbaut de Vaqueiras 392, 2 (B/S, 546)
MSS: E 209, P 44, R 3.
Base Text: E

You have now heard who Raimbaut de Vaqueiras was and how and through whom he came to occupy a position of honor. But now I want to tell you about how, after the good marquis of Monferrat had made him a knight, Raimbaut fell in love with Lady Beatriz, the marquis' sister and the sister of Lady Alazais de Saluces.[1]

He greatly loved and desired her, though always careful never to let her or anyone else know about it. He greatly enhanced her reputation and noble standing and brought her many admirers from near and far, and of both sexes. And she paid him great honor with the way she received him. He was dying of desire and fear, for he didn't dare ask her for her love or show any signs that he had any interest in her love.

But, like a man tormented by love, he came before her one day and told her that he loved a gracious, young and noble lady with whom he had an intimate relationship; but so much did he fear her great nobility and honored position that he did not tell her or show in any way how much he loved her, or ask for her love. He begged her in the name of God and Mercy to give him some advice as to whether he should speak his heart and will and ask her for her love or whether he should die concealing, fearing, and loving.

This noble lady, Lady Beatriz, upon hearing what Raimbaut was saying, and knowing Sir Raimbaut's desire for love--for she had already noticed much earlier that he was dying, languishing with desire for her--

was touched by love and pity and said to him: "Raimbaut, it is only fitting that every fine lover who loves a noble lady should bring her honor and fear in order to show her the love that he feels for her. But rather than dying, I would advise him to tell her of the love and desire that he has for her and to beg her to take him on as her servant and friend. You may be assured that if the lady is cultivated and courtly she will not think less of him or think him dishonorable but, rather, will admire him more and think of him as a better man. To you in particular I would advise that you speak your heart to the lady that you love and tell her about the desire you have for her and ask her to take you on as a servant and knight; for you are such a knight that there is not a lady in the world who shouldn't willingly take you on as her servant and knight. I have seen Lady Alazais, the Countess of Saluce, accept Peire Vidal as an admirer; and the Countess of Burlatz, Arnaut de Marueill; Lady Maria, Gauselm Faidit; and the lady of Marseille, Folquet de Marseille.[2] This is why I advise and authorize you, on my word and with my guarantee, to ask her, to beg her for her love.

Sir Raimbaut, when he had heard the advice and guarantee that she was offering, and the permission that she was granting, told her that it was she, from whom he had sought and asked for advice, that he loved in this way. And Lady Beatrix told him that it was good that he had come and was trying to do well and speak right and make himself worthy. She said that she wanted to take him on as knight and servant and that he should strive to do his best. Raimbaut therefore strove to speak well and do as he should, and to advance Lady Beatrix as much as he could.[3] And he composed this love song which is written like this:

(Love) Now demands from me her customs and duties...
392, 2:1)

---

[1] This Lady Alazais, who is identified as Lady Beatrix's sister, is the same love interest that the razo author attributes to Peire Vidal. Thus, perhaps, the confusion in attributing the next song (364, 47) to Raimbaut. Notice also that both Raimbaut and Peire are said to have shared a special relationship with the lord; both are said to have been his 'dressing-master/valet.'

[2] It would appear that this razo author either knew the other razos and the information they contain or that he is the author of many of the other razo texts.

³ Note again that what is couched in erotic terms (desire, fearing, dying, loving) turns out to be another case of the poet being hired on to sing the lady's praises.

Song 392,2 Raimbaut de Vaqueiras: " Era.m requier sa costum'e
son   us..."
             Source: Linskill, 145.
             MSS: A 162, C 124, D 106-367, D^c 252, E 184,
                  J 6, M 103, N^2 12, P 13, R 61-512,
                  Sg 47 (#2), T 188, U 73, a^1 324,
                  O 26 (anonymous).
             Other English translations: Linskill, 147.

1. Love, for whom I sigh and moan and lie awake,
   Now demands from me its customs and duties,
   For I have sought counsel from the noblest lady in the world
   And she told me to go as high as I can above me
   And love the finest lady there is, for she is my guarantee   5
   That this will bring me honor, renown and benefits, not
       damages.
   Since she is the most highly reputed lady in the world,
   I have placed in her my heart and my hope.

2. No one has ever loved a lady so highly placed
   Or noble as I; and since I can find no one to equal her,   10
   I turn my attentions to her and love her, on her counsel,
   More than Thisbe loved Pyramus.
   Joy and merit put her before all others.
   To those who are noble she is gracious and welcoming,
   And to the others she appears haughty.   15
   She is generous with her wealth and sweet of manner.

3. Never did Perceval feel greater joy
   When he took the armor from the knight in red
   At the court of Arthur than I feel with her counsel.
   But she kills me like Tantalus was killed: 20

For My-Lord forbids me to have what she gives me in
   abundance,
She who is esteemed, courtly, perfect,
Rich and noble, young and well-spoken,
Of good sense and beautiful appearance.

4. Beautiful lady, I was as brave or braver than   25
   Emenadus at the assault of Tyre
   When I asked you for the lock of hair
   And you gave me counsel concerning your love.
   But more renown and honor should fall to me,
   For my courage was greater in the realm of love.   30
   And that's the kind of courage your lover should show:
   Let him share your happiness or die for you.[1]

5. May My-Englishman never blame or accuse me
   If for her sake I leave Orange and Montélimar;[2]
   Thus may God give me advice about her beautiful body, 35
   For the best of ladies rank below her in worth.
   Even if I were the king of England or France
   I would go off to fulfill all of her commands,
   For in her is my heart and my desire
   And she is the thing for which I have the greatest desire. 40

6. Beautiful-Knight, in you I have placed my hope;
   And since you are the most worthy in the world,
   And the most esteemed, I should suffer no damages;
   For you gave me your counsel and acted as my guarantee.

7. Lady Beatrice of Monferrat enhances her reputation 45
   For all good deeds always pass before her.
   That is why I gild my songs with her praise
   And advance my career with her beauty.

---

[1] The numerous references to other texts in this song attest to Raimbaut's learning. Piramus and Thisbe he would have known through Ovid's *Metamorphoses* and perhaps through contemporary French versions; Tantalus must also have come through Ovid or contemporary glossaries of mythological material. From the reference to Perceval, we can assume that he knew of Chrétien de Troyes' rather recent romance or an earlier, unknown version of

tale; and Emenadus is the hero who captures Tyre in the Old French *Roman d'Alexandre* (Linskill, 151).

[2] Englishman is generally taken to be a senhal for Boniface de Montferrat, Raimbaut's principal patron. Note, however, that he addresses him as a woman in this passage.

72/62. Raimbaut de Vaqueiras

Attributed falsely to Raimbaut; in fact, the razo was written to explicate:

Peire Vidal 364, 47 (B/S, 462).
MS: R 3.

And it so happened that the lady went to bed with him, to sleep with him. The marquis, who loved her so much, found them sleeping and was very angry. Like a wise man, he did not wish to touch them but took off his cloak and covered them with it. He then took Sir Raymbaut's and left with it.[1]

When Sir Raymbaut got up, he understood what had happened. He took the cloak from around his neck and went straight to the marquis. He knelt down before him and begged for his pardon. The marquis saw that Raymbaut knew what had happened and he remembered all the pleasure that Raymbaut had given him on so many occasions. Since the marquis responded in ambiguous terms, --so that no one would understand this request for pardon, saying that he pardoned him for having returned what he had stolen,-- those who were listening thought that he was talking about the coat that Raymbaut had taken.[2] Thus the marquis pardoned him and told him that he should never go back to thieving; and only those two understood what was really being said.

After this incident, it came to pass that the marquis with all his retinue went off to Romania, with the full support of the Church, where he conquered the kingdom of Salonica. And Sir Raymbaut was made a knight due to the fine deeds he accomplished. And there he was given a great amount of land and a great fortune and it is there that he died.

And he composed a love song about what had happened with the sister which he sent to Sir Peire Vidal and which says:

> They have already said so much good about the marquis...
> (364, 47: 1)

And here you will find some of his works.

[1] This account of the nightly visit to the lovers' bedside is an obvious allusion to the visit of King Marc to the lovers' hut in Béroul's *Tristan* (lines 1975-2030).

[2] Boutière and Schutz (463) note that the word play is on 'rauba', meaning both theft and robe. Thus while the marquis and Peire are discussing Peire's having gone back to thieving, i.e. stealing his wife, the rest of the entourage understands that Peire has returned to the marquis his stolen robe. It has earlier been established (in razo 70) that Raimbaut and Peire Vidal (see razo 59) are both the favorites of their patrons and are given privileges beyond what other poets receive.

Song 364, 47　　Peire Vidal: "Tant an ben dig del marques..."
　　　　　　　　Source: D'Arco Silvio Avalle, 107.
　　　　　　　　MSS: C 40, D^a 162-564, D^c 249, E 30, I 40, K 28, N 100, Q 70, R 65-547.

1. They have already said so much good about the marquis,
   The coarse and refined joglars both,
   And everything they say is so true,
   That I don't know what I can say about him.
   His worth, however, is the source　　　　　　　　5
   From which good reputation is born and begins to grow;
   Valor is renewed there,
   And it makes one speak his true praises.

2. If the King of Aragon
    Hadn't taken away my happiness,   10
    I'd now be enjoying fine and full joy
    With the ladies from Carcassonne.
    Their deeds and manners,
    The knights and counts,
    And the barons and vavassors,   15
    All these do me good and bring me pleasure.

3. This is why the Lombards have conquered me:
    Because he/she called me "dear sir";[1]
    I have never seen another archer
    Let fly his arrow with more surety or skill.   20
    I am struck unfailingly in the heart
    With a square-blade of charm
    That was forged in the fire of love
    And tempered with sweet pleasure.

4. Eyes and thick black lashes,   25
    And the nose, like the handle of a cross-bow:
    This is the bow that, with just one
    Quick glance, delivers such a blow
    That no shield can offer protection.
    Since it is her pleasure to conquer me,   30
    I don't consider it a disgrace
    If the mighty conquers the mightier.

5. Her beautiful body is so justly proportioned
    And her words so gay and pleasing
    That there is no knight in the world   35
    Who wouldn't want to see her.
    She has the words and deeds and look
    Of someone from Mombello and Argence,
    The coloring of someone from Monrozier
    And her living quarters are in Vallflor.[2]   40

6. Her wealth is a thousand times double
    That of the story of the chessboard;
    For from her true and fine renown
    Not a thing is missing.
    Since she grants me, without delay, my wishes,   45
    There is more for me there than in Provence;

> For I now have more honor here where I am,
> And a man must opt for what's best.

7. And if My-Brother knew[3]
   Who was keeping me in her employ, 50
   Steel axes couldn't keep him
   From coming to see her.
   There he would find, without fail,
   A sweet fruit with honored seed
   And a court of worthy lords 55
   With one attractive archer.[4]

[1] This song provides an excellent example of a case in which the song is manifestly dedicated to the praise of a man (the marquis, cited in the first line) but which then switches to praise of a lady. Here, however, the transition is less clear than in other examples, and at this point the listener would have had to assume that the singer was still referring to the presumably male marquis.

[2] These town names are probably metonymical references to people that inhabit them. Mombello, for example is found in the lands of Montferrat and would thus refer to Boniface or a member of his family (Avalle, 109).

[3] "Fraire" is likely a senhal for another poet given what follows. "Sweet-Fruit" in line 54 may be another. Peire also uses "Fraire" in songs 364: 24 and 40. It can also be found in Raimbaut d'Aurenga's song 389, 32; in Pons de Capdoill's song 375, 16; and in Bertran de Born's song 80, 34 (Stronski, *Folquet*, 31). Paden et al. identify "Fraire" in Bertran de Born as being a reference to Guillem de Berguedan, Bertran's brother in poetry (Paden et al., 291).

[4] Gender ambiguity is again underlined by the use of "semensa" in line 54, one of whose primary meanings is semen. Thus, the "sweet fruit" could be a reference applicable to both genders.

73. Raimbaut de Vaqueiras 392, 9 (B/S, 465)
    MS: P 44.

You have by now heard who Rambaut was and where he was from and how the Marquis of Monferrat made him a knight and how he loved the Lady Beatrix and lived in a state of joy due to her love.

Listen now to how he experienced for a brief time a great sadness. This was on account of the false and jealous people who don't like love or courting ladies, and who were saying things to Lady Beatrix while around other ladies. This is what they were saying: "Who is this Rambaut de Vaqera, even if he has been made a knight by the marquis, that he should go courting a lady as nobly born as you are? Be warned that it brings no honor to you, not to you or the marquis." They said so many evil things, here, there and everywhere (as vile people are wont to do), that Lady Beatrix became angry with Rambaut de Vaqera. When Rambaut asked for her love and begged for her mercy, she did not hear his prayers but told him instead that he should go court some other lady who might be better for him and that he would hear nothing more from her. This was the source of the sadness that Rambaut had for a short time, as I told you at the beginning of this "rason."

So he gave up singing and laughing and all the other activities that should have been pleasing. And this was a great shame. And all this happened because of the scandal-mongers' talk, as he says in a stanza of the stampida that you will hear.[1]

During that time there came to the marquis' court two joglars from France who were excellent fiddlers. One day they were playing a stampida which the marquis, the knights, and the ladies all loved. It did not lift Rambaut's spirits at all, however, and the marquis noticed this and said to him: "Lord Rambaut, why is it that you do not sing or rejoice when you hear such beautiful sounds from a fiddle and see before you a lady as beautiful as my sister, who has taken you on as her servant and is the most noble lady in the world?" Sir Rambaut answered that he wouldn't do a thing. The marquis knew why he was sad and said to his sister: "Lady Biatrix, for love of me and all of these people, I want you to deign to ask Rambaut, in the name of your love and grace, to cheer up, to sing and be happy like he used to be." Lady Biatrix was so courtly and of such good grace that she comforted him and asked him if he couldn't cheer up for the sake of their love and compose a new song.

And so Rambaut, for the reason that you have just heard, composed the stampida which goes like this:

>   Not the feast of May
>   Nor the leaves of the beech
>   Nor the song of the bird   nor the gladiola flower
>   Can please me,
>   Gay and noble lady,
>   Until I get   an express message
>   From your beautiful   body, which tells me of
>   A new pleasure   that love brings me
>   And new joy,
>   And brings me closer
>   To you,   true lady,
>   And until he falls
>   From his wound,
>   The jealous one, before he can get rid of me... ((392, 9: 1-14)

This stampida was composed to fit the notes of the stampida that the joglar was playing on his fiddle.

[1] An "estampida" is a rhythmic dance song. This particular song is the only example of the genre in Provençal and may very well have been taken over from a French jonglar and fitted with new words, as the razo author tells us.

Song 392, 9   Raimbaut de Vaqueiras: "Kalenda maia..."
               Source: Linskill, 185.
               MSS: C 125, M 106, R 62-519, Sg 49,
                   M 250 (anonymous).
               Other English translations: Blackburn 135; Linskill
                   187; McPeek, 153.

1.   Not the feast of May
           Nor the leaves of the beech
     Nor the song of the bird nor the gladiola flower
           Can please me,

    Gay and noble lady,   5
Until I get   an express message
From your beautiful   body, which tells me of
A new pleasure   that love brings me
     And new joy,
     And brings me closer   10
  To you,   true lady,
     And until he falls
     From his wound,
The jealous one, before he can get rid of me.

2.   My beautiful friend,   15
   For God's sake, let it never happen
That a jealous man   should laugh over my demise,
    For he would pay a high price
    For his jealousy
If two such lovers   were parted;   20
For I would never   again be joyous,
Nor would joy without you do me any good.
     Such a route
     Would I take
That no one would ever see me again.   25
     That day
     Would mark my death,
  Noble lady,   if I were to lose you.

3.   How could a lady be lost,
    Or returned to me,   30
If I didn't   first have her?
    No man or woman becomes a lover
    Just through thought alone.
But when one who loves is changed into a lover
The honor is greater   the longer it grows.   35
The look of love alone can get the talk started.
     But in the nude
     I have never
  Held you   or gotten anything else from you.
     I have wished for   40
     And trusted
  In you   without any other help forthcoming.

4.   It will be a long time before I feel joy again
       If ever I should leave you,
Beautiful-knight,   in anger;   45
       For nowhere else is my heart
       Attracted, and nowhere am I pulled
By desire,   for I desire nothing else.
To the scandal-mongers that would bring pleasure,
       I know it,
Lady, for otherwise   they won't be cured.   50
       Such a one will return
       When he hears of
My demise,   to thank you for it
       And to watch you.
       He studies you,   55
Imagining things which make my heart sigh.

5.   It begins so sweetly
       But shines beyond all others,
This worth of yours, Lady Beatrice,
       And then grows greater.   60
       In my opinion
Your power   is garnished with merit
And fine words   that never deceive.
You hold the seed of deeds of renown,
       Knowledge,   65
       Patience,
You have these   plus judgement
       Without argument;
       You clothe
Your worth   in benevolence.   70

6.   Gracious lady,
       Each one praises and speaks of
Your worth,   which is so pleasing;
       And as for anyone who forgets you,
       His life is worth little to him.   75
This is why I adore you, distinguished lady,
For I have chosen you as the most noble,
And the best: of perfect reputation,
       Courted,
       Served,   80

290

More noble than Erec's Enide.
I've composed,
Finished,
Sir Englishman, the estampida.

74/79. Raimbaut de Vaqueiras 392, 31

Commented upon in a razo concerning Guillem del Baus. See razo number 79.

75. Folquet de Marseille 155, 23 (B/S, 474)
MSS: E 198, N^2 22, R 1.
Base text: E

Folquet de Marceilla loved the wife of his lord, Sir Barral, Lady Alazais de Rocamartina. He sang and composed his songs about her and was very careful to see that no one knew about this love, for she was the wife of his lord and this would be considered a serious crime.[1] The lady accepted his prayers and songs because of the great praise he dedicated to her.

Sir Barral had two sisters of great wealth and nobility: one was named Lady Laura de Saint Jorlan, the other Lady Mabelia of Ponteves, and both lived with Sir Barral. Folquet had such close friendships with both of them that it seemed as if he were courting both of them for their love.

Lady Alazais thought that he was courting Lady Laura and that he loved her; she therefore accused him of it and this was reported to him by many knights and many men. She then gave him his leave, for she did not want to hear his pleas and verses any more, and told him that he should leave Lady Laura and expect no further goods or love from herself.

Folquet was very sad and mournful when his lady dismissed him and so he gave up conversation, singing and laughing. For a long time he was in a state of great sorrow, moaning over the bad luck that had come his way, for he was losing his lady, whom he loved more than anything else in the world, for the sake of another whom he did not love, except out of courtliness.[2]

It was over this state of sorrow that he went to see the Empress, the wife of Sir Guilem of Monpeslier, who was the daughter of the emperor, Emanuel, and who was considered the head and supreme guide of all nobility, courtliness and learning. He complained to her about the bad luck that had come his way. She comforted him as much as she could and begged him not to be sad or despair but said that he should compose and sing songs about her love.

And so, because of the beseechments of the Empress, he composed this song which says:

My song springs from such courtly circumstances
That I cannot fail... (155, 23: 1-2)

---

[1] According to much of the theory of 'courtly love,' based largely on Andreas Capellanus' northern French treatise on love, love can only exist between individuals married to other people, never between the two members of a married couple. The razo author may be suggesting the same thing here, but he acknowledges that such a liaison between a high-born lady and poet was not at all acceptable in real practice and would be severely punished.

[2] The author here distinguishes between ladies one loves and ladies one sings about. It is clear from the context that Folquet may sing about these two sisters in standard courtly terms but that that does not at all imply that he 'loves' them. Both have been identified, but as sister-in-law and cousin, not sisters (Stronski, 144; B/S, 477).

Song 155, 23 Folquet de Marseille
Source: Stronski, 19.
MSS: A 66, B 45, C 4, D 43-150, D^c 245, E 2, F 46, G 5, I 63, K 48, M 30, N 57, O 79, P 9, R 42-357, S 37-23, T 227, V 86, W 188, c 13, b^1 6.

1. My song springs from such courtly circumstances
   That I cannot fail.
   In fact, I should do better this time
   Than ever before; and do you know why?
   Because it's the empress who invites me to compose. 5
   It would be so wonderful to give myself up to her
       If she would permit it;
   But since she is the pinnacle and root
       Of good manners
   It isn't right that my intelligence should be 10
   Weak or slow in responding to her call.
   Thus, I must double my ingenuity.

2. And if ever before in my song I spoke
   About scandal-mongers, who are hated by God,
   I still want to denounce them completely; 15
   May God never forgive them
   For they said things that were never true.
   Because of that, the one I obey
       Turns her back on me
   And believes that I have turned 20
       My thoughts to another.
   I am dying over this grievous error
   And lose what I love in perfect fashion
   Over the unsubstantiated things they are saying.

3. Still this doesn't make me lose hope, 25
   For I have always heard
   That a lie cannot be hidden forever
   Without dying at some point.
   Once the truth overcomes the false accusation,
   It will be proven and recognized 30
       How true to her I am.

293

>   For I so submit and bend to her,
>   And so willingly,
>   That my firm heart and my good sense
>   Are engaged in a dispute over loving her   35
>   And each of them thinks his love is stronger.
>
> 4. If mercy does not come to support me
>   What shall I do? Will I ever be able to leave her?
>   Not me; for I have already learned how to die,
>   And now it would be only too welcome.   40
>   Within my heart I contemplate her face,
>   And contemplating it, I languish;
>   For she told me
>   She will not give me what I've been asking for
>   For so long.   45
>   This doesn't slow me down though;
>   Instead, my suffering is doubled
>   And I die, all mixed-up.
>
> 5. Shall I then love her in secret
>   Since I see she will never deign to take me on?   50
>   Yes, I will, for in my heart I contemplate her
>   And I know I will have to go on doing so whether I want to or
>   not.
>   The heart holds the body in prison
>   And keeps it so oppressed and conquered
>   That it doesn't seem to me   55
>   That it will ever allow it to leave!
>   And so I wait
>   To see how I might conquer her through endurance,
>   For long suffering and mercy can win out
>   Where force and ruse are useless.   60
>
> 6. Sir/Lady Aziman, I would be glad
>   To die sweetly for my My-Lord,
>   Since in either case, I will die.[1]

---

[1] Aziman is a senhal used by Bernart de Ventadorn and Bertran de Born as well as by Folquet. Stronski (*Folquet*, 28) says that Aziman was used by Folquet and Bertran de Born to address their songs to one another.

76. Folquet de Marseille 155, 27 (B/S, 478)
MS: N² 22.

I have already told you about Sir Folquet de Marceilla: who he was, where he came from, how he advanced in merit and nobility, how he lived his life on earth and how he left it, how he loved the wife of his lord, Sir Baral, and how he composed for her many beautiful songs about merit and resentment, and how he never had any joy or pleasure from her.

Now I want to tell you how he later fell in love with the Empress, the wife of Guillem de Monpellier, she who was the daughter of the Emperor of Constantinople, whose name was Manuel. She was the one who was sent to King Anfos of Aragon, as I told you in the other text.[1] It was about her that he composed this song, which says:

> An overweening desire
> Has established itself within my heart... (155, 27: 1-2)

He was so unlucky that at the same moment that he fell in love with her, she was accused of having done her husband, Guillem de Monpellier, wrong. He believed these charges and sent her away, away from him, and off she went. Folquet was sad and mournful and desolate over this, and said that he would never again be joyful because he missed her:

> The Empress, who was raised by youth
> Into the highest ranks;
> And if her body hasn't been violated
> It will show
> How a madman found a way to disgrace himself...
> (155, 27: 56-60)

---

[1] B/S note that this passage appears to refer back to razo 18 to Bertran de Born's song 80, 32, a text which recounts the same story using similar expressions in the same order. From this, B/S conclude that the two were likely composed by the same author (B/S, 479). Guillem de Montpellier had, in fact, repudiated Eudossia, the daughter of the Emperor of Constantinople, in 1187.

Song 155, 27   Folquet de Marseille: " Us volers outracujatz..."
                Source: Stronski, 46.
                MSS: A 66, B 45, C 4, D 42, E 6, G 7, I 65, K 49,
                    M 28, N 61, Q 22, R 43, T 229, V 88, c 14.

1. An overweening desire
   Has established itself in my heart,
   Though my hope doesn't tell me
   That it can ever be fulfilled,
       So high are its pretensions.   5
   But my good sense doesn't tell me
   I should despair either;
   So I am split in two:
       Not giving in to despair
       And not daring to have hope.   10

2. I feel as if lifted on high
   Toward the one before whom my power is so small.
   This is why fear chastises me:
   For daring like this works
       Against many people.   15
   But there's one consoling thought that keeps me joyful:
   That she might come over to the other side
   And show me that humility
       Has her so much in its power
       That some good could come to me from all of this.   20

3. My heart is so fixed there
   That a lie seems like truth
   And pain seems like pleasure;
   Yet I know that it's true
       That a good effort can win out.   25
   This is why I beg you, worthy lady,
   That you allow me only this--
   And then I will be nobly paid--
       That you let me go on wishing for
       The joy I desire to see.   30

4. It seemed to me a case of madness
   And excessively daring desire
   When, with just one look,

She overtook me so quickly
   That in secret   35
There came to my heart such desire
That I fell in love.
Since then, however, this feeling has multiplied with such
      force
   That morning and evening
   It makes me suffer sweetly.   40

5. I don't feel as if I've wronged you
   In any way, except perhaps in that I lack the learning
   Needed to pay you compliments.
   I believe it is because I have lost all measure
      In loving you loyally   45
   That my intelligence now fails me.
   If, however, the matter were to be judged fairly,
   I should not be blamed;
      For this kind of ignorance
      Should be considered a compliment.   50

6. Singing doesn't please me any more;
   May abstention do me some good!
   But retirement and indifference
   Would be joy and solace to me
      Now that the empress is gone,   55
   She who was raised by youth
   Into the highest ranks.
   And if her body hasn't been violated,
      It will show
      How a madman found a way to disgrace himself.[1]   60

7. Ah, sweet and agreeable thing,
   May humility overcome you;
   For no other joy can please me
   And I haven't the wit or learning
      To want anything else.   65

8. I have expelled so many sighs
      That day and night
   I lose my power through sighing.

[1] OR: "And if her body (heart) hasn't been killed, it will bear the proof that a madman..." Folquet may to be saying that if she hasn't been killed or disfigured through rape, her beauty will be so evident that Guillem's desertion of her will prove him to have acted like a fool.

77. Folquet de Marseille 155, 20 (B/S, 480)
MS: N^2 22.

Not very long after Sir Folqet had fallen into a state of torment and sorrow over the lady who had gone away and left Monpellier, Sir Baral, his lord and the lord of Marceilla, the one man he loved more than any in the world, died. The grievous sorrow he already felt over his lord Sir Baral's wife, who had died, and the Empress who had gone away, were doubled. He then composed this plainch which says:

> Like one who is so burdened
> With unhappiness that he feels no pain,
> I feel neither grief nor sadness... (155, 20: 1-3)

Song 155, 20   Folquet de Marseille: "Si cum cel q'es tan greujatz..."
　　　　　　　Source: Stronski, 61.
　　　　　　　MSS: A 66, B 45, D 43, I 63, K 48, N 63, P 9, Q 21, R 52, V 89, a 113.

1. Like someone who is so burdened
   With unhappiness that he feels no pain,
   I feel neither grief nor sadness;
   It's like I've lost hold of myself.
   This blow I've received so exceeds any other   5
   That my heart cannot bear to think about it;

Nor can any man know of its magnitude
   Without having experienced it himself.
   It's of Sir Barral, my good lord, that I speak,
   For now, if I sing or laugh or cry,   10
   I don't care about it the way I used to.[1]

2. I think I've been bewitched
   Or fallen into some error
   When I can't find around me his great worth,
   Which kept us here in honor.[2]   15
   For just as a magnet
   Attracts iron and lifts it toward itself,
   Many was the heart, though weighty and beaten down,
   That he straightened out and led to merit.
   Whoever took from us renown, joy and honor,   20
   Wit, generosity, luck and riches,
   Is little concerned with our advancement.

3. Ah! How many are now dispossessed
   Who once were rich in his love;
   And how many died on that day   25
   When he died and was buried?
   Never were so many dead seen buried in one piece of land!
   Even those who just heard the mention of his name
   Expected to gain from it,
   So esteemed was his reputation.   30
   For he knew how to use his good name to raise up
   The small and make them great, and make the great greater,
   Until the point that the circle couldn't enclose him.[3]

4. Ah, my sweet and private lord,
   How can I speak your praises?   35
   For like a surging river
   That flows with greater force at the point where it is emptied,
   Your praises grow just in thinking about them;
   And I find there is always more to be done.[4]
   It's similar to your giving: 40
   Your desire to give grew
   As more people came seeking.
   But God always gave you back a thousandfold
   As he does to good givers.[5]

5. Now, at the height of your glory,   45
   You have fallen like a flower
   Which, once it has been seen at its loveliest,
   Fades all the more quickly.
   But with such a image God shows us
   That we must love only him   50
   And hate the miserable world
   Through which man passes like a pilgrim.
   For any merit or wisdom,
   Except for that which follows his commandments,
   Turns into dishonor and folly.   55

6. Beautiful lord God, who doesn't like to see
   The death of any sinner,
   And who, in order to kill theirs,
   Suffered your own death in peace,
   Let him live with the saints up there,   60
   Since you did not wish to let him stay down here.
   May you deign to pray for him,
   Virgin, you who pray to your son on behalf of so many.
   It is because he helps them
   That the best men can retain hope   65
   In your precious and merciful prayers.

7. Lord, it's a great miracle
   That I can sing about you at a moment like this
   When I really should be crying.
   But I already cry so much just thinking about you!   70
   And because of that many troubadours will soon have
   Spoken more praise of you than I have,
   When it's I who should be saying a thousand times more.

---

[1] OR: " he doesn't appreciate me the way he used to."

[2] i.e. He kept us living in style with gifts and goods.

[3] Ms. R gives the last word as 'gazans' rather than 'garans,' meaning: "He couldn't contain the profits." The line as translated seems to suggest that the spiraling effect that results from his generosity is positive and that the closed circle, or limited economic system (as in hoarding), is negative.

[4] i.e. that the praising of En Barral can never be completed.

[5] His giving resembles a cornucopia. See note 3.

78. Folquet de Marseille 155, 15 (B/S, 482)
MSS: E 197, N² 22, R 1.
Base text: E

When the good King Anfos de Castela had been defeated by the King of Marroc, whose name was Miramamolin, and this latter had taken over Calatrava and Salvaterra and Castel de Dompnas, there was great mourning and sadness throughout all of Spain on the part of all those good people who heard the news because Christianity had been dishonored and because of the setback entailed by the fact that the good King had been defeated and lost some of his lands.[1] Miramamolin's people often entered into the good King Anfos' kingdom to steal and pillage. The good King Anfos sent his messengers to the Pope, asking him to implore the barons from the kingdom of France and the kingdom of England and the King of Aragon and the Count of Toulouse to help them.

Folquet de Marceilla, who was a close friend of the good King of Castela and had not yet gone into the order of the Sistel, preached a sermon to encourage the barons and good people, saying that they should help the good King Anfos and showing them the honor that would come to them from helping the King and the pardon that they would have from God.

And here is the song that he composed like a sermon and which says:[2]

Henceforth I know of no reason... (155, 15: 1)[3]

---

[1] Anfos of Castela is Alphonse VIII of Castile. Miramamolin is the Spanish version of the Arabic title: Amir-el-Memenin, Head-of-the-Faithful. Calatrava was a fortress defended by the military order of the Cistercians. When it was lost, the Cistercians moved to Salvatierra. Salvatierra was also lost and the Christian forces only regained momentum with the famous battle of Las Navas in 1212. After that victory, Alphonse VIII appealed to Pope Innocent III and a crusade was proclaimed (Stronski, 148-52; B/S, 484).

[2] The razo author characterizes this crusading song as belonging to a different, and didactic, genre in modifying the verb with the phrase "... like a sermon." This is the only such categorization in the razos.

³ Folquet himself entered the Cistercian order in 1200 at the Abbey of Le Thoronet, five years after the loss of Calatrava. He later was named Bishop of Toulouse and became infamous as a partisan of the crusading forces that destroyed the Southwest in search of heresy (B/S, 473). Dante accorded him a place in Paradise less than a century after his death (d. 1231) (*Paradiso*, IX, 67-108).

Song 155, 15 Folquet de Marseille: " Hueimais no·y conosc razo..."
Source: Stronski, 70.
MSS: A 67, B 46, C 6, D^a 165, E 2, I 64, K 49, N 61, P 7, Q 22, R 13.

1. Henceforth I know of no reasoning
Behind which to hide
If we now want to serve God,
For he did so much for us
That he was willing to suffer the consequences himself. 5
First, he lost the Sepulcher
And now he is letting Spain slip away
Because we came up with some excuse down there.
Here, at least, we fear neither the sea nor the wind.
Alas! How could we feel the call any more strongly 10
Unless he were to return right now to die for us again?

2. He made to us a gift of his own self
When he came to deliver us from our wrongs;
And he determined that for that act we should be grateful
When he gave himself over for us as ransom. 15
Therefore, anyone who wants to live through death,
Let him now publicly give his life for the God
Who gave up his life and redeemed it through his death.
Man, too, must die, though he never knows how.
Oh, anyone who lives his life without fear of death lives
    badly. 20
We know that this life, which we are so eager to hold on to,
Is bad and that to die like that is good.

3. Listen to what a mistake those people are making
And what they will be able to answer.

Each of them wants to safeguard and serve his body,   25
Which no man can preserve
From death, for any amount of money;
And they don't give a thought to the soul,
Which can be saved from death and torture.
Let each weigh in his heart whether I speak the truth or not,
And afterwards he will have a greater desire to go.   31
And let no worthy man be concerned about the question of poverty;
It's enough that he undertake this voyage for God to show his mercy.

4. At least he can keep his heart pure,
And he can arm himself with that;   35
God and our King of Aragon
Can provide him with the rest.
I don't believe he could ever let down
Any man who goes off with a worthy heart
Since we so rarely see him fail to be there for others.   40
He should never let God suffer any losses
For God will honor him if he serves him honorably.
This year, if he wills it, he shall be crowned here below
Or up above, in heaven: he will not fail to gain one or the other.

5. The Castilian king should pay no attention to crazy talk;[1]
Nor should he turn back   46
Because of losing; on the contrary, he should be thankful
To God, who extended to him his summons,
For it's through him that God wishes to advance his cause.
Any army that doesn't have God on its side will come to nothing;   50
And his regal reputation will be worth a hundredfold
If he takes God right now as his companion in arms.
God wants nothing but recognition;
Provided that he shows no pride before God,
His reputation will be honored and envied.[2]   55

6. The life and renown that one seeks from the foolish crowd
Fall to ruin more easily, the higher one's status.
Let us then build on firm ground

> The kind of reputation that holds together when the other is crumbling.
> May all man's renown, joy, and praise reside in 60
> His deep reflection on all that God does for us.
>
> 7. Beautiful-Magnet, we see that God is awaiting you,[3]
> For he would like to win you over honestly.
> He keeps you in such honor that I am very pleased.
> Don't ever make him change the good wishes he holds for you. 65
> Let it be you who changes, for it's a hundred times better
> For a man to bow down himself than to be thrown down by force.

[1] The reference is to Alphonse VIII, as mentioned in the razo.

[2] One can note similarities between the language of service and recompense used in this religious context and the terminology used by the troubadours in discussing their service and expectations of reward.

[3] See note 1 to song 155, 23 under razo 75 for the identification of Aziman with Bertran de Born.

79/74. Guillem del Baus (Raimbaut de Vaqueiras) 392, 31 (B/S, 485)
MS: H 47

Guilelm del Bauz, the prince of Orange, robbed a merchant from France and took from him a large number of goods while he was on his route.[1] The merchant went to the King of France to complain. The King told him that he could not do justice for him because he was too far away from the site: "But I give you my word that you should do whatever you can to get even, no matter what the means, if it works."

The bourgeois went off and had a counterfeit copy of the King's seal made. And he had letters written in the name of the King addressed to Sir

Guilelm del Bauz, inviting him to come to the King and promising him a great many goods, honors and gifts. When Guilelm del Bauz received the letters he was very happy and made a great many preparations to go to see the King.

He departed and on the way passed through the city of the merchant whom he had robbed, though he did not know where that merchant had come from. And the bourgeois, when he found out that Sir Guilelm was in the city, had him taken captive, along with his companions.[2] So Guilelm agreed to return all that he had taken and to make up for all his damages. Then back he went, poor and defeated.

He then went off to pillage a property that belonged to Sir Aimar de Pitheus, which is known as Osteilla.[3] But when he was crossing the Rhone in a boat, Sir Aimar's fishermen captured him.

Sir Rambauz de Vaqeiras, who shared with Guilelm the mutual name of "Engles", composed these stanzas about this affair:

Everyone is begging me to attack you, Englishman,
For the mad expedition from which you have returned mad,
And for which any other man would have been ruined.
But you are of such noble and high-born heart
That you know how to hide your madness,
Which no one defends; and if those men from Estela
Had been French, you would have taken your revenge,
For the King gave you nothing and is criticized for it...
(392, 31: 1-8)

---

[1] Guilem is Guillem IV de Baux. He was the husband of Barrale, the daughter of En Barral, the Viscount of Marseille and patron of numerous poets (notably Folquet de Marseille, see above). He was a poet and two examples of his verse are known. He and his brothers are said to have protected several poets, including Raimbaut de Vaqueiras and Perdigo. The confusion in attributing this song to Raimbaut (see razo 74) may stem from the fact that his vida states that Guillem was his first patron. The property of Vaqueiras would, in fact, have been within Guillem's realm. (B/S, 487)

[2] Note the wealth and power that this merchant wields.

³ Aimar de Pitheus was also a poet. Some verses he exchanged in partimens with Raimbaut de Vaqueiras and Perdigo have been conserved. He was from Poitiers (B/S, 487).

Song 392, 31   Raimbaut de Vaqueiras: "Tuich me pregon, Engles, qe vos don saut..."
Source: Linskill, 268.
MSS: D^a 210-774, H 47.
Other English translations: Linskill, 269.

1. Everyone is begging me to attack you, Englishman,
   For the mad expedition from which you have returned mad,
   And for which any other man would have been ruined.
   But you are of such noble and high-born heart
   That you know how to hide your madness,   5
   Which no one defends; and if those men from Estela
   Had been French, you would have taken your revenge,
   For the king gave you nothing and is criticized for it.

2. I am really amazed at you, Sir Raimbaut,
   That you are so angry with me;   10
   For in no time you will be recognized as being crazier
   Than Peirol, who is thought to be an imbecile.[1]
   Go off then to the king of Barcelona
   And the others, as you have determined to do;
   For you are more in love with money and a hand-me-down
       outfit   15
   Than Sir Conoguz is with Lady Falcona.[2]

3. Englishman, it's a good thing Sir Aimar came to the skirmish,
   For the fishermen would have taken you like a pike!
   I'm not at all saying that you were ever really beaten,
   Except of course for those blows that came from counter-
       blows.[3]   20
   And it doesn't hurt him any if the king didn't, and doesn't, give
       you anything,

Or if you believed in the bourgeois' seal,
That honest man over whom you started all this.
Sir Aimar would be like the Good God, who is quick to forgive.

[1] Raimbaut de Vaqueiras' father is called "Peirors" in the vida and is said to be mad. Linskill hypothesizes that this line in the song is the source of the reference in the vida (Linskill, 270). He also points out that "pirol" and "arnaut" are synonyms in Languedoc. The entire line would then be a pun as in: "...Peirols qe hom ten per arnaut" (Imbecile that men take for an imbecile).

[2] Guillem accuses Raimbaut of being only interested in money, a typical charge directed against troubadours. Conoguz may be a senhal; there is jongleur addressed by that name in a cobla by Uc de Saint Circ (Linskill, 270-71). The story of Conoguz ("Known") and Falcona is unknown. Especially as it is phrased as an insult, it may be a facetious reference as in: "...than to have known the love of Lady Falcona," or it may be in some way obscene, punning on the particle "con" (cunt) within the words: Conoguz and Falcona.

[3] This highly ambiguous account of the incident seems to imply that Englishman started the skirmish and was injured only by the blows returned to him by the other person acting in self-defense. It could also be facetious, meaning that Englishman was only hit by his own blows, in ricochet. Aimar (Ademar of Pitheus, according to the razo), who came to help him, is also aware that Englishman is guilty.

80a. Guillem de Cabestaing 213, 5 (B/S, 537)
MSS: H 21, R 3, P 50.

Version H and R (H translated with additional details from R in italics)

Guillem de Capestaing was a noble lord of a manor from the county of Roussillon, just at the border of Catalonia, and which is under the jurisdiction of the King of Aragon. He was noble, courtly, learned, a fine knight at arms, highly esteemed by all the good people and greatly loved by the ladies. He was also a good composer of songs.[1]

He fell in love with a noble lady who was the wife of a rich baron of that land whose name was Raimon de Castel Roussillon. Sir Guillelm de Capestaing was his vassal. He loved her for a long time and paid her court and composed his songs about her. She loved him so much that she made him her knight. For a long time he had great joy from her and she from him. But Sir Raimon de Castel Roussillon was told that Sir Guilelm loved his wife and that she loved him. He became jealous of her and of him and locked her in at the top of a tower. He had her closely guarded and did and said many unpleasant things to her. G. de Capestaing fell into a great sorrow and sadness over this and composed this song which says:

> The sweet consternation
> That Love often brings me... (213, 5: 1-2)

And when R. de Castel Roussillon heard the song that Sir G. had composed, he understood it in such a way that he believed it was composed about his wife *for it says in one stanza:*

> *All that I do out of fear*
> *You must accept in good faith*
> *Even when I do not see you.* (l. 28-30)

And these words he understood, for Sir G. was not able to see her. So he *(the husband)* summoned G. to a talk to take place before the castle of Capestaing. *He led him outside, far from the castle,* and *like a traitor* cut off his head and put it in a hunting sack. He cut his heart out from his body and put it in the sack with his head. He returned to the castle where he had the heart roasted and had it brought to his wife's table *for the lady loved heart of venison,* and he had her eat it without knowing what it was she was eating, *all the while pretending to eat it himself.* When she had eaten it all, R. stood up and told his wife that what she had eaten was the heart of Sir G. de Capestaing and he showed her the head and asked her if it had been good to eat. She listened to what he was asking her and what he was telling her and saw and recognized the head of Sir G. de Capestaing. She answered that it had been so good and tasty that she would never allow any food or drink to take from her mouth the flavor that the heart of G. de Capestaing had left there. When R. de Castel Roussillon heard what she was saying, he ran at her with his sword. She *was afraid and* fled toward the door of the balcony *(the windows of the tower)* and he came running behind her. The lady let herself fall from the balcony *(threw herself from the window)* to the ground below and broke her neck *(and died)*. The news of this misfortune spread throughout Catalonia and all the lands of the King of Aragon, King Anfos, and all the barons of those lands. There was great sadness and mourning over the death of Sir G. de Capestaing and the lady because of the way R. de Castel Roussillon had so shamefuly killed them.

The relatives of Guilelm and the lady and all the courtly knights of that country and all the lovers assembled and waged a war of fire and blood against R. de Castel Roussillon. King *Anfos* of Aragon came to that land when he heard about the death of the lady and the knight and took R. de Castel Roussillon prisoner and took away his castles and lands and had Guilelm de Capestaing and the lady placed in a monument at the door of a church *of San Ioan* in Perpignan in a rich city on the plain of Roussillon which belongs to the King of Aragon. For a *long* time all the courtly knights and *noble* ladies of *Catalonia and* Roussillon and Cerdagne and Conflent and Ripoll and Peiralada and Narbonne celebrated each year *the anniversary of their deaths* and all the fine lovers of both sexes prayed to God for their souls *asking him to have mercy on them*. Thus, *as you have heard*, the King of Aragon captured Raimon de Castel Roussillon, took from him all his earthly goods, destroyed his castles and put him to death in prison. He gave all his possessions to the relatives of Sir Guilelm de Capestaing and the lady who died for him.

The song for which he died begins:

The sweet thought
Which love often grants me...

And here are some of his works.

---

[1] The vida identifies the lady as Saurimonde of Perialada. Such a lady is documented as having married a Raimon de Castel-Rossello in 1197. Most of the place names in the razo can be verified in the region of Perpignan, Narbonne and Roussillon. Two of Guillem's songs are addressed to "Sir Raimon." According to the records, however, Saurimonde cannot have been killed by her husband as she lived to marry a second time. Boccaccio used this tale for the ninth story of the fourth day of his *Decamerone*.

80b/3. Guillem de Cabestaing 213, 5 and Bernart de Ventadorn 70, 1

Version of manuscript P (P 50):

My lord Raimon de Rousillon was a noble baron, as you know. He had as his wife lady Margarida, the most beautiful lady known in those times, and the most highly esteemed by virtue of all her good qualities, all her merits and all her courtliness.

It happened that Guillelm de Castaing, the son of a poor knight from the castle of Castaing, came to the court of my lord Raimon de Roussillon and presented himself before him, asking that he be made a valet of his court, if it pleased him. My lord Raimon, when he saw how beautiful and gracious he was and how he seemed to be from a good background, told him that he was very welcome and that he should stay at his court. Thus Guillem lived there with him and was so excellent at behaving in a suitable fashion that the common people and the important ones all loved him. He was able to advance himself to the point that my lord Raimon wanted him to serve as his wife Margharida's young squire; and so it was done. Then Guillem made an effort to excel even more in word and in deed. But, as is wont to happen in matters of love, Love came and decided to assail Lady Margharida with its assaults and to heat up her thoughts. G.'s actions and words and appearance so pleased her that one day she could not hold back from saying: "Now tell me, Guillelm, if a lady showed you signs that she loved you would you dare love her?" Guillem, who had already realized what was going on, answered frankly: "I would, my Lady, though only if the signs were true." "By Saint Johan," said the lady,"you answered that like an honorable man, but now I should like to test you to see if you will be able to know and recognize those signs which are true from those which are not." On hearing these words, Guillaume answered: "Let it be as you wish, my Lady." Then he began to think, and love started up a dispute within him, and the thought that Love sends to his chosen ones entered deeply into the heart. From then on he was the servant of Love. He began to compose gay and gracious verses, dances, and love songs that are lovely to sing. There were many of them, and most were dedicated to the lady for whom he was singing. Love, who does reward her servants when they please her, decided to give her servant his due. She began tormenting the lady so grievously with thoughts and worries about love that she could not stop thinking, day or night, about the nobility and talent that had been so abundantly given to Guillelm and which resided within him.

One day it happened that the lady took Guillelm aside and said: "Now tell me, G., have you noticed my signs and have you decided whether they are true or false?" G. answered: "Lady, may God be with me, from the moment that I became your servant there is no thought which enters my heart which is not of the finest ever born and the truest in word and in appearance. This I believe and will believe all my life." The lady responded: "G., I am telling you, with God's protection, that you will never be deceived by me; nor will your thoughts ever have been in vain." She opened wide her arms and kissed him gently, in the bedroom in which they were seated, and there and then they began their love affair.

It hadn't gone on for long when the scandal-mongers, whom God hates, began talking about their love and started conjecturing about the meaning of the songs that G. was composing, and saying that he was paying court to Lady Margarida. They went around saying it so much, on high and on low, that it reached the ear of Lord Raimon. He was very hurt and grievously angry because it meant he was losing his companion whom he loved so, and also because of the disgrace to his wife.[1]

One day it happened that Guillelm had gone off to hunt with his sparrowhawk, accompanied by only one page. My Lord R. inquired as to his whereabouts and a valet told him that he had gone off to hunt with his sparrowhawk; and another, who knew where he was, told him: "In such and such a land." Raimon then went and had himself covertly armed, had his horse brought to him and went off alone on the road to the spot where Guillelm had gone. He rode for so long that he found him. When G. saw that he had come, he was greatly amazed and immediately had evil thoughts. He came forth to meet him and said: "Lord, it is good of you to have come. But how is it that you are alone?" Lord Raimon answered: "G., I have gone out looking for you so as to spend some pleasant time together, just you and I. Haven't you caught anything?"
--"Oh, me, Lord? Hardly anything at all for I have hardly found a thing and, as the proverb says, 'He who finds little, can only get little', as you well know."
--"Let's leave that subject now," said Lord Raimon. "Tell me the truth, by the faith that you owe me, about all the things that I should like to ask you."
--"In the name of God, Lord," said G., "if there is anything to say, I will certainly say it."

--"I don't want you to give me any denials or justifications," said Lord Raimon. "You will tell me the entire truth about each thing I ask you."
--"Lord, since you wish it, ask me," said G., "and I will tell you the truth."
So Lord Raimon asked Guillelm:
--"If God and faith mean anything to you, have you a lady for whom you sing and for the love of whom you are tormented?"
Guillelm answered:
--"Lord, how could I sing if Love didn't have a hold on me? You should know, Lord, in all truth, that Love has me entirely in her power."[2]
R. answered:
--"I am very willing to believe that, for otherwise you couldn't sing so sweetly. But please, I want to know. Tell me who your lady is."
--"Oh, Lord, for God's sake," said G., "be careful of what you ask me. Is it right that one should disclose the name of his love? You tell me, for you know what Sir Bernard de Ventadorn says:[3]

> My good sense helps me out on one account:
> Never has any man asked me about my joy
> That I didn't willingly lie to him about it.
> For it doesn't seem like the proper thing to do--
>   On the contrary, it's foolish and childish--
>   That a man who has been blessed with love
> Should want to open his heart to another
> If it can't do him any good or be of service to him... "
>
>   (70, 1: 17-24)

Lord Raimon responded:
--"I pledge that I will help you in any way within my power."
R. went on so much about it that G. answered: "Lord, you may as well know that I love the sister of Lady Margarida, your wife, and I think that she feels the same about me. Now that you know it, I beg you to help me or at least that you do nothing to hinder me."
--"Take my hand and my faith," said R., "that I swear and pledge to you that I will help you in any way possible within my power." And thus he promised on good faith. When he had finished with his promise R. said:
--"I want us to go there together, for it is close by."
--"By all means," said G, "in the name of God."
Thus they went on their way to the lady's castle.

When they got to the castle, they were warmly received by Sir Robert de Tarascon, the husband of my Lady Agnes, my Lady Margarida's sister; and by my Lady Agnes as well. Lord R. took Lady Agnes by the

hand and led her into a bedroom. There they sat down on a bed. Lord R. said: "Now tell me, sister-in-law, by the faith which you owe me, do you love someone with a true love?" She said: "Yes, lord."
--"And who is that?" he asked.
--"This I absolutely cannot tell you. And why should I go on telling you stories?"
Finally, he begged her so much that she said she loved Guillelm de Cabstaing. She said this because she saw that Guillelm was sad and deep in thought and she knew perfectly well that he loved her sister. Seeing this, she was afraid that R. might be thinking badly of Guillelm. This revelation brought R. great happiness. The lady explained the whole story to her husband and he told her that she had done well and he gave her his permission to do or say anything necessary to keep G. out of trouble. So the lady did so. She called G. into her bedroom all alone and spent so much time with him there that R. thought that he must be getting from her the pleasure of love. He found this all very pleasing and he began to think that what he had been told was not true. What more can I say? The lady and Guillelm came out of the bedroom, the supper was prepared, and they all ate in great happiness. After supper, the lady had a bed readied for the two of them near the door of the bedroom, so that in one way or another R. would think that G. was spending the night with her. The next day they all dined at the castle in great happiness and after the dinner, they left with great ceremony and returned to Roussillon. As soon as R. could get away from Guillelm, he went straight to his wife and told her all that he had seen go on between G. and her sister.

All that night the lady felt a heavy sorrow over this and the next day she sent for G., gave him a poor welcome, and called him a liar and a traitor. G. begged for her mercy, like a man not guilty of what he was being accused of, and told her everything that had happened, word for word. The lady summoned her sister and through her learned that G. was not guilty. On account of all this, the lady told him and commanded him to compose a song in which he would show that he loved no other lady but her. And so he composed this song which says:

> The sweet thought
> Which Love often grants me
> Makes me recite about you, Lady,
> Many pleasing verses.
> Pensive, I gaze upon
> Your noble, precious body,
> Which I desire,

Without letting it show.
Though I may wander,
For your sake, I never abandon you
But go on yielding to you
With fine, loving sentiments.
Lady in whom beauty is brought to perfection,
Many times I forget myself
For I praise you and implore your mercy... (213, 5: 1-15)

And when R. de Rossillon heard the song that G. had composed about his wife, he summoned him for a talk outside the castle, cut off his head and put it in a hunting sack, cut his heart from his body and put it in the sack with the head. Then he went back into the castle and had the heart roasted and carried to his wife's table, and he made her eat it without knowing what it was. When she had eaten it, R. stood up and told his wife that what she had eaten was the heart of G. de Cabstaing. He showed her the head and asked her if it had been good to eat. She heard what he was asking her; saw and recognized Sir Guillelm's head, and answered that it had been so good and tasty that never again would anything eaten or drunk remove from her mouth the taste that Sir G.'s heart had left there. R. ran at her with his sword. She fled to the door of the balcony, threw herself off, and broke her neck.

This evil deed was known throughout Catalonia and in all the lands belonging to the King of Aragon, King Anfos, and all the barons of those lands. There was great sorrow and mourning over the deaths of Sir Guillelm and the lady, because of the horrible way in which R. had brought about their deaths. The families of Sir G. and the lady got together, along with all the courtly knights of that land and all the lovers, and waged a war of fire and blood against R. The King of Aragon came into the land when he learned of the deaths of the lady and the knight. He took R. prisoner, took away from him his castles and lands and had G. and the lady placed in a monument before the door of a church in Perpignan, a city on the plain of Roussillon and Cerdagne which belongs to the King of Aragon. For a long time all the knights of Roussillon and Cerdagne and Conflent and Ripoll and Peiralada and Narbonne celebrated each year the anniversary of their deaths, and the fine lovers of both sexes prayed to God for their souls. Thus the King of Aragon took R. prisoner, took away all his possessions, put him to death in prison, and gave all his possessions to the families of Sir G. and the the lady who died for him. The city in which G. and the lady were buried is named Perpignan.[4]

¹ Raimon's behavior in this razo is just the opposite of what is called for within the fiction of fin'amor. He does not allow for the love between his wife and her lover and behaves like a *gelos* in the way that he reacts to the court rumors. It is interesting that in this passage his first reaction to the news of the affair is hurt over losing the love of his favorite valet, Guillem. Only secondarily does he react to the fact that the love-object is his wife, and then the anger springs from the fact that she will face public disgrace, rather than that she loves someone else.

² Such a statement is a topos of fin'amor rhetoric, but the vida to Uc de Saint Circ (who may well have composed both that text and this) belies that fiction by declaring that Uc wrote some love songs by feigning that he was in love (B/S, 240 and Egan, 110).

³ This is the only razo in which the song of another poet is cited, other than in cases where two poets collaborated on a song, as in a tenso. The fact that it occurs in this particular razo is further evidence that this longer narrative from manuscript P represents a departure from earlier techniques of composition and a turn toward more sustained narratives in which elements from different sources are joined. This move lead directly to the narrated prose tales of the Italian *Novellino* and later to Boccaccio.

⁴ This version is clearly based on the same model as the preceding one but differs in that it adds incidents and characters. The tale of the eaten heart was probably a known folk tale at the time. Its roots have been traced by Matzke, 1911, and it was also used for the story line of the contemporary French text, *Roman du Castelain de Couci et de la Dame de Fayel*. Dante and Boccaccio used the motif in the *Vita Nuova* and the *Decamerone*, respectively (Burgwinkle, 1989).

Song 70, 1   Bernart de Ventadorn: "Ab joi mou lo vers e.l comens..."
              Source: Appel, 3.
              MSS: A 88, B 56, C 47, D 19, D^c 248, F 20, G 9, I 27, K 16, L 19, M 37, P 17, V 51, a 87.
              Other English translations: Nichols, 41.

1. In joy the song takes form, starts up,
   And in joy it remains and finishes.
   And only if the ending is good
   Will I consider the beginning good.
       Joy and happiness come to me   5
       Through that good beginning;
   That's why I should be thankful for the good end,
   For it's at the end that I see all good deeds praised.

2. If joy both empowers and conquers me
   It's a wonder I can stand it;   10
   For I never say a word, or let it be known
   Who it is that makes me so gay and joyful.
       It would be hard to find a true love
       That is without fear and doubt;
   For one is always afraid of failing before the thing
       he loves.   15
   That's why I don't dare summon the courage to speak.

3. My good sense helps me out on one account:
   Never has any man asked me about my joy
   That I didn't willingly lie to him about it.
   For it doesn't seem like the proper thing to do--   20
       On the contrary, it's foolish and childish--
       That a man who has been blessed with love
   Should want to open his heart to another
   If it can't do him any good or be of service to him.

4. There is no more annoying, deceitful   25
   Or villainous thing a man can do,
   In my opinion, than to turn to spying on
   Another's love or friends.
       You pests! What good does it do you
       To cause me strife and worry?   30
   Everyone wants to do well at his job:
   You are destroying me but I don't see you getting any joy in
       return.

5. Boldness is well suited to a woman
   Surrounded by miserable people and wicked neighbors;
   And if a bold heart doesn't give her strength   35
   It's hard for her to remain worthy and excellent.

This is why I am begging that beauty,
In whom I've placed my faith, to keep this in mind:
May she never change or alter her course because of talk;
For the enemies I have, I make them die of jealousy.   40

6. I never thought, while kissing her lovely mouth,
That in kissing me she could betray me;
For with just one sweet kiss she kills me,
If there isn't another after it to cure me.
For it seems to me to be like   45
Peleus' lance:
No man could recover from just one blow
If he didn't manage to be struck a second time.[1]

7. Beautiful lady, your noble body
And beautiful eyes,   50
Your sweet glance, clear face,
And lovely manners have conquered me;
For when I really consider it,
I can find no one your equal in beauty.
Either you are the noblest lady one could ever find in this
world   55
Or I'm not seeing clearly through these eyes that look upon
you.

8. Beautiful-Sight, I have no doubt
That your reputation is growing,
For you know how to do and speak such pleasing things
That no man can prevent himself from loving you.   60

9. I am sure to have happiness,
For I have placed my hope in such a lady
That whoever speaks ill of her couldn't lie more vilely,
And whoever speaks well of her couldn't speak a more
beautiful truth.

---

[1] The reference to Peleus recalls Ovid's *Remedium amoris* 47-48: Vulnus in Herculeo quae quondam fecerat hoste, / Vulneris auxilium Pelias hasta tulit" (Nichols, 177).

Song 213, 5   Guillem de Cabestaing: "Lo dous cossire..."
Source: Långfors, 13.
MSS: A 84, B 53, C 212, D 103-357, E 144, F 33, H 21, I 105, K 89, L 102, R 96-803, S 227-147, T 258, U 130, V 98, v, 36, a^1 275, b^1 6, e 124, Q 111 (Cirardus), Q 6 (anonymous).
Other English translations: Blackburn, 191, Smythe, 174.

1. The sweet thought
   Which love often grants me
   Makes me recite about you, Lady,
   Many pleasing verses.
   Pensive, I gaze upon   5
   Your noble, precious body,
   Which I so desire,
   Without ever letting it show.
   Though I may wander,
   For your sake, I never abandon you   10
   But go on yielding to you
   With fine, loving sentiments.
   Lady in whom beauty is brought to perfection,
   Many times I forget myself,
   For I praise you and implore your mercy.   15

2. May the love you forbid me
   Forever hate me
   If ever I turn my heart
   To another site of courtship.
   You have taken from me laughter   20
   And replaced it with worry.
   There is no man who suffers
   A more painful martyrdom than I.
   For you, whom I most covet
   Amongst all the ladies in the world,   25
   I must disavow and deny;
   I must make it appear that I have fallen out of love.
   All that I do out of fear
   You must accept in good faith,
   Even when I do not see you.   30

3. In my memory
   I hold on to your face and sweet laugh,
   Your worth,
   And beautiful, smooth, white body.
   If I were as true to God   35
   In my faith,
   There's no doubt I'd pass
   From life straight into paradise.
   For here I am, my heart
   Given over to you without reservation,   40
   And no other joy attracts me.
   There isn't a lady wearing the veil
   With whom I'd sleep as compensation,
   Or for whom I'd act as lover,
   That I'd prefer to your simple greeting.   45

4. Every day I am uplifted by
   Desire; your manners,
   To which I incline,
   Bring out the best in me.
   It seems as if your love controls me,   50
   For even before I ever saw you
   It became my intention
   To love you and serve you.
   And that is how I have remained:
   Alone, without any help   55
   From you; you for whom I've given up
   Many others' gifts: let him who wants them take them!
   I'd rather wait for you,
   The source of my joy,
   Even without any public promise.[1]   60

5. Before agony takes flame
   In my heart,
   May mercy descend
   Upon you, Lady, and love.
   Let joy bring you to me   65
   And banish these sighs and tears.
   May neither rank nor wealth
   Forbid me access to you.
   All other rewards are forgotten
   If mercy does not intercede on my behalf.   70

    Oh, sweet and beautiful thing,
    It would have struck such a blow for sincerity
    If you had either loved me or refused forever
    When first I implored you;
    For now I don't know where things stand.   75

6. I can find nothing about your worth
    To argue with;
    May mercy for me overtake you
    So that honor will be yours.
    May God never hear me   80
    From amongst His supplicants
    If ever I should consent to take the income
    Of the four major kings
    Just because mercy and good faith
    Have failed to do me any good before you.   85
    For I could never leave
    You, in whom I have placed
    My love; and if ever you should accept that love
    With a kiss, and it should happen that you liked it,
    I would never wish to be apart from you.[2]   90

7. Nothing you ever want,
    Frank and courtly lady,
    Could ever be so forbidding
    That I wouldn't do it for you
    Before even thinking of anything else.   95

8. Sir Raimon, the beauty
    And good things that are found in My-Lord[3]
    Have taken me and hold me captive.

[1] The familiar motif of economic loss that results from serving a lady who does not come through on her promises. There is only the vaguest resemblance between the situation outlined in the razo and the content of this song.

[2] Again, the alternative to continuing devotion to the lady is presented in sexual and economic terms. Guillem says he would rather be with his lady than sleep with others or be rich as a king, things he apparently desires and threatens to get elsewhere.

[3] OR: the riches that reside within...

81. Lanfranc Cigala 282, 14 and Guillelma de Rosers 200, 1
    (B/S 571)
    MS: P 48.

Now I am going to tell you --and it's a rich tale you're listening to-- about what happened to some knights, owners of a rich castle. They were rich in heart and mind, and at arms and in possessions; young and beautiful in body; rich in love, in courting ladies and at all pleasing tasks, skillful at arms and masters at war. More than all the other lovers, they loved two beautiful, noble and learned ladies in true love; and for them they accomplished many agreeable deeds, such as one does for the love of ladies: beautiful courts, beautiful tournaments, rich gifts and beautiful receptions. They made themselves highly esteemed and the news of their noble doings spread near and far. They were more loved by their ladies than any knight who lived at that time.

These ladies lived in another castle, three leagues away from their knights. One day these ladies sent their messengers to those two knights, telling them and asking them, in the name of their love, to come to see them that night; and each of them said that he would go, but neither one knew about the other. The two brothers were at that time involved in a war with some strong barons from that area and they were fearful for their castle. They had agreed between themselves and promised that they would never both leave the castle for any reason, regardless of what should happen, and that there would always be one of them at the castle to guard it and to serve the noble men as they came and went from their castle. Thus each one of them was thinking of going to ask the other's permission, in a case of such dire need, to go off on his route that evening, and each told the other about his message. The first one began to swear then, saying that nothing in the world could keep him at home that night and the second one did the same. Neither of them wanted to agree to stay home for the sake of the other's entreaties or the needs of the castle, and so they both went on their way. You should know that the weather was awful; there was rain and wind and snow and it was like that right up to nightfall. And so they made sure the castle was well-protected.

Then they went off together. They had not gone far when they heard some knights coming from the other direction. They got off the road, close by a bush, and heard the knights saying: "May God grant us a good lodging tonight!" To which another responded: "If God watches over the two brothers, we will have everything we need and will be welcomed, honored and served; for they are the noblest and most courtly knights in the world. Other than for them, we wouldn't find a lodging anywhere within three leagues of their place."

This plaint caused the two brothers both happiness and sadness: happiness over the good things they had heard said about themselves, and sadness that there was not at least one of them at the castle. Because of this, each begged the other to turn back and return to the castle and between them they had an argument. Finally one of them went back and said that he was returning out of love for his lady.

Lanfranc Cigala heard all about this affair, just as it had happened. This is why he asked Lady Guillelma in a poem which of the two was more deserving of praise: the one who turned back to serve the knights or the one who went on to see his lady. And over this set of circumstances he composed a tenso which says:[1]

> Lady Guillelma, there were once many knights
> Wandering about on a stormy night
> Lamenting in their language about finding lodging.
> Two barons, who were rushing off
> To lovemaking with their ladies, heard them.
> One turned back to help those knights;
> The other ran off to his lady.
> Which of the two did better in performing his duty? (282, 14: 1-8)

[1] B/S note that this razo, about an Italian troubadour, is marked by an abundance of Italianisms within the Occitan text and was therefore most likely composed in Italy, perhaps expressly for manuscript P. The lady in question, Na Guillelma, has been identified as Guillerma of Rougiers, from the region of Saint-Maximin, who spent time in Genoa. These are the only verses she is known to have written (B/S, 575).

Song 282, 14 and 200, 1
        Lanfranc Cigala and Guillelma de Rosers: "Na
        Guillelma, maint cavalier arratge..."
        Source: Branciforti, 172.

MSS: I 159, K 145, M 263, O 93, a 542.
Other English translations: Bogin, 178.

1. Lady Guillelma, there were once many knights
   Wandering about on a stormy night
   Lamenting in their language about finding lodging.
   Two barons, who were rushing off
   To lovemaking with their ladies, heard them.   5
   One turned back to help those knights;
   The other ran off to his lady.
   Which of the two did better in performing his duty?

2. Lafranc, my friend, it is my opinion
   That the one who stayed on course to his lady brought his
      travels to a better end.   10
   The other one performed well; but His-Lord
   Cannot judge his fine heart as clearly
   As the other, who sees on the spot, with her own eyes,
   That her knight has observed his promise.
   One who does what he says is worth much more   15
   Than one who changes his heart from one thing to another.

3. Lady, if you will permit me, every act of goodness
   That the knight committed was motivated by love;
   For by his courage, he saved those others from damages and
      death.
   No man can truly possess courtliness   20
   If it hasn't come to him through love.
   This is why His-Lord should show him a hundred times more
      honor
   Than if he had come to see her: for through his love for her
   He saved so many knights from torment.

4. Lafranc, you've never argued as foolishly as you do now   25
   About that knight and what he did.
   For you had better face it: he committed a serious crime
   When the desire to serve touched his heart,
   For he did not serve His-Lord before any other.
   From her he would receive gratitude and pleasures;   30
   Then, for her love, he could serve whenever he wanted,
   In many good locations, and never fail in his mission.

323

5. Lady, I beg your pardon if what I say seems crazy,
   But I now see evidence of what I used to think about ladies:
   That the only pilgrimages you like your lovers to make   35
   Is the one that leads straight to you.
   Yet when one wants to train a horse for jousting,
   One must lead him along using moderation and good sense.
   It's because you rush your lovers along so rudely   39
   That their powers fail them and resentment overcomes you.

6. I'll say it once again, Lafranc: a knight had better
   Give up all signs of folly the very day
   That he would take as his master
   A beautiful and worthy lady of noble birth.   44
   For in his home they would have offered generous service
   Even if he hadn't been there. Then each one defends him
   For he knows that he is so cowardly
   That in his hour of greatest need his powers would fail him.

7. Lady, I have had the power and the courage,
   Not to use against you, but to conquer you in bed.   50
   I must have been crazy to pick a fight with you;
   But what I want is to have been conquered by you, by
      whatever means.

8. Lafranc, this much I will grant you and agree to:
   That I feel so full of heart and courage
   That with all the ingenuity that a lady has to defend herself,
   I will defend myself against the bravest there is.[1]   56

---

[1] The evolution of this song from a tenso on a hypothetical subject to an exposé of sexual domination makes it one of the most interesting of the 'discussion' songs. The equation of the lover and the horse, coupled with the repeated references to the lover's powers failing him, suggest multiple alternative meanings.

The Garland Library of Medieval Literature

Series A (Texts and Translations); Series B (Translations Only)

1. Chrétien de Troyes: *Lancelot*, or *The Knight of the Cart*. Edited and translated by William W. Kibler. Series A.
2. Brunetto Latini: *Il Tesoretto (The Little Treasure)*. Edited and translated by Julia Bolton Holloway. Series A.
3. *The Poetry of Arnaut Daniel*. Edited and translated by James J. Wilhelm. Series A.
4. *The Poetry of William VII, Count of Poitiers, IX Duke of Aquitaine*. Edited and translated by Gerald A. Bond; music edited by Hendrik van der Werf. Series A.
5. *The Poetry of Cercamon and Jaufre Rudel*. Edited and translated by George Wolf and Roy Rosenstein; music edited by Hendrik van der Werf. Series A.
6. *The Vidas of the Troubadours*. Translated by Margarita Egan. Series B.
7. *Medieval Latin Poems of Male Love and Friendship*. Translated by Thomas Stehling. Series A.
8. *Bartbar Saga*. Edited and translated by Jon Skaptason and Phillip Pulsiano. Series A.
9. Guillaume de Machaut: *Judgment of the King of Bohemia (Le Jugement dou Roy de Behaingne)*. Edited and translated by R. Barton Palmer. Series A.
10. *Three Lives of the Last Englishmen*. Translated by Michael Swanton. Series B.
11. Giovanni Boccaccio: *Eclogues*. Edited and translated by Janet Smarr. Series A.
12. Hartmann von Aue: *Erec*. Translated by Thomas L. Keller. Series B.
13. *Waltharius* and *Ruodlieb*. Edited and translated by Dennis M. Kratz. Series A.
14. *The Writings of Medieval Women*. Translated by Marcelle Thiébaux. Series B.
15. *The Rise of Gawain, Nephew of Arthur (De ortu Waluuanii Nepotis Arturi)*. Edited and translated by Mildred Leake Day. Series A.
16, 17. *The French Fabliau:* B.N. 837. Edited and translated by Raymond Eichmann and John DuVal. Series A.
18. *The Poetry of Guido Cavalcanti*. Edited and translated by Lowry Nelson, Jr. Series A.
19. Hartmann von Aue: *Iwein*. Edited and translated by Patrick M. McConeghy. Series A.
20. *Seven Medieval Latin Comedies*. Translated by Alison Goddard Elliott. Series B.
21. Christine de Pizan: *The Epistle of the Prison of Human Life*. Edited and translated by Josette A. Wisman. Series A.
22. *The Poetry of the Sicilian School*. Edited and translated by Frede Jensen. Series A.

23. *The Poetry of Cino da Pistoia.* Edited and translated by Christopher Kleinhenz. Series A.
24. *The Lyrics and Melodies of Adam de la Halle.* Lyrics edited and translated by Deborah Hubbard Nelson; music edited by Hendrik van der Werf. Series A.
25. Chrétien de Troyes: *Erec and Enide.* Edited and translated by Carleton W. Carroll. Series A.
26. *Three Ovidian Tales of Love.* Edited and translated by Raymond J. Cormier. Series A.
27. *The Poetry of Guido Guinizelli.* Edited and translated by Robert Edwards. Series A.
28. Wernher der Gartenaere: *Helmbrecht.* Edited by Ulrich Seelbach; introduced and translated by Linda B. Parshall. Series A.
29. *Five Middle English Arthurian Romances.* Translated by Valerie Krishna. Series B.
30. *The One Hundred New Tales (Les Cent nouvelles nouvelles).* Translated by Judith Bruskin Diner. Series B.
31. Gerald of Wales (Giraldus Cambrensis): *The Life of St. Hugh of Avalon.* Edited and translated by Richard M. Loomis. Series A.
32. *L'Art d'Amours (The Art of Love).* Translated by Lawrence Blonquist. Series B.
33. Giovanni Boccaccio: *L'Ameto.* Translated by Judith Serafini-Sauli. Series B.
34, 35. *The Medieval Pastourelle.* Selected, translated, and edited in part by William D. Paden, Jr. Series A.
36. Béroul: *The Romance of Tristran.* Edited and translated by Norris J. Lacy. Series A.
37. *Graelent* and *Guingamor:* Two Breton Lays. Edited and translated by Russell Weingartner. Series A.
38. Heinrich von Veldeke: *Eneit.* Translated by J. Wesley Thomas. Series B.
39. *The Lyrics and Melodies of Gace Brulé.* Edited and translated by Samuel Rosenberg and Samuel Danon; music edited by Hendrik van der Werf. Series A.
40. Giovanni Boccaccio: *Life of Dante (Trattatello in Laude di Dante).* Translated by Vincenzo Zin Bollettino. Series B.
41. *The Lyrics of Thibaut de Champagne.* Edited and translated by Kathleen J. Brahney. Series A.
42. *The Poetry of Sordello.* Edited and translated by James J. Wilhelm. Series A.
43. Giovanni Boccaccio: *Il Filocolo.* Translated by Donald S. Cheney with the collaboration of Thomas G. Bergin. Series B.
44. *Le Roman de Thèbes (The Story of Thebes).* Translated by John Smartt Coley. Series B.
45. Guillaume de Machaut: *The Judgment of the King of Navarre (Le Jugement dou Roy de Navarre).* Translated and edited by R. Barton Palmer. Series A.
46. *The French Chansons of Charles D'Orléans.* With the Corresponding Middle English Chansons. Edited and translated by Sarah Spence. Series A.

47. *The Pilgrimage of Charlemagne* and *Aucassin and Nicolette*. Edited and translated by Glyn S. Burgess and Anne Elizabeth Cobby. Series A.
48. Chrétien de Troyes: *The Knight with the Lion*, or *Yvain*. Edited and translated by William W. Kibler. Series A.
49. *Carmina Burana: Love Songs*. Translated by Edward D. Blodgett and Roy Arthur Swanson. Series B.
50. *The Story of Meriadoc, King of Cambria (Historia Meriadoci, Regis Cambriae)*. Edited and translated by Mildred Leake Day. Series A.
51. *The Plays of Hrotsvit of Gandersheim*. Translated by Katharina Wilson. Series B.
52. *Medieval Debate Poetry: Vernacular Works*. Edited and translated by Michel-André Bossy. Series A.
53. Giovanni Boccaccio: *Il Filostrato*. Translated by Robert P. apRoberts and Anna Bruni Seldis; Italian text by Vincenzo Pernicone. Series A.
54. Guillaume de Machaut: *La Fonteinne amoureuse*. Edited and translated by R. Barton Palmer. Series A.
55. *The Knight of the Parrot (Le Chevalier du Papegau)*. Translated by Thomas E. Vesce. Series B.
56. *The Saga of Thidrek of Bern (Thidrekssaga af Bern)*. Translated by Edward R. Haymes. Series. B.
57. Wolfram von Eschenbach: *Titurel* and the *Songs*. Edited and translated by Sidney M. Johnson and Marion Gibbs. Series A.
58. Der Stricker: *Daniel of the Blossoming Valley*. Translated by Michael Resler. Series B.
59. *The Byelorussian Tristan*. Translated by Zora Kipel. Series B.
60. *The Marvels of Rigomer*. Translated by Thomas E. Vesce. Series B.
61. *The Song of Aspremont (La Chanson d'Aspremont)*. Translated by Michael A. Newth. Series B.
62. Chrétien de Troyes: *The Story of the Grail (Li Contes del Graal)*, or *Perceval*. Edited by Rupert T. Pickens and translated by William W. Kibler. Series A.
63. Heldris de Cornouaille: *The Story of Silence (Le Roman de Silence)*. Translated by Regina Psaki. Series B.
64. *Romances of Alexander*. Translated by Dennis M. Kratz. Series B.
65. Dante Alighieri: *Il Convivio (The Banquet)*. Translated by Richard H. Lansing. Series B.
66. *The Cambridge Songs (Carmina Cantabrigiensia)*. Edited and translated by Jan M. Ziolkowski. Series A.
67. Guillaume de Machaut: *Le Confort d'Ami (Comfort for a Friend)*. Edited and translated by R. Barton Palmer. Series. A.
68. Christine de Pizan: *Christine's Vision*. Translated by Glenda K. McLeod. Series B.
69. *Moriz von Craûn*. Edited and translated by Stephanie Cain Van D'Elden. Series A.

70. *The Acts of Andrew in the Country of the Cannibals.* Translated by Robert Boenig. Series B.
71. *Razos and Troubadour Songs.* Translated by William E. Burgwinkle. Series B.

For Product Safety Concerns and Information please contact our EU representative GPSR@taylorandfrancis.com
Taylor & Francis Verlag GmbH, Kaufingerstraße 24, 80331 München, Germany

www.ingramcontent.com/pod-product-compliance
Lightning Source LLC
Chambersburg PA
CBHW070722020526
44116CB00031B/1091